FLOW

by Julia F. Christensen, PhD

FLOW For Dummies®

Published by: **John Wiley & Sons, Inc.**, 111 River Street, Hoboken, NJ 07030-5774, www.wiley.com

Copyright © 2026 by Julia F. Christensen. All rights reserved.

Media and software compilation copyright © 2026 by John Wiley & Sons, Inc. All rights reserved, including rights for text and data mining and training of artificial technologies or similar technologies.

For general information on our other products and services, please contact our Customer Care Department within the U.S. at 877-762-2974, outside the U.S. at 317-572-3993, or fax 317-572-4002. For technical support, please visit https://hub.wiley.com/community/support/dummies.

Wiley publishes in a variety of print and electronic formats and by print-on-demand. Some material included with standard print versions of this book may not be included in e-books or in print-on-demand. If this book refers to media that is not included in the version you purchased, you may download this material at http://booksupport.wiley.com. For more information about Wiley products, visit www.wiley.com.

Library of Congress Control Number: 2026942043

ISBN 978-1-394-35112-1 (pbk); ISBN 978-1-394-35113-8 (epub); ISBN 978-1-394-35114-5 (epdf)

Printed and bound by CPI Group (UK) Ltd, Croydon, CR0 4YY

C9781394351121_090626

The manufacturer's authorized representative according to the EU General Product Safety Regulation is Wiley-VCH GmbH, Boschstr. 12, 69469 Weinheim, Germany, e-mail: Product_Safety@wiley.com.

Contents at a Glance

Table of Contents

CHAPTER 8: Imagination, Aesthetic Emotions, and the Right Intentions 167

CHAPTER 9: Avoiding Mind-Hooks While Seeking Flow 195

CHAPTER 10: Stringing It All Together: Owning Your Flow 215

PART 3: INTEGRATING FLOW INTO DAILY LIFE 223

CHAPTER 11: Reaching Flow While Learning a New Language 225

CHAPTER 12: Finding Flow with Athletic Movement 245

CHAPTER 13: **Finding Flow with Arts and Crafts**. 267

CHAPTER 14: **Flowing on the Page** 285

very problematic behaviors for tapping into flow so that you can avoid them on your pathway to flow.

This book is for everyone — for busy business people, parents, students, artists, professionals from all walks of life. And that's because anyone can benefit from flow. You don't need any particular expertise because your brain already knows flow and has been able to find flow since birth. You just need to find your way back there, with curiosity and some willingness to play and experiment with what works best for your brain.

Finding ways to focus and appease our brain today is becoming a paramount need that everyone should care about — for private life and for business. A flow-practice frees up the mind space and generates not only flow when you want it, but also increases your wellbeing, health, and productivity. In this book, I offer science-backed, hands-on advice about how to do that.

About This Book

Flow For Dummies is a practical guide that includes simple strategies to use activities that you love as tools so that you can improve your ability to find flow when you need it. Having access to flow can help strengthen your ability to focus, grow your resilience, bolster feelings of self-worth, and improve your health and well-being. And very likely, it can also boost your productivity levels. I stay away from abstract theory and complicated instructions in this book. It's structured in a way that you can read it all in one go, or only those chapters that are most important for you. You can find out about:

- What flow is, who finds flow easily, and what to do if you don't

- The science supporting how eight behaviors can help guide you to flow, along with three behaviors that can prevent you from finding flow

- Expanding your roster of potential flow activities and reverse-engineering the flow state

- How to include a flow practice in all different kinds of lives and situations

How to Use This Book

You can read this book from the front to back cover. Or, you can browse individual chapters at your heart's content. If you let it, your mind will likely find the right pages for this point of your life.

I'd give one piece of advice though, if I may. I know flow well, but in writing this book, I've been surprised over and again at how it all links together. This has allowed me to build the chapters on each other. Different from my first book on flow, *The Pathway to Flow (Vintage)*, this *Flow For Dummies* takes a completely practice-based approach. So, if I may, I'd recommend: take advantage of this layered presentation of information that I've crafted for you through the five parts of this book:

>> **Part 1: Getting Acquainted with Flow Basics:** Chapter 1 starts out with the essentials to introduce you to the science of flow. You can read about the neuroscience of the ten Flow Elements (proposed by the father of flow-research, Professor Mihaly Csikszentmihalyi), in Chapter 2. Chapters 3 and 4 discuss what makes a person prone to flow, as well as how body and brain relate when it comes to finding flow.

>> **Part 2: Reverse-Engineering Flow:** Chapters 5 through 8 present what I call the eight Guiding Stars of Flow, behaviors that can enhance your chances of finding flow if you include them in your life. Chapter 9 outlines three behaviors that I call mind-hooks, whose neurobiological effects can prevent you from finding flow. In Chapter 10 and Bonus Chapter 2, you can get started at putting your flow practice together and identifying the types of absorption that you can find.

>> **Part 3: Integrating Flow into Your Daily Life:** Chapters 11 through 14 and Bonus Chapters 3–5 stroll through types of activities with which you can potentially find flow. For each of these activities, I look at how to apply the eight Guiding Stars of Flow to that particular activity and how to stay clear of the three mind-hooks.

- **≫ Part 4: Flowing to the Next Level:** If your life is complicated, Chapters 15 and 16 and Bonus Chapter 6. These
  chapters cover stressful and complicated life situations,
  offering tips on how to build a small flow practice that can
  make all the difference for your peace of mind, preserving
  your productivity levels and good spirits, despite what's
  going on around you.

- **≫ Part 5: The Part of Tens:** The chapters in this section can
  offer you inspiration about how to get started with a flow
  activity and all the benefits of flow.

Foolish Assumptions

If you picked up this book, I know that you want to make a change
for the better in your life (or the life of someone you care about)
and that you want to start with clear and practical principles. In
writing this book, I've come to appreciate the *For Dummies* style
very much because it forced me to present the scientific evidence
in a way that you can apply straight away to your life.

Although flow is for everyone, so this book is for everyone,
I made a few assumptions about who you are. Any one of these
descriptions might apply to you:

- ≫ You last experienced flow in childhood.

- ≫ You experience flow sometimes and want more of it, but
  you have no clue how to flow when you want it.

- ≫ You're in a stressful or even life-changing situation where
  you feel that you don't have any control over what happens
  to you (incarceration, immigration, asylum, disease, and so
  on), and you want a healthy and positive break from it all.

- ≫ You know flow well in one aspect of your life, and you want
  to apply flow to another activity.

- ≫ You lost the ability to find flow with your once-beloved flow
  activity, and you want it back.

>> You're convinced you don't have time for flow.

>> You think flow is an idle passe-time.

>> You're human.

Icons Used in This Book

Throughout this book, you'll see different icons that I use to highlight important information. Here they are — together with a brief definition of what each of them means:

The Tip icon highlights information that can give you a leg up in your flow pursuit.

The Remember icon highlights things to keep in mind while you investigate flow and your flow chances.

The Warning icon highlights information about potential pitfalls and missteps that you should avoid in your quest for flow.

The Technical Stuff icon indicates content that dives a little deeper into the science of flow; information that you don't need in order to find flow but that can spark your interest.

Beyond the Book

At Dummies.com, you can find materials that go beyond the contents of this book. Just enter "Flow For Dummies" in the Search text box and search to access this book's online Cheat Sheet. It includes questionnaires and worksheets that can help you determine how easily you can tap into flow, given your personality type, as well as what aspects of your life to lean into more for flow. The Cheat Sheet also offers some easy-to-use advice about developing your flow practice.

Online Bonus Chapters

A lot can be said about flow — and many activities can be *flowable.* I therefore offer you six bonus chapters online, found at `www.dummies.com/go/flowfd`:

- **»** **Bonus Chapter 1:** Selecting Cues and Setting Boundaries

- **»** **Bonus Chapter 2:** Healthy and Unhealthy States of Absorption

- **»** **Bonus Chapter 3:** Tapping into Foods, Flavors, Textures, and Scents

- **»** **Bonus Chapter 4:** Flowing in the Office

- **»** **Bonus Chapter 5:** Unlocking Your Flow with Performative Arts and Jobs

- **»** **Bonus Chapter 6:** Discovering Neurodiversity and Flow

1

Getting Acquainted with Flow Basics

Explore what the flow state is and what it feels like.

Break down the science, myths, and real-world value of flow.

Assess your personal tendencies, strengths, and barriers to entering flow.

Get your brain, body, and environment to work together to make flow possible.

Chapter **1**

Putting Flow in a Nutshell

Welcome to your pathway to flow. No matter who you are, you've likely experienced flow at some point in your life. At least, you probably remember it from your childhood, when you spent hours lost in play; where time and space disappeared around you, and you later remerged, feeling great. Because you picked up this book, I suspect you want more of that special state but can't really seem to get it. No matter whether you're someone that hasn't felt flow since childhood, or you're a stressed businessperson, a busy parent, a professional artist, or a barista, if you wonder where your flow went, this book is for you.

I'll be your guide on this pathway to flow. I'm a psychologist and neuroscientist, and I've spent the last 15 years working within international research institutions at the intersection of the arts and sciences. As a former professional dancer, I've known flow all my life. But I write this book as a scientist to share the science of why flow doesn't have to remain this elusive state that happens to you by chance — or that doesn't happen at all. In this chapter we will get acquainted with what flow is, why it benefits us, and how finding back your flow is possible.

Identifying the Benefits of Flow

In this chapter, you can stroll through the science of flow, see how to distinguish it from other good and bad states of absorption (more on that distinction in Chapters 9 and Bonus Chapter 2, found at `www.dummies.com/go/flowfd`), and why real flow makes you feel so incredibly good. Astonishing scientific discoveries in the recent past reveal that tapping into flow regularly makes people healthier, happier, and nicer to be around.

As an unexpected side effect of having a regular flow practice, you may also become more productive in your work, face less risk of developing burnout, and feel more intrinsically motivated in your chores. And, tapping into flow regularly tends to make people develop a more optimistic outlook on life, kick-starting this little motor called satisfaction in your mind. Satisfaction can propel you forward, even against all odds — and strengthen something inside you that psychologists call *resilience* (successfully adapting to difficult or challenging life experiences). You can read all about the benefits of flow in Chapter 2.

Flow is for everyone: You simply need to know how to get started. And after you start that practice, you can see how its effects ripple through your life — creating feelings of self-confidence, self-relevance, and meaning.

Discovering flow

To clarify what I'm talking about when I talk about flow, *flow* is a state that unites the following ten elements (which I discuss in detail in Chapter 2), according to the father of flow research, the Hungarian scientist Professor Mihaly Csikszentmihalyi. You're in flow when you're actively doing something and you:

>> Are completely concentrated and absorbed in the activity

>> Have clear goals about what you want to achieve

>> Get clear signals that tell you whether you're doing the activity well or need to adjust — you feel in control

>> Feel a transformation of time (time zips by or slows down)

>> Do what you do because of *intrinsic rewards* (because you enjoy and feel satisfaction from doing the activity)

>> Feel effortlessness in what you're doing and perhaps you feel part of something bigger than yourself

>> Find the task neither too easy nor too difficult — there is a skills-challenge balance

>> Feel fully immersed, like your actions and attention have merged, and you're part of the activity itself — perhaps you feel you *are* the movement or otherwise feel you lose yourself in the action

>> Stop experiencing repetitive, looping thoughts and mental replay of the past — rumination recedes

>> Feel in control and escape the unpredictability of life — worries recede

Don't we all want more of that?

Knowing what flow feels like doesn't necessarily move you any closer to how to get that special feeling. And that's where this book comes in. You can reverse engineer the state that you want by using the newest evidence from psychology and neuroscience. In Chapter 5, I give an overview of eight behaviors that can guide you to flow, and in Chapters 6 to 8, I reveal the science of each of them. In Part 3 and in Bonus Chapters 3 and 4 found at `www.dummies.com/go/flowfd` you can then read about all eight behaviors applied to about 20 different activities and hobbies.

Searching for flow

No matter who you are, having flow in your life has positive effects. Science shows that regular flow helps make people healthy in mind and body, more balanced, and more productive. Population-based assessments show that the *Cox hazard ratio*, a statistical measure of a person's risk of developing a disease over time, suggests that people who experience flow regularly have a lower risk for some mental and physical ailments, such as burn out and heart disease.

In a 2024 study by a group of scientists, including Dr. Miriam Mosing and her student Emma Gaston at the Max Planck Institute for Empirical Aesthetics in Frankfurt, they combed through a large dataset that contained information about thousands of individuals to see whether the risk of receiving a diagnosis of something bad was different in flow-prone people and people who aren't prone to flow. (Flip to Chapter 3 for discussion of flow-proneness.) They found a correlation between being flow-prone and having fewer medical issues:

- **Depression:** Sixteen percent lower risk

- **Anxiety:** Sixteen percent lower risk

- **Schizophrenia:** Fourteen percent lower risk

- **Bipolar disorder:** Twelve percent lower risk

- **Stress-related diseases:** Nine percent lower risk

- **Cardiovascular disorders:** Four percent lower risk

Everyone struggles with something; no matter who you are, life can be tough. For instance:

- Work demands productivity and loyalty, regardless of all adversity.

- Family demands quality time, solutions, and a constant flow of good vibes (or cash).

- Institutions insist on their cumbersome bureaucracy, regardless of your family duties, neurodiversity, or feelings of overwhelm.

- Your body wants a good amount of exercise, care, and healthful food to function properly — especially if you're north of 50 or have a chronic health condition.

In the turmoil of the many things that your life demands of you, you can struggle to drop your attention into a fountain of creative focus, feel good, and live out your full potential.

Regular flow makes it possible to have a happy, productive life. And that's because of some very welcome side effects of the delicious feeling of being in flow. For example, scientific assessments reveal:

>> Regular flow experiences train your attention to last; you can reclaim your focus in other domains of your life.

>> The flow after-glow makes you better able to handle what feels like too much if you don't have flow; your perspective changes. You become more optimistic.

>> If you can experience flow during your work, sport, or art, you can improve both your creativity and productivity; you can think outside of the box.

>> When you have flow experiences, you can rekindle your energy and sense of authentic self. You come back to yourself, which stokes your *intrinsic motivation* (feeling enjoyment and satisfaction simply from doing the activity, not from an outcome).

>> Flow can return a feeling of agency over your life, healing a troubled mind; you take back control, even just for a little while.

The Do's and Don'ts of Flow

So, how do people achieve flow? In the past decades, neuroscientific research has uncovered eight behaviors that anyone can do to help them find flow, which I call the Guiding Stars of Flow (I introduce these behaviors briefly in the section "Discovering flow," earlier in this chapter). And research also points to three behaviors that you should avoid while you try to find flow (which I call the Gods of Mind-Hooking, discussed in detail in Chapter 9). In Part 3, I unpack all these helpful and unhelpful behaviors in relation to particular flow activities and Bonus

Chapters 3 and 4 (found at www.dummies.com/go/flowfd), string it all together.

You can't just decide to copy these behaviors, and then have flow. It's not that easy. You need to tailor the behaviors to your own life, depending on who you are, what work you do, and what hobbies you enjoy. In Part 4, I discuss ways to apply the Guiding Stars of Flow to different kinds of lives — busy lives, lives on the edge, and in Bonus Chapter 5 (www.dummies.com/go/flowfd), you can discover flow and neurodivergent lives.

Some people can tap into flow particularly easily. I talk about what makes someone flow-prone in Chapter 3. But you don't have to be flow-prone to achieve flow. These eight Guiding Stars of Flow have a strong effect on your brain and body, and can help you set the settings for flow in your mind.

Feeling Flow (Whoever You Are)

Anyone and everyone can tap into flow. That's why I wrote this book. Archeological evidence (which you can find details about in Chapter 2) suggests that humans have always sought flow, by crafting, hunting, dancing, drawing, storytelling, athletic pursuits, music-making, and so on.

Appreciating the benefits of flow revealed through modern scientific research (see Chapter 2), flow may have brought those human ancestors who tapped into flow regularly some advantages — including emotional regulation and the ability to deal with a complex life, full of stresses (maybe that sounds familiar to you). However, you may have some road blocks on your pathway to flow, which I talk about in the following sections.

Dismissing the myth of the genius

People often talk about flow as something creative folks have in common; a curious, all-absorbing state of mind where they feel amazing and can be incredibly productive and creative at the same time.

Take a look at the following list of achievements that have impacted humanity, created by individuals whose minds found flow by doing what they did (but remember that finding flow doesn't mean that you will or have to create something amazing):

>> **The printing press:** Invented by Johannes Gutenberg (around 1450) and started off exponential literacy development. This first printing press is the reason that you can pick up a copy of a book you love or haven't yet read and be surrounded by a library of printed books.

>> **Antibiotics and vaccines:** Improve the health and well-being of millions. Maybe antibiotics saved your life when you had a terrible infection, or perhaps your great-great-grandmother survived as a child because she received a vaccine for a deadly illness.

>> **Moving pictures:** In 1895, the Lumière brothers created the first ever motion picture. Whatever your favorite movie, consider it brought to you by the Lumières.

These accounts of how other peoples' creative flow led to excellence, societal impact, and Nobel prizes might wow you. But those glorious stories can also alienate you from your own potential for tapping into flow and being creative with what you do. If you expect to invent the next big thing, you have too high expectations! The myth that you have to be a genius to find flow definitely doesn't help you find flow. In Chapter 2 (and in many subsequent chapters!) you'll hear me repeat that for tapping into flow, your goal can never be success or a final prize. Focusing on extrinsic rewards and aims makes reaching flow impossible.

Preventing self-sabotage

To prevent self-sabotage that can happen if you buy into the myth of the genius (see the preceding section), remember:

>> **Everyone faces uncertainty.** The human mind loves a hero's story, and looking back at history, it can often seem that everyone always knew what they were doing and why until they gloriously reached their goal. But in reality,

everyone goes through a string of failed attempts, slippery slopes, and mysterious crossroads. You need to figure out how to deal with uncertainty. As you can read about in Chapter 16, you need to set up a flexible practice and not get ahead of yourself.

>> **Don't aim for fame.** The famous people discussed in the preceding section didn't know they'd achieve what they did. And certainly many more people with dreams and goals never receive recognition (even if they achieve their goals). Anyone can benefit from being in flow, even if the outcomes of their activities remain unknown to the wider world. For flow, make peace with being an unknown hero.

>> **Avoid flow-sabotage from the people and popular culture around you.** Families are a huge flow-stopper. In German, there is a saying that goes something like this: 'either you're perfect at it or you better don't do it'. A second-century Greek physician called Galen preached that 'Laziness breeds humors of the blood!' and he'd certainly have grouped 'flow' within mental states to be avoided. There are people who believe that spending time on being in flow for us mere mortals is a waste of time, or that you are lazy and should be frowned upon, if you do. While we experience popular culture around us — 'social learning' takes place inside our brain.

To prevent socially induced self-sabotage, you need to keep a few points in mind about humanity's social brain (I look more closely at the social components of the brain in Chapter 6). Your social brain compels you to fit in:

>> **Stressing your brain by not conforming:** When you behave differently than your social group, your brain can switch on a bizarre drama-queen soap opera about loneliness before your inner eye to warn you about social exclusion.

>> **Rewarding your brain by following the group:** Evolutionarily ancient circuits in your brain lights up in reward activity when you conform to a social norm. That's why people crave fitting in — it's rewarding to do so.

Your social brain can make your group very strong (that's great!). However, its drama-queen nature can also lead you to self-defeating behaviors that prevent you from achieving your goals just so that you can fit in (that's bad!).

Remember: These processes are beyond your conscious control. You need to trick them — which you can do if you have the right knowledge about the brain.

Voices outside and inside your head may tell you that you can't really get into flow, creativity, and other fun mental pursuits. Listening to that narrative is a form of self-sabotage.

Recognizing Flow-Proneness

Scientists have measured peoples' flow-proneness by using specifically designed and validated tests since the mid-2000's (you can read more about these studies in Chapter 3). Researchers asked and answered questions such as these:

>> Are flow-prone people more intelligent than others? (No.)

>> Do flow-prone people have a special personality? (Yes.)

>> Do the brains of flow-prone people have unique features? (Yes.)

These findings provide those who aren't flow-prone with reassurance for three reasons:

>> You don't need to be specifically intelligent to find flow. Einstein may well have been very intelligent, but that wasn't what made him flow-prone.

>> Knowing your personality type, gets you a step closer to understanding whether you can easily find flow. With that information, you can tailor your personal pathway to flow, taking into account the needs of your personality type.

>> If you know how brains differ in terms of flow potential, you can prepare yourself constructively (see also Chapter 4).

In Chapter 3, you can look at different personality traits and how they impact your experience of flow. If you have many of the personality traits that make someone flow-prone, your personality may be conducive to flow. If you still don't get flow regularly, you can use this scaffolding to get you more. On the other hand, if you don't have many (or any) of these traits, consider how to keep those aspects of your personality in check when you seek to tap into flow.

Identifying Non-Flow Healthy States

In addition to flow, you can find plenty of practices circling about in the self-help space — and different terms that describe them, all revolving around different states of mind, consciousness, and degrees of absorption. At first glance, these states of mind or practices can seem close to flow:

>> Meditation and mindfulness

>> Yoga flow

>> Trance

>> Reverie, daydreaming, and mind-wandering

>> Sleep and dreaming

I discuss the similarities and differences of all of these practices in detail in Chapter 10 and Bonus Chapter 2, which is found at `www.dummies.com/go/flowfd`. Sometimes, your brain may not even register a real difference between these practices.

WARNING

Sometimes, one practice or mindset simply works for you, while the other just doesn't. You can find flow with many different activities — yoga or meditation, for example — if that particular activity helps you find the ten Flow Elements (which you can read about in Chapter 2). But if you don't feel the Flow Elements with an activity, you likely can't use it to find flow.

On the Cheat Sheet found at `www.dummies.com/go/flowfd` you can find a potential flow activity, and Part 3 offers some specific activities that may appeal to you.

Avoiding Unhealthy Mental Absorption

Some activities nudge your brain into a state of highly absorbing arousal, yet it can disrupt your peace of mind, making finding flow almost impossible:

>> Media flow

>> Rumination (sticky thinking)

>> Obsessive-compulsive disorder (OCD)

>> Alcohol- or drug-induced time-warp

Chapter 9 explains absorbing activities that prevent flow. I call them *mind-hooks*. In Bonus Chapter 2 (`www.dummies.com/go/flowfd`), I show you how to identify unhealthy absorption and how to aim for the real thing.

Differential Diagnostics

Take a look again at the 10 Elements of Flow by Professor Mihaly Csikszentmihalyi covered earlier this chapter in the section "Discovering flow." You'll find that while some of the above activities tick some of the 10 Flow Elements on the list, they don't unite all of them. More differences:

>> **Creative mindset:** One difference between flow and all of the above is the creative mindset that comes with flow — you are creating something. Just like you can create a dance sequence, you can certainly also create a yoga

sequence or a specific meditation routine. This requires
a high level of mastery in these disciplines which most
people never reach. Start with something more tangible.
See Part 3 for ideas of flow activities that may work for you.

>> **Skills-challenge balance:** Just sitting or copying poses is
not going to get your mind to tap into flow. This is where
Flow Element 7 becomes important — the skills-challenge
balance. As we will see in Chapter 7, an important ingredient of flow is mastery and technique. Once you master the
technique of a skill, it's a bit like learning a language (see
Chapter 11). First you learn individual words (poses or
movements in yoga or dance, notes in song and music, and
so on), then you learn to combine them into sequences
(the sun greeting in yoga — the combination of Grade 1 in
the Royal Academy of Ballet system; the tone ladder in
music and song).

>> **No spirituality:** The largest difference between medita-
tion, mindfulness yoga and flow is that there doesn't have
to be any spiritual component in flow at all, no enlightenment path, no greater power. While in flow you can
certainly feel like something has taken you over, or that
you're part of something bigger than you. But what is likely
going on is that the skill you're using is controlled by your
implicit memory systems that we will speak about in
Chapter 7. Your brain is executing automated skills that
you have perfected through technique practice, which now
rewards you with unconstrained, effortless *doing*. This is
part of the action-awareness fusion of flow (see Chapter 2).

>> **Flow is not a basic need:** Clearly, when we sleep, time and
space disappear around us, like when we're in flow.
However, sleeping is a basic need, if we don't, we collapse.
Brief, we cannot function if we don't sleep. Flow is also
healthy — but it's not flow that makes you healthy, but
what it does to your body while you're in flow, getting rid of
stress hormones, for example. Organizing thoughts,
escaping ruminative and other sticky thoughts.

Find out how the brain 'makes' the 10 Flow Elements in
Chapter 2.

Creating a Better Tomorrow

Having a flow practice in place before life gets tough can really benefit you physically and mentally. One of the best gifts that parents can give to their children is introducing them to a flow practice early on. That way, the child has the right habits logged inside their brain to get them to flow when things turn awry.

But it's never too late to start a flow practice. Your brain has *neuroplasticity*, meaning the capacity for building new neural connections, from birth till death.

Building the Right Memories

Developing a flow practice that allows you to stay present has advantages:

Who creates a beautiful present that they like and cherish, later has a beautiful past to look back to. We construct our memories, with every single day of our life. Memories are built via neural connections between cues that reach our eight senses, our feelings, thoughts, insights . . . Memories are stored via electric impulses in a structure called the 'temporal poles' in your brain. — If you touch your temples and let your fingers slide slightly toward the back of the head — that's where they are. And it's where that dance, that surprise, that birthday, that trip to . . . sits for you to revisit that bubble of blissful being.

Unfortunately, your brain has what psychologists call a "negativity bias." You're much better at remembering negative events. It's an evolutionary left-over, a mechanism that ensured that our ancestors would remember negative stuff quickly, and would be very fast to act upon it — for survival. While you cannot override this ancient mechanism, you can make sure, regardless of how tough your life is, that you create many, many fine little memories of feelings of achievement and well-being — now. One way to do this is via a flow practice.

Perhaps right now, the worst that ever happened to you was the death of a pet. But life moves on, and even the most protected individuals will, at some point in their life, face stuff not going the way they want or events traumatizing them. A regular flow practice is part of what makes a person resilient, able to deal with hardship. (See Chapter 2 for more benefits of flow.)

If you're currently in a situation of hardship, Chapters 15 and 16 guide you in developing a flow practice while life is unpredictable or very stressful.

Understanding the Science of Flow

So, what happens in the brain when you're in flow? Science doesn't know for certain. One of the difficulties of studying flow in the lab is flow itself. You can recreate many behaviors in the lab and study them (sleep, yoga, trance, and so on). But for the mind to tap into flow, you must meet a series of prerequisites that researchers struggle to recreate in the lab at the time I'm writing.

You can also find flow's neural patterns in other states of mind, meaning they're not specific to flow. What science knows so far about flow and the brain is that no one system in the brain creates flow. Rather, flow seems to be the result of a careful interplay between processes that you can stoke through your behaviors — which I introduce in Part 2 as the eight Guiding Stars of Flow (as well as the three Gods of Mind-Hooking that you need to avoid).

I use the words *may*, *some*, and *perhaps* quite a lot throughout this book. Scientific findings provide evidence, but humans have to interpret that evidence (and that interpretation isn't always correct). Studying flow scientifically comes with many complexities.

All over the world, researchers are currently designing experimental setups and tasks to get people to feel flow in the lab.

STUDYING FLOW IN THE LAB CAN BE DIFFICULT

Trying to study flow in a scientific lab is like trying to fix a watch with a hammer: it is impossible. We have not yet found the best scientific methods to study flow. For example, some people need a specific ritual that contains familiar cues around them to achieve flow, such as specific smells or sights, such as incense or a *drishti* stone. Or you may need to do particular movements to get yourself into flow, such as the repetitive movements of your arms in a tennis serve, the steps of a dance, or the actions of your fingers on the piano keys. In a lab, you get submerged in completely new cues, and your movements are constrained.

Besides, you can also find it hard to tap into flow while you wear an itchy *electroencephalogram* (EEG) cap (the electrodes attached to the EEG cap provide scientists with information about the distribution and timing of your brain's electrical activity during a task or during flow), or while lying inside the huge tube of a hammering functional Magnetic Resonance Imaging (fMRI) machine (which monitors how and where the blood flow in your brain changes during a task — or during flow).

Because of the difficulty of studying flow in the lab, scientists have invented many different methods to try to investigate flow. These variations have caused a bit of a problem to the field of flow research. In 2022, Clara Alameda and her colleagues from the University of Granada in Spain reviewed 25 studies that used neuro-imaging techniques (such as EEG and fMRI) to study what happens in the brain during flow (including when people did arithmetic tasks, read a novel, walked on a tightrope, or played video games). They found that they couldn't easily identify a true pattern of results because the studies had such diverse methods and variability in the quality of their research designs. These results even included contradictory findings.

So, the evidence that scientists have about flow and the brain is, in fact, somewhat mixed. Hopefully you can use this book as a bit of a guide to help you navigate this evidence and find your flow.

Chapter **2**

What Makes Flow *Flow?*

You can easily escape a tough life by going clubbing, spending time on social media, or drinking alcohol. You can find many things that absorb your attention, many of which feel very good. Besides, for most people, flow is something that mostly happens by chance, not something that you can experience whenever you want to. The long of the short is that not all forms of absorption are linked to the amazing physical and mental health benefits that studies have shown flow to provide. Why does flow feel the way it does and have all these benefits? What's going on in your brain when you're in the state of flow, and how can you recognize it? And can you really reach true flow whenever you want to?

In this chapter, you'll discover the ten core elements of flow that will allow you to craft a flow tool for your daily life. I suspect that I'll have to convince you of the utility of such a tool. That's why I'll also show you what happens in the brain that powers those elements. Finally, you can trace echoes from the past — how archaeologists have uncovered the practices of our long-gone ancestors that tell us ancient tales of flow from the dawn of human civilization.

Finding the Value of Flow

The study of *flow* is still a young field in science, but the first evidence makes a good case for its benefits. When you attain flow, you become more productive, reach your full capacity, concentrate intensely, expand your creativity, and become more efficient.

You also improve your skill (because you repeat the actions of your skill, build routines and stamina, thus honing your abilities; see Chapter 6); feel intrinsically motivated (because you stoke your imagination and aesthetic emotions, as discussed in Chapter 8); maintain self-control (because you stay clear of *mind-hooks*, meaning the wrong states of absorption, which you can read about in Chapter 9 and Bonus Chapter 2 (`www.dummies.com/go/flowfd`); and boost your mood (because you activate restorative processes in your brain and body, and stoke feelings of achievement and self-confidence, discussed in Chapters 4 and 16).

TIP

You can also see social benefits if you seek flow: You can connect with a community and combat feelings of loneliness. If you enjoy baking, threading pearls on a string, organizing spreadsheets, knitting, or painting, you may be surprised by how many others enjoy the same thing, who are looking for someone like you to hang with. After you engage in an activity that really works for you, doors to secret worlds start opening. Like Harry Potter, you'll suddenly know which stones to tap in the train station to pass into that parallel world and find your crowd. See Chapter 6 for more about how the social systems of your brain affect flow.

The Ten Elements of Flow

Mihaly Csikszentmihalyi (1934–2021), a Hungarian-American psychologist, coined the term *flow* to describe the state of complete absorption and enjoyment that leads to peak performance and fulfillment. To understand more about what incredible magic happens in our body and brain when we're in flow, the following sections outline the ten Elements of Flow that describe perfectly what it *feels like* to be in flow. Csikszentmihalyi assembled these elements from the evidence of decades of psychological experiments and surveys. The following sections take a look at these elements through the lens of modern neuroscience.

As your read through the neuroscience behind the ten Elements of Flow, you can see that your brain is doing *a lot* all at the same time when you're in flow. I suspect that you'll also start feeling that you really want this state, but don't know how to get there. Don't worry, that's what Chapters 6 to 8 will be about. Here, we're looking at what it feels like to be in flow, so we know what we're aiming for, and why.

Flow Element 1: Getting completely absorbed in the activity

You're working on that mandala, Excel spreadsheet, or formula, and you don't hear the doorbell ring. You don't smell the pizza is turning to carbon in the oven, nor sense that your partner is staring at you for a response. You're in your own world. Scientists call this state *sensory decoupling.* Sensory decoupling is part of the flow state (and other absorption states), and it happens when your brain creates an internal shield from the outside world and attends very closely to one thing. Your brain deems as irrelevant all other information that your senses provide it with from your physical environment.

When you're not in a state of sensory decoupling, whenever a loud sound, light, or other cue to your senses occurs, your brain's regular activity on an *electroencephalograph* (EEG; a device that looks like a swimming cap and has electrodes embedded. Scientists use it to measure the brain's electrical activity) shows a spike. Neuroscientists call this spike the *N100* because it happens roughly 100 milliseconds after the onset of unexpected cues — which occurs *before* we're consciously aware of the cue, reflecting how fast our brain's sensory and attentional processing is, and how much about it remains outside of our awareness. However, in a state of sensory decoupling, you have a much lower N100 spike. Sensory decoupling helps you focus your attention to the exclusion of the world around you. You're absorbed into your bubble of bliss.

You can increase your chances of sensory decoupling by using techniques that block your senses while you seek flow. For example, when you try to concentrate:

>> Face in a direction that doesn't contain cues that you know can distract you (such as e-mails, social media, colleagues, family, to do lists, or foot items).

>> Wear a hat that has a brim to block visual information.

>> Wear headphones and use specific frequencies for your ears (*white noise* to block high-frequency distractions like traffic, *pink noise* to achieve a soothing consistent background, or *brown noise* for concentration and for blocking low-frequency sounds — google examples and see what works best for you).

>> Make sure that you feel neither too cold nor too hot, and wear clothes so comfortable that you hardly notice them to prevent your skin receptors from sending signals to your brain, distracting it.

>> Quash thirst and hunger; otherwise, your *interoceptive sense* (the sense of your body from within) will let you know and interfere with your focus.

>> Avoid strong, delicious, and disgusting smells. Your brain is hard-wired to respond to them, breaking your absorption.

Flow Element 2: Having clear goals about what you want to achieve

When you flow, you have the feeling of acting with intention. You know what you're doing and why.

You don't see the goal of what you're doing as the final outcome (the grand novel, the closed deal, the best choreography, the end of the list of e-mails, the final proof, the full dataset, the award-winning performance). You do have an ultimate goal, of course, but you don't get ahead of yourself.

When you're in this goal-directed action, the associative systems in your brain start conspiring to let you tap into flow. These systems span the cerebral cortex and connect with many deep structures, such as your memory systems and your sense of self. You start tapping into your intuitive systems for creation. You may have a final working goal hovering before your inner eye, which could be something like, for example:

>> Playing a particular song

>> Threading beads to make a bracelet

>> Writing 400 words for your novel

>> Finishing ten e-mails

>> Writing justification for the purchase of an item (*not* the final event that you need the item for!)

The immediate goals within the activity become literally the next step in front of you:

>> The current bar in the song

>> The current sentence that you're writing

>> The current stitch in the embroidery

>> The current step in the choreography

TIP

So, where do you put your focus while you set your intention? Use your imagination — check out Chapter 8 to see why this approach works. Briefly, imagine this: You're just the messenger. You're working *for* the product that you're currently creating, to improve it, to make it wonderful, you're helping it. The famous Italian master Michelangelo once said, "I saw the angel in the marble and carved until I set him free."

Help your creation into this world, so that it can take flight. You're its guide. Build a relationship with it, like with a lover or a friend. You two are a unit, and you're collaborating on getting it out into the world. This mindset can allow you to identify the small, immediate goals that you need to aim for.

Flow Element 3: Receiving reliable feedback about how it's going

When we're in flow, we have clear *learning signals* (these rewarding feelings of 'cha-ching — I did it') that ping our reward system when a move, stitch or other little next move works out. *Dopamine,* a neurotransmitter that is out and about in our brain, acts as a learning signal for our brain that encodes the link between a cue and a reward, making sure you go back there and do the same move *like that* again, to get another hit of the dopamine kick. As your brain threads together all those little wins and feeds them into your memory systems (aka "learning"), this also hold your attention throughout a task.

For Flow Element 2 to work, you need to have a clear intention (see the preceding section) and don't get ahead of yourself. (Don't worry, we'll see more about how to do that in Chapter 8!)

The reliable feedback comes from the action itself, to your brain. It's none of the following (which may never happen anyway): praise of others, the look of the final product, the final full piano album that will beat Lang Lang in the charts, your boss making you employee of the month, your opera performance at La Scala. So, the reliable feedback is never the final, glorious product, it's not applause nor praise from others, and it's never the final, sharable selfie. Reliable feedback happens when your senses perceive the immediate effect of your actions, *while you do them,* and your brain realizes that what you're doing is right (or not), so you either adjust your next move or keep evolving.

Use the feedback from your senses purposefully. You have eight senses, so you have plenty of sources across your body for reliable sensory feedback:

>> **Sight:** You see that the stitch you're making on the item looks right, and you continue to the next stitch. If you're a sighted individual, you probably rely hugely on your sense of vision for reliable immediate feedback on what you're doing. You can train your vision to detect subtle differences in surfaces, colors, textures, and so on, so that your sight gives you reliable feedback on how your task is going.

>> **Hearing:** You hear the note that you just struck, and a good feeling engulfs you briefly; you sense your voice hit the tone that you want it to, and you continue up the scale. People can tune their ears to look out for the subtlest of changes in the sounds of the activity that they're engrossed in.

>> **Touch:** The dough you're kneading feels right to your fingers, and with every knead, it's changing; the clay under your fingers changes shape at every move on the potter's wheel. The same goes for sand castles, silk paper flowers, etc.

>> **Taste:** Your sense of taste tells you whether you're mixing ingredients of teas, dishes, sauces, or drinks in the right direction. For example, some tea sommelier hobbyists find flow in their morning rituals, training their sense of taste to detect the tiniest of nuances when they mix the herbs from their balcony herb garden.

>> **Smell:** While you arrange dried flowers into a potpourri, you notice the change of scent in the air. You work on the composition, perhaps adding some drops of essential oils that fit the colors and the textures of the potpourri elements. Many jobs and hobbies require people to use their sense of smell to figure out whether they're getting the results they want, such as florists and odor judges that test fragrances or hygiene articles — not just cooks, perfumiers, and wine sommeliers!

>> **Interoception:** The sense of your body from within; your heartbeat, hunger, chill, warmth, emotions, and so on. It's the sensation that bubbles up to your conscious mind while you re-read your latest sentence that tells you it feels right — that it properly conveys your story character's emotion. Or, it's the sensation of reading a text and understanding what's going on. People vary hugely in how attuned they are to their interoception. Some people rely heavily on that internal compass, others never feel their body from within. It's totally fine — use what works for you.

>> **Exteroception:** The sense of your body in space. Where are you? In a large room? A small one? High up? Underground? Your dance routine is going well — you're facing the correct direction in the choreography — How does your body tell you that? Via *exteroceptors,* specialized nerve endings located close to the surface throughout your body, in your eyes, nose, mouth, skin, and ears. They help your brain map and understand the world that surrounds you.

>> **Proprioception:** Your sense of your limbs and movements with regards to each other. It tells you that you did your swing-dance turn just the way you wanted, or that you're

finding the right grips in the bouldering gym, and so on. You have *proprioceptors* — special nerves that give you a sense of your body's positioning — scattered throughout your body, in muscles, joints, tendons, ligaments, and skin. They're a type of *mechanoreceptor,* nerves that tell you about the mechanics of your body, integrating it all into a sense of your body's position and movements of your limbs.

Focus on figuring out how to detect those little wins whispered to you via your senses — and lean into them. Trust them for the reliable feedback communication that they provide. I feel them in my chest, bubbling up via my interoception, while my body tells me, "Okay, this works." For example, while I write these lines, I focus my mind's eye only on the next couple of words, while the general goal of the section hovers somewhere at the back of my mind. I aim for it without trying to grasp onto it. When my hands get tired from typing, I go back and read the paragraph, listening to how the sentences sound inside my head, whether my inner voice keeps stumbling over a word. If so, I edit. Then, I continue. If I have a stale feeling about a sentence, I delete it and try again. It's like leveling out the walls of a clay vase that you're turning between your hands on a potter's wheel. Just let it roll on and on, until you feel that it all has the right shape. The repetitiveness of your movements while you perform your task also helps your brain tap into flow (which I talk about in the sections about Flow Elements 4 and 8).

Flow Element 4: Feeling a transformation of time (time zips by or slows down)

Flow makes the clock speed up or slow down. Actually, what really happens is that your brain plays a funny game when you're fully engrossed in something — and it's all because of dopamine again. Your brain has some expectations about how often it gets a dopamine shower (basically, each time stuff that you do works out for you — a bit like what we saw earlier this chapter, in Flow Element 3). And during flow (and other states of absorption, such as scrolling on social media), it gets loads of dopamine, which messes with your internal clock. Your brain suddenly gets more hits of dopamine, which gives it the impression that time has sped up.

Repetitive movements help you enter this meditative space. It comes naturally to people who have a routine or a ritual that gives them flow. Starting from when you brush your teeth in the morning, to the movements of your craft, to driving your car, editing your spreadsheet — these movements on repeat can all act as washing machines for your mind, cleaning it up for creative flow, and in so doing, they are also speeding up the inner clock so that time seems to fly.

Flow Element 5: Doing what you do for intrinsic rewards

When you choose the activity that you want to use for flow, make sure that you get something *personally* from it, that you can find something in it that satisfies *you*. If you can't immediately see what about an activity qualifies, perhaps modify the activity until you feel joy in doing it.

Psychologists call this personal attachment the *self-relevance* of an activity. When you do something that's self-relevant, systems of your brain activate that sit deep down toward the limbic system in your brain, which plays an important role in affective processing, so, in your emotions and in remembering what gave you these emotions. When you have this attachment to an activity, *doing* that activity now reaches into your sense of self, your emotions and personal memories — and conspires with your brain's reward systems.

Add colors, sounds, movements, or other cues that you *like to* what you're doing. Don't shy away from using a golden keyboard to type or pink gloves while you write. Whatever works.

By making sure you *like* it, you generate intrinsic motivation, simply because it connects the reward with what makes you, *you*. You can find out more about the different parts of the reward systems and why stimulating those shared pathways with our sense of self provide an important Element of Flow in Chapter 4.

Some science suggests that people who do things for the enjoyment of the activity itself have better mental health, better moods, and are often quicker in mastering the activity.

Flow Element 6: Feeling effortlessness in what you're doing

Why do some tasks feel like such a drag, while you perform others completely effortlessly? The reason why we feel so effort-less when we're in flow feels seems to be that the activation patterns in your brain change in three surprising ways. When you're in flow:

>> **Your brain's reward system is very active.** Dopamine and norepinephrine are neurotransmitters that make your brain sharpen its focus on the current task. Nothing escapes you, and when you can act optimally, things get easy.

>> **Self-referential thinking decreases.** You stop thinking about yourself, your personal memories and to-do's. Systems in your brain that you use for self-referential thinking deactivate when you experience flow, as when you read a book you love.

REMEMBER

Normally, self-referential thinking is a good thing because it makes you aware of your position in the world. In some mental health conditions, people can't quite place them-selves in the world; they feel that they don't belong. But during flow, this losing yourself a little frees you from the bounds of existence — no wonder things feel lighter!

>> **Self-conscious emotions dissipate.** When you tap into flow, you stop feeling embarrassed. Humans are very social creatures. You're hard-wired to fit in and conform. Neurological systems around the *insula,* a neural structure toward the middle of your brain, take care of social emotions. If you do something that others consider a little strange, these systems in your brain shriek "Danger!" and your mind gets very distracted. When you're in flow, the activity in those systems lessens, and your self-consciousness dissipates.

Flow Element 7: Finding the balance where it's neither too easy nor too hard

Do you know this feeling when you are doing a task and the challenge of the task and your skill-level are perfectly matched? This delightful hovering in-between neither-too-easy-nor-too-difficult keeps our attention engaged, our motivation fueled and gives us loads of feelings of accomplishment.

A good flow activity creates the opportunity to never really be done learning it perfectly. It will always offer you a new challenge. In this situation, your brain's *neuroplasticity* (its ability to form new connections) is constantly being stimulated. You keep learning — and that means more dopamine showers, more reward. Our brain simply loves to be kept moving, challenged, expanding.

People may ask you, "Don't you already know how to do that?" or "Aren't you soon done with learning all the steps?". However, here's the secret: for flow, you actually never *want* to be done. You *want* to be able to keep finding new challenges, new things to learn — this can also help you focus on the here and now.

For example, say that you're in the standing warrior yoga pose. You're not just statically standing there. Although you look very still from the outside, you let your inner eye run through your body, making micro-adjustments while you go (looking for these little wins, bubbling up via your proprioception and interoception, discussed in the section "Flow Element 3: Receiving reliable feedback about how it's going," earlier in this chapter). Let your breath help you; keep breathing. (Hello, interoception — am I holding my breath?) Your inner eye can start evaluating at your feet and make its way up:

>> What's the pressure of your heel and toes on the ground, and is that pressure evenly distributed? (Hello, proprioception — do I have pains or stretches down there at the foot?)

>> Are you slumping inward onto the inner side of your feet? Start correcting that, little by little.

>> Is your knee aligned between your upper and lower thighs?

>> In what direction are your hips with regards to space? (Hello, exteroception — am I aligned with the wall?)

Here are two important aspects of finding a flow activity:

>> **Find a task that's just right.** To be able to tap into flow, don't choose a task that's too easy, nor one that's too difficult. If you feel bored, you'll tire and disengage; and if you feel out of your depths, you'll get anxious and your mind will jump around like a rabbit. Both states are useless for tapping into flow.

>> **Keep challenging yourself.** With some tasks, you plateau at some point. If you know that you'll likely plateau in the activity you do, find ways to add layers of complexity to it so that you can help your brain find challenge with it.

Whatever activity you flow in, keep a skills-challenge balance so that you're feeding your brain's neuroplasticity — constantly. Give your brain opportunities to grow, literally.

TIP

Dancers know this inner work well, as do singers, actors, and musicians. Perhaps ask one of them why they'll never know it all for their craft, why they can always find a new challenge — how do they do that? How do they deal with never being done learning something?

While you focus on these little successes, speeding up your inner clock so that it feels like time flies, looking for new challenges also keeps you humble (and this helps with loosing yourself in the activity a little, as mentioned earlier, in "Flow Element 6: Feeling effortlessness in what you're doing"). It doesn't matter whether you're drawing, painting, doing pottery work, writing, calculating, solving formulas, or coding; you can always find technical aspects that you can work on to correct your movements or to take what you make to the next level.

WARNING

Challenge yourself within the activity without becoming competitive or needing to prove something to anyone. See Chapter 9 for more about how to avoid the *mind-hook competitiveness*, a mental state that metaphorically hooks you to the ground and prevents you from flow.

Flow isn't only for drummers and poets. Whatever your task, achieving flow carries myriad benefits and you can tap into it by making sure you stoke the skills-challenge balance. For example:

>> **Working in spreadsheets:** Challenge yourself tirelessly to find ways to make them more ergonomic, faster to parse, more aesthetic to look at, and so on. Challenge yourself to design a spreadsheet so that you or anyone using this spreadsheet doesn't feel any negative emotion. Only positivity allowed — how can you achieve that? Focus on answering that question.

>> **Managing processes:** Get creative and optimize your processes; make them understandable and digestible for anyone who needs to go through them. Make it your duty to design your processes so that people emerge from them quickly and easily. Don't let users get stuck — that's your challenge. Perhaps you need to do some user-experience experiments for that? Well, off you go.

Flow Element 8: Experiencing a fusion of actions and awareness

Have you ever felt like you *are* the movement when you're in flow? If you haven't, get ready for it. It's wonderful. Two mechanisms in our brain are responsible for this feeling — the perception-action loop and brain network synchrony.

The perception-action loop

Normally, your brain perceives the chance for an action and then follows the action, a process called the *perception-action loop.* Our senses help our brain update our actions all the time. A gap exists between the cue that signals the action opportunity and the action itself. It's not a very large gap, of course, otherwise everyone would move around like they're in a stop-and-go movie. The gap is in the milliseconds range, and our actions are (mostly) fluid. However, when in flow, this gap gets even smaller or disappears entirely. So, your brain perfectly strings together perception and action when you're in flow.

To help shorten this gap, you have at least two tools at your disposal:

>> **Create the movement habits of your craft in your brain.** I talk about *habit loops,* which are very helpful for automating actions, in Chapter 5. In Chapters 6 and 7, you can find discussion about the science behind how routine and technique practice can help you create the right habit loops that can shrink the perception-action gap. In Bonus Chapter 1, you can explore the cues that help you achieve this.

>> **Use your imagination.** The imagination is a collaboration between large-scale brain networks spanning your motor, memory, and perceptual systems, and your sense of self. The imagination helps you string together the actions of your craft better than any verbal or written instruction ever could, reducing the gap between perception of the instruction and the action that you take on your product or activity. See Chapter 8, where I explain the neuroscience of the imagination.

Brain network synchrony

When in flow, large brain networks synchronize; or the synchronization of these systems makes us tap into flow. Scientists aren't quite sure which leads to the other.

It seems that synchrony happens when cognitive control systems, including also the systems that control our attention and our movements, connect with the deep reward systems. The synchronization of the electric energy of the brain across these systems is thought to make skills and information more easily accessible. And this may help our brain tap into flow.

The brain gets 'things in order' so that it can be more efficient. Think of when you want to make a cake. You need various ingredients, so you put everything out on the kitchen table in front of you before you start. You don't have to stop mixing ingredients to go search the cupboards and drawers for the next item in the recipe. When you're doing your flow-activity, your brain quickly activates the connections to the different skills that it knows it needs for the task and gets them all ticking to the same beat. Much more efficient, if they all coordinate.

Without knowing anything about the brain, our ancestors intuitively used two tools to make their brain synchronize networks, and you can use these tools, too:

>> **Rhythm:** From the moment that you're born, your brain synchronizes to external beats. You're hardwired to bob along to rhythms. Rhythm has a coordinating, synchronizing effect on your brain and body that you can use. Rhythm can become a flow trigger because of its repetitiveness and its synchronization effect on the brain, whether your flow activity is dancing to music, or listening to music while you write, clean, create spreadsheets, and so on. See Chapters 6 and 7 for more information on the effect of routines and rhythms on your brain.

>> **Social connection:** For some activities, moving in synchrony with others or attending to the same thing as others (to a piece of music, a director, a movie, etc.) in the same room makes your heart rates and other physiological rhythms synchronize. This synchronization happens naturally in a dance, music, or signing context. However, any creative activities that you can practice socially can eventually help you synchronize your brain's systems if you make sure to attend to the same thing as a group (look at, listen to the same thing). You can find more on the effect of social connection in Chapter 6.

Flow Element 9: Losing ruminative thought loops

Rumination is the incessant spiraling of thoughts about negative things that have already happened. In contrast, *worrying* is the incessant thinking about what might happen. Rumination often focuses on the past, while worrying focuses on the future. And neither is in an individual's control and both of them are poison for flow. (See the following section for discussion of worrying.)

Ruminating takes the form of thoughts like, "If only I hadn't done that" or "Why did I say that?" You may mentally replay silly but negative experiences from the past, such as unpleasant interactions or embarrassing mistakes. The most common triggers for this carousel of thoughts are other people. According to some studies, 38 percent of people ruminate daily and 26 percent ruminate several days a week; and 50 percent of people who ruminate do it for more than 20 minutes each time that they do.

When you ruminate, you prompt a hyperactivation of the systems that deal with self-referential thinking and your memory systems, especially of negative memories. Therefore, rumination is a very absorbing state of mind — just not a very healthy one.

How does flow help to remove ruminative thought loops? Flow instead pulls you into the present by filling the reward system with sweet dopamine hits that give you feelings of joy, satisfaction, and accomplishment. Flow also deactivates those self-referential systems (which you can read about in the section "Flow Element 6: Feeling effortlessness in what you're doing," earlier in this chapter).

Flow tasks distract your mind from the gloom, especially if you make sure that your flow activity includes as many senses as possible. You can use *flow triggers,* meaning cues that you associate with the feeling of being in flow, so that, when you see them again, they remind your mind of the feeling and open the gates to feel it again — see Chapter 10 and Bonus Chapter 1 for suggestions.

Flow Element 10: Feeling in control and escape the unpredictability of life

Uncertainty makes people worry — some people more than others. The eerie unpredictability of life can get to everyone. Worrying about stuff can drain your last energy reserves (a very human reaction).

In a community survey among 2,136 people, Dr. Jeannette Golden from St Patrick's Hospital in Dublin, Ireland, found that 79 percent of the people worried regularly (only 21 percent hardly ever did!), 37 percent worried excessively, 20 percent worried in an excessive, uncontrollable way, and 6.3 percent met the criteria for a diagnosis for generalized anxiety disorder (GAD).

Worrying is one of the diagnostic symptoms of GAD, but that's a separate beast. If you suspect that you're among the 6.3 percent of excessive GAD-level worriers, please see your medical provider for a referral to a psychological professional.

In Dr. Golden's study, leaving out the 6.3 percent who had GAD, the more people worried, the more they were also likely to have depressed moods. Clinical psychologists call the mechanism by which this happens *learned helplessness.* Through years and years of trying to control worries by flexing their mental biceps alone (and never succeeding), these people's brains have learned that they are never going to make it — they have *learned* that they are helpless. Of course, they are not helpless, it is just their brain giving them this wrong impression. But the more you try to control stuff in your head, the more helpless you feel. Worries focus on the future; and the future is, by design, unreachable *now.*

Dr. Golden also found that men worry less than women. (Gentlemen: This is your chance to support your ladies! Go for some flow together. Remove the unpredictability.) And according to the study, worrying declines with age.

Lucas S. LaFreniere and Michelle G. Newman, psychology professors from Pennsylvania State University, asked a group of participants to track their worries and to check whether those worries came true. Based on this study, 91.4 percent of worries didn't come true. So, you have good reasons not to worry. However, few people can successfully not think about what worries them (which I talk about in the sidebar "Why you can't just decide to stop thinking," in this chapter).

Using flow to combat worries is a very human thing, and some anthropological and psychological research suggests that humans have always used flow to deal with an uncertain world. Why does that work? Well, our brain is a prediction engine. It likes what it knows. It has observed how the world, and the people in it, generally behave. Small stuff that happens (or doesn't happen) around us can make us worry: You feel quite certain that if you press the button on the light switch, the light will go on. If it doesn't, things didn't go to plan.

This not-going-to-plan situation sets your brain on edge, especially if you have many of these incidents around you — and perhaps not all of them are so unimportant like a light switch that doesn't work. More complex expectations about social behaviors can also be a source of worries. If you wave at someone, you expect them to wave back; if they don't, you may start worrying why they didn't. These 'not-going-to-plan-moments' are called *expectation violations.* When in flow, things *do* work out — as a result, we feel in control. Worries subside.

Social media can present you with a type of expectation violation like someone not waving back at you, but on steroids. Rejection, ghosting, not receiving likes, contact requests and comments on social media can make you worry big time. Step away from social media, or you'll never find flow. (And, no, scrolling doesn't count as a type of healthy flow; check out Bonus Chapter 2 and `www.dummies.com/go/flowfd` and Chapter 9 in the book.)

You can combat worries by doing something, which returns agency and a feeling of being in control to your brain. The control doesn't necessarily have to relate to the thing that you're worrying about (that's often not possible, anyway). However, just making that orchestra of neurons in your brain jam in perfect predictability calms your nervous system and nudges your mind back from the edge. To combat the expectation violations around you for a little while, knit that scarf, dance that dance, bake a cake, edit that spreadsheet, build that bridge on the model train track, or sing that song.

Repetitive movements, including doing creative activities that you know and love, return the feeling of predictability to your brain. Play a drum rhythm on your table or a real drum. This borrowed predictability can soothe worries. See Chapter 6 for more information about how you can borrow predictability for your brain.

Try to create moments in your day in which you don't just react to what happens to you, such as when you respond to e-mails or clean up the dishes. When you're reacting to demands — whether from your environment, other people, or a specific situation in front of you — the situation dictates most of your actions, so you're not in control.

If you don't yet know of anything in your life that can combat the effects of uncertainty on your brain, I have two tips for you:

>> **Write.** Perhaps decide to do 20 minutes of expressive writing two to three times per week (see Chapter 14). Professors James Pennebaker and Joshua M. Smyth give a wonderful overview of how to best take up expressive writing in their book *Opening Up by Writing it Down* (Guilford Press). The repetitiveness of the act of writing can act as a pacifier for your brain. Along with the ritual of the writing itself, you can combat uncertainty before you know it — and off you go, flow. See more about the effects of movements, rituals, and routines in Part 2 of this book.

>> **Get aesthetic.** Aim to give your mind *aesthetic emotions* (what you feel while evaluating a cue, such as awe at a masterful painting, feeling moved by a piece of music, admiring the beauty of a mountainscape, and so on; see Chapter 8). You probably know the feeling of walking out of the cinema and suddenly feeling different. The aesthetic experience of watching a movie that impacted you allows you to see your life in a new light. Psychologists refer to these experiences as *self-transformational.* Aesthetic emotions are part of that experience and have the power to crack open unexpected doors within you, and within these snaps of light, you might discover ways to change your life so that you feel more in control.

WHY YOU CAN'T DECIDE TO JUST STOP THINKING

Ruminative thoughts (discussed in the section "Flow Element 9: Losing ruminative thought loops," in this chapter) and worries (see the section "Flow Element 10: Feeling in control and escape the unpredictability of life," in this chapter) act as some of the chief culprits for lack of flow in a person's life. They simply can occupy too much of your mind space to let your creative soul take flight. It sounds so easy to just let flow guide you so that you can find your stability that get optimal performance in life and business.

(continued)

(continued)

Flow has this power and potential, for sure; however, you can't find focus by trying to follow the well-meaning advice "Just stop thinking about it." This inability has a fascinating neuroscientific reason.

When you actively try to not think about something, one part of your brain needs to keep reminding another part of your brain (where you store what you're supposed to stop thinking about) that it has to stop thinking about that thing. This constant reminder causes the thing to be thrown in and out of your awareness, so it's always somewhere on your mind.

Let me give you some science about why this happens. Fascinating research conducted by psychology professor Daniel Wegener and others during the 20th century showed that the more they insisted research participants should stop thinking about something, the more that something kept catapulting in and out of their awareness — even after the experiments had ended.

From a neuroscientific perspective, if you could simply tell your brain to stop thinking about something or tell it to empty itself like pulling the plug from a bathtub, it would be dangerous. Your brain is (and has to be) always *on*. You need many of the systems of your brain to keep you alive. And remembering forbidden things is part of that self-protection. The rule-based systems of our brain keeps the information active in the memory systems, while the impulse control systems wag an index finger to remind you that you shouldn't think about this information.

Also, the human brain reacts with magnetic interest to things that are forbidden, a basic form of reinforcement learning (as when behaviors are shaped by their consequences). If you can't have something, that something becomes very attractive to your mind — you remember it more than you would if you hadn't tagged it as forbidden. This just means that your brain works the way it should.

In order to effectively get something off your mind, use your body to play your *body orchestra* (all the interactions between body and brain that we will cover in Chapter 4) or trick it into playing a different movie in your head by changing what you're currently doing. Parts 2 and 3 of this book can help you develop your flow practice so that you can change the way you *feel* (flow!) by what you *do*.

A Brief History of Flow

Many thinkers before psychologist Mihaly Csikszentmihalyi (discussed in the section "The Ten Elements of Flow," earlier in this chapter) have contemplated this strange state of flow, sometimes under different names. From their different perspectives (artistic, psychological, and philosophical), they all agree that humans need this state of mind to disconnect from a tough life, boost their mood, health, motivation, sociality . . .

For example, William James (1842–1910), known as the father of psychology, called flow *altered states of consciousness* in which we're entirely immersed, effortlessly focused, and feeling delightfully connected. The Renaissance painter Albrecht Dürer was described as someone who could be immersed in the most pleasant reverie — which was a catalyst for his creativity. The philosopher and writer Friedrich Nietzsche (1840–1900) was convinced that to be truly fulfilled, we all need to lose ourselves in our favorite activity regularly. And Abraham Maslow (a psychologist from the mid-1900s), who proposed the *hierarchy of needs* (the idea that our motivation is determined by which of our needs are fulfilled — only basic needs, or also self-realization needs), called flow *peak experience*, a state of mind that makes you feel connected, awed, expanded, euphoric, and whole.

Stepping back in time

In 1930, at the Yuzhniy Oleniy Ostrov burial site in Russia, 200 kilometers (about 124 miles) from the Finnish border, a large team of archaeologists found the remains of about 177 prehistoric individuals. Over and over again, they found rows and rows of elk teeth, neatly aligned, as if on a string. The leather strings had long disintegrated, but bits of garments remained beneath the elk teeth. The archaeologists at the time couldn't make sense of what they were looking at and the evidence lay dormant in archives for decades.

Almost 100 years later, the archaeologist Dr. Riitta Rainio collaborated with the artist Juha Valkeapää to return some life to these mysterious garments. Likely these two felt some flow together while they created these garments as authentically as possible, in the same way that those individuals living at the end of the last Ice Age in Russia probably did.

The modern examiners couldn't easily understand how the prehistoric people used the elk teeth — what archaeologists call *use-wear*. When archaeologists perform *traceology* (the science of examining in the traces from the past that are left on objects from using them), they usually find that everyday objects have cuts, scratches and little chipped edges. Not so for these mysterious teeth; they had regular, neatly distributed traces across them. No matter what the archaeologists did, they couldn't reproduce this pattern with modern elk teeth, even when they sewed them onto a shirt and moved around with them.

Finding a movement match

After creating these elk-tooth garments (see the preceding section), the examiners noticed the sound that the teeth made when scraping against each other during a movement. They started moving rhythmically, and the elk teeth created a soothing jangle sound.

You can watch a video of Juha Valkeapää and Dr. Riitta Rainio on YouTube performing a dance, dressed in garments that have rows of elk teeth sewn onto them.

What the interdisciplinary team discovered, after hours of rhythmic dancing, was that the modern elk teeth now showed very similar use-wear to the original artifacts. The prehistoric people had been dancing! Those mysterious traces on the artifact elk teeth in all likelihood occurred because of grinding, scraping, and rattling together while the person wearing the garment danced.

The only difference was that the scratches on the old teeth were much deeper than those found on the modern recreation, which suggests that the prehistoric garment-wearers performed the motions that the modern team did for much longer — they must have danced for many hours to achieve such deep scratches in the teeth (or they had many dance sessions through the years).

Figuring out why they might dance

So, why would prehistoric people spend their hard-earned calories on dancing and also put themselves at risk? When you dance, you burn between 4 and 11 calories per minute, depending on the dance style, and your heart rate goes up over 140 beats per minute (BPM) — it's an aerobic exercise. Also, if you dance around and make noise while doing so, predators and enemies can spot you incredibly easily.

An important additional experience that the researchers took from this Stone Age rattle was how absolutely mesmerizing and trance-inducing they found listening to this sound. Researchers experienced the feeling, whether they were watching and listening to the dance or actually doing it. But they reported an amplified feeling if they were doing the movements themselves. The elk-teeth could provide cues to eyes, ears, and the sense of touch to push the dancers' minds off into flow.

Likely, without being aware of it, prehistoric humans used these elk-teeth on strings to help rid themselves of the stress hormones of an uncertain life. Long before neuroscience would tell humanity that flow can make you healthier, prehistoric humanity already knew.

Identifying Flow Triggers

Modern people can only speculate what human ancestors did and why. However, the cues that they left can help you on your quest to flow. From what you can see in the archaeological record, our ancestors probably used flow triggers such as sounds from elk teeth jangling together and rhythmic movements. Many spiritual and religious practices today, in fact, have elements of a flow practice that you can borrow from.

For example, consider creating an altar for your flow practice more about flow altars in Chapter 10, a place where you always return to perform the repetitive movements of your task, improve your technique with a ritualistic routine (good for the 10 Flow Elements, especially for the one discussed in the section "Flow Element 7: Finding the balance where it's neither too easy nor too hard," earlier in this chapter). Instrumentalize your senses! Use your senses like a tool to create associations between a sensory cue and the flow feeling. For example, always use the same:

- >> **Colors:** Golden laptop, silver beads, pink scarf, blue wool.

- >> **Sounds:** For example, rhythmic drums or white noise.

- >> **Tactile sensations:** Wear a certain type of clothes, touch specific objects, and so on.

- >> **Smells:** Incense, perfume, fresh air, or whatever scent you love and want to make part of your flow ritual.

- >> **Tastes:** Always drink a certain tea or coffee; eat a certain type of food only while going for flow. Or a specific type of candy — liquorice?

- >> **Movements:** *Proprioception,* repetitive or elegant movements can help you create a freer mind and doing those movements will remind your mind of that *free*dom.

- >> **Time and place:** Performing your task at the same time each day so that your body feels the same (*interoception,* meaning the sense of your body from within), and the same place so that you perceive a familiar location (*exteroception,* which is the sense of space).

TIP

Modern neuroscience has shown that if you repeatedly pair sensory cues with the activity that gives you flow, then your brain associates the cue and the flow. Psychologists call this process *associative learning.* After you develop this association, the cues can help you tap into flow. I talk much more about how to craft these associations in Chapters 5 and 6.

Likely these activities had a meaning to our ancestors beyond the functional because we find them in all cultures, all over the world and in all human societies. Attaining a trance-like flow state could serve a spiritual objective. But it's also possible that our ancestors sought flow from these activities, whether they knew it consciously or not. They recognized how flow activities had an organizing effect (like a type of meditation) on individuals and the group, so they sought these states on purpose (you can find more information about the social effects of group flow in Chapter 6).

Chapter 3

Getting to Know Your Flow Potential

Choosing the right settings for your flow begins with taking time to reflect on yourself and your life. What are your daily routines? Who's important in your life? Do you like being around people, or are you an introvert? What do you like to do? Ask yourself, if you were a character in a novel, how would a reader describe you? What are your flaws? What's your defining experiences — positive or negative — that still shape your motivations today? Building awareness of who you are and what motivates you doesn't just provide a good exercise in self-reflection; it can also help you build your pathway to flow so that you can plant cues that you like along that path.

This chapter examines what makes certain people flow-prone and what doesn't. One of the aspects of flow-proneness that I discuss is how certain personality traits may make finding flow harder, and how other personality traits can make it so much easier.

At www.dummies/flow, you can also find a validated personality questionnaire that can guide you in understanding more about your flow potential — how easy or hard you may find tapping into flow right now, considering your personality. You'll also see a *flow-proneness* questionnaire that can give you further guidance on your pathway to flow.

Why Flow Comes Easier to Some

Flow-proneness is a thing — flow simply comes more easily to some people than to others. But being prone to flow doesn't make you smarter or more talented. Instead, it often comes down to a mix of personality, habits, and the way each person's brain is wired. Some people are naturally more flow-prone; others need to be more intentional about creating the right conditions to flow.

In the following sections, you can look at various factors that contribute to flow-proneness.

Dopamine: Your brain's motivational tool

Dopamine — a neurotransmitter that plays a role in mood, motivation, learning motor control, and pleasure — has become a buzz word in the self-optimization space. People talk about *dopamine detox* or *dopamine junkies*, suggesting that dopamine is something naughty that feels really good, but that you should have only in moderation. Well, dopamine has loads of super important functions in your brain and body, so you can't (and shouldn't) eliminate it.

Dopamine is mainly "made" in the *midbrain* and *substantia nigra*. It is implied in processes in different parts of the brain, such as the *prefrontal cortex* where it fuels cognitive operations (working memory, decision-making, planning, etc.), in the *substantia nigra* where it contributes to motor control or in the hypothalamus where it is involved in the regulation of hormones. But thanks to its ability to govern reward-seeking behavior and motivation it is often mentioned in relation to your brain's reward system. A special portion of this system, called the *striatum*, guides your behavior.

The striatum uses dopamine as a form of positive reinforcement, encouraging you to repeat behaviors that worked out. And your striatum contributes to evaluate your decision-making by running the numbers: It weighs options against each other, and suddenly, one option feels like the correct one to your conscious mind. Dopamine's role in the striatum doesn't make you a pleasure junky; rather, it helps you manage and regulate your behavior in a functional and coherent way. For the striatum, dopamine is the gasoline that keeps the production plant going.

These processes largely happen outside of your awareness. Therefore, through your choices and behaviors, you have to set the right conditions in your brain so that it all works in your favor — and doesn't become pleasure-junkiness. You can read more about your *body orchestra* (the idea that because brain and body are linked, you can 'play' neurobiological processes to a certain degree, through your behavior) and how to tune it for flow in Chapter 4 and in Part 2.

Exciting research by neuroscientist Dr. Örjan de Manzano suggests that the striatum also plays an important role in flow-proneness. It seems that the striatal system and its dopamine link to flow in two ways:

>> **Staying motivated:** With a steady source of fuel, dopamine keeps the inner flame alive, building *intrinsic motivation* for a task (where you engage in the task for the sake of the task itself, and not for some ulterior motive, such as gains — see the section "Flow Element 5: Doing what you do for intrinsic rewards " in Chapter 2).

>> **Controlling your dopamine:** The striatum helps you control impulsive behaviors and maintain positive affect by controlling the level of dopamine. It recaptures the dopamine via specific receptors, helping you avoid emotional ups and downs.

Imagine the striatal system sitting deep in your brain, covered in little trumpet-shaped openings that suck up a dopamine molecule like a vacuum when it comes passing by. Those little vacuums are the all-important receptors taking care of stabilizing affect and impulses.

When the striatum recaptures dopamine, the relative balance of the amount of dopamine that is still out and about makes your attention last and enables emotional stability and a continuous focus in a task.

Dr. Örjan de Manzano and his colleagues used a neuroimaging technique called positron emission tomography (PET) to see whether they could identify differences in the brains of people who are flow-prone, and people who aren't. Their experiment followed these steps:

1. **Twenty-five people filled in several flow questionnaires.**

   These questionnaires were designed to determine how flow-prone a person was.

2. **Each person was scheduled for a PET scan.**

3. **Before entering the scanner, each participant received an injection that contained a radioactive tracer called raclopride** (it is radioactive but completely safe to use).

   This tracer binds itself to *dopamine D2* (that's a type of dopamine receptor in the striatum).

4. **The results showed that the more dopamine D2 receptors in the striatum, the more flow-prone a test participant was.**

   So, if you have more dopamine receptors in your striatum, it seems you can more easily find flow. Other research has suggested that these receptors help a person have a less-jumpy attention span, stable emotions, and positive feelings.

How do you get more dopamine receptors? It's a contested subject and difficult to say. But research shows that regular exercise can help you get a balanced, less impulsive mindset. You can find more about your brain's need for movement to set it up for flow in Chapter 6. *Spoiler:* Make sure you have enough aerobic exercise in your life!

Further research by Dr. de Manzano and his colleagues suggests that some people are just lucky: They're born with more dopamine D2 suckers in their striatum.

Genes and flow-proneness

Two exciting studies have examined the link between genes and flow:

>> **Twins:** You might know that monozygotic twins share 100 percent of their genetic information. For that reason, monozygotic twins allow researchers to study the influence of genes on a particular trait — for example, flow-proneness. If one twin is flow-prone, how likely is it that the other twin is also flow-prone? A study Dr. Miriam Mosing and her colleagues, looked at 444 monozygotic twin pairs from Sweden and found that flow-proneness was 29 to 35-percent heritable — which means that it is a moderate level of heritability.

>> **The genes for dopamine D2 receptors:** Flip back to the preceding section for discussion of these receptors. The gene that codes for the dopamine D2 receptors (DRD2 C957T rs6277) affects how many D2 receptors exist in the striatum; specifically, how many copies of that gene a person has. In a sample of 236 Hungarian genetically unrelated adults, Dr. Mate Gyurkovics (at the time of Eötvös Loránd University, Budapest) and colleagues found that those participants who carried two copies of this particular gene were more flow-prone than those who carried only one copy. So, the more D2 receptors in the striatum, the more flow-prone a person is.

Interestingly, lower dopamine D2 receptor density in the striatum is also linked to certain personality traits, such as more risk-taking and novelty-seeking. Perhaps it's not surprising that more dopamine receptors make a person less impulsive and able to focus.

REMEMBER

The heritability estimate in the twin study was only moderate. And currently, the science about whether specific genes code something in the brain that make a person flow–prone is quite mixed. So, don't worry about whether you have the genes for flow! Research suggests that a lot of the variance in flow–proneness occurs because of environmental factors — for example, whether you create an environment conducive to you developing a flow habit in your brain. See Part 2 of this book for how to do just that.

The Big Five Traits: Personality and Your Path to Flow

Does a particular personality type find flow easier than other personality types? Probably, yes. But don't despair if you think you don't have an easy-flow personality; the science shows that these links are only moderate and you can develop your flow practice regardless of your personality type — you just need to tailor it to *who you are*. More on that tailoring in Parts 2 and 3 of the book.

Everyone has the big five personality traits:

>> **Openness to experience:** how curious, open to try new things, adventurous are you?

>> **Extroversion:** how outgoing, energetic, assertive and sociable are you?

>> **Agreeableness:** how cooperative, empathetic, compassionate are you?

>> **Conscientiousness:** how organized, responsible, and diligent are you?

>> **Neuroticism:** how emotionally irritable, anxious and sensitive are you?

People just have different relative amounts of each trait. So, for each individual, the dials of the different traits are set a little differently. For example, scientific research has shown that people who play music, as a hobby or professionally, have particularly high levels of neuroticism. They also tend to be very open and extroverted.

Recreational and professional dancers often are also very open and extroverted. But dancers tend to have low levels of neuroticism — lower than the general population, and much lower than a lot of musicians. The personality of a business founder is usually very conscientious, open, and extroverted, and they tend to score low on neuroticism.

The bars in Figure 3-1 show a free representation of the results from two studies: Study 1 is by Karen L. Kuckelkorn and colleagues from 2021 about musicians' personality. Study 2 is by myself, Julia F. Christensen and my colleagues from 2024 about dancers' personality profiles. Values for the five personality traits (conscientiousness, openness to experience, extraversion, neuroticism and agreeableness) of people who do not play music nor dance are represented as "0" on the y-axis (the vertical line), so that the bars represent how much musicians and dancers are different from people who do not practice these two types of activities. (Please note that these graphs were produced as estimations — they don't represent the true values from the articles.)

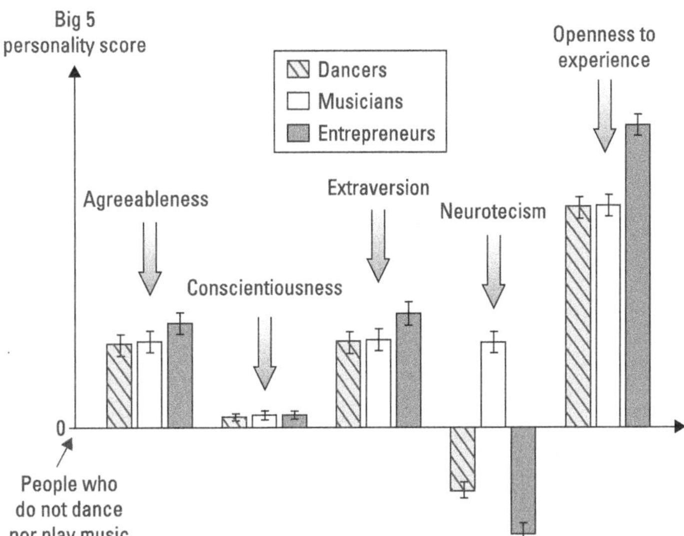

FIGURE 3-1: Big five personality mixing desk.

If you can figure out where your dials are, you can get one step closer to finding a flow activity that works for you. At the end of the chapter there is a personality test for you to investigate, where your dials are.

This personality-trait conversation relates to normal personality dispositions, not personality disorders, where the dials have gone far beyond the mixing board.

You can find the questionnaire at `dummies.com/flow`.

Neuroticism

If you're neurotic, you tend to experience negative feelings and thoughts more often than people who score low on neuroticism; you have constant negative self-talk going on in your head. Also, a neurotic person tends to be anxious, self-conscious, and irritable, and they find it hard to deal with stress, frustration, loss, and threat.

Data shows that highly neurotic people may also be more prone to depression and anger. If you're really high up there on the neurotic spectrum, you have severely impaired emotion regulation. Scientific assessments show that high neuroticism is associated with less life and work satisfaction and a higher risk for burn out. If you're very neurotic, you might fare well in jobs that require a lot of attention to detail and clear boundaries. These kinds of jobs can set your certainty-loving brain at ease.

The poet Suzy Kassem says, "Doubt kills more dreams than failure ever will." The multiple worries of the neurotic mind keep popping up before their mind's eye about what might happen, breaking the continuous focus that a person needs for flow. This constant worry makes *sensory decoupling* (separating your internal experiences from the world around you — see the section about "Flow Element 1: Getting completely absorbed in the activity" in Chapter 2) difficult, and therefore, halts *absorption* (focusing deeply on your internal world). Besides, ruminative and worrisome *thought loops* (in which your brain focuses on what has happened or might happen, see the section about "Flow Elements 9 and 10" in Chapter 2) are particularly hard to break in the neurotic mind, which also makes flow difficult to reach.

Because of the protective effects of regular flow against burnout and its boost to life satisfaction, if you score high on neuroticism, you definitely need flow. And a loving, kind attitude toward that part of your personality can help you on that path because science shows that positive affect is a flow booster too.

Acknowledge neuroticism when you see it in your actions and thoughts; greet it like a friend who worries too much. Some research shows that changing your self-talk to the pronoun *you* (instead of *I*) can reduce stress. Why? Speaking to yourself as *you* magically changes your mind's perspective in a way that lets you see the path to a more positive self-regard more clearly. Perhaps combine this pronoun shift with an expressive writing practice. (Flip to Chapter 14 to find out more about expressive writing for flow.)

REMEMBER

High neuroticism isn't the only culprit for lack of flow experiences; both dancers (who usually score low on neuroticism) and musicians (who tend to score high) are very flow-prone and have flow as a major part of their lives.

Conscientiousness

Highly conscientious people are disciplined (but not perfectionistic!), organized, responsible, hardworking, and thoughtful, and they generally enjoy engaging in controlled goal-directed actions, which can help them excel at work and in life.

ACQUIRED NEUROTICISM

Perhaps you used to think of yourself as someone who's definitely *not* neurotic. But somehow, the descriptions in the section "Neuroticism," in this chapter, ring true. If you recently experienced high levels of loss of control, of insecurity in job and life, you may have an increased level of neuroticism. Usually, research shows that personality traits are pretty stable across life. However, some studies have shown that if you have a high level of job insecurity, over time, you may become more neurotic, and less conscientious and agreeable. So, even if you're not born neurotic, you can acquire neuroticism because of life circumstances.

If you fall into the acquired-neuroticism category, practice an activity that, through its familiar, repetitive movements and rituals, brings you back to yourself and reminds you of who you really are. Check out Chapter 6 to find out why repetitive movements can act as washing machines for the mind. And in Part 4, you can see how to adapt flow to different life situations.

If you score high on conscientiousness in the big five personality traits (see the section "The Big Five Traits: Personality and Your Path to Flow," earlier in this chapter and the questionnaire at the end of the chapter), science shows that you tend to have good health, positive aging, and good emotional regulation skills for self-control. These self-regulation skills usually help acquire useful skills and knowledge — something that scientists call *human capital* — not in an economic sense, but in terms of resilience and problem-solving ability. Plus, also these two characteristics of conscientious people make them flow-prone:

>> **Persistence:** They calmly approach tasks and persist until they understand — this helps them solve things step by step.

>> **Achievement:** They enjoy setting a realistic but challenging goal that keeps them engaged but doesn't stress them out. They know how to design tasks so that they get clear feedback signals from the activity, and they remain within the skills-challenge balance (two Flow Elements discussed in Chapter 2).

In a job context, conscientious people enjoy both their actual role and extra-role actions (relying on their intrinsic motivation) — something that employers love about them.

If you don't score high on conscientiousness, perhaps look at the descriptions in the preceding list and see whether you can implement some of those actions in your own life. Avoid perfectionism, though. Especially if you score high on neuroticism, remain malleable.

How Other Personality Factors Influence Flow

Other than the five main personality traits (discussed in the section "The Big Five Traits: Personality and Your Path to Flow," earlier in this chapter), other elements of personality can influence how prone you are to flow, including anxiety, *alexithymia* (difficulty labeling and interpreting emotions), emotional intelligence, and optimism. The following sections talk about these factors and their link to flow.

Anxiety

Anxiety is a state of unease, dread, or fear. When we experience anxiety, we usually also have physiological reactions in our body — our heart races, the hairs on the back of our neck rise, our hands grow cold, or our knees feel like they're made of jelly.

Anxiety is bad for flow because of it comes with *hypervigilance* (a heightened alertness for potential threats around you), while you need *sensory decoupling* (preventing external cues from affecting your internal experiences) for flow. When hypervigilant any potentially dangerous cue goes straight to central relay stations of your brain (your *amygdala* and the *thalamus*), grabbing your attention and disturbing what you're currently doing. You can't find flow if your brain is constantly drawing your attention elsewhere.

Scientists use the Positive and Negative Affect Schedule (PANAS) to distinguish between trait anxiety and state anxiety:

>> **Trait anxiety:** You have a tendency to respond with anxiety to things that happen. This trait can cause a problem for finding flow, in general, because your mind is roused from its absorption all the time, and you're probably prone to worry. But if you can find it, flow can definitely help you unwind and relax. Make sure to build a strong flow habit. Check out Part 3 for flow activity options to choose from.

>> **State anxiety:** Your anxiety is likely due to something specific that recently happened, which poses a problem for finding flow right now (even if flow now could help calm you down again). If you already have a flow habit in place, turn to it — pick up that knitting pouch and clean your mind of the stress hormones. Flow helps build resilience to life's ups and downs.

ANXIETY IN THE BODY

In a study published in 2013 in *Proceedings of the National Academy of Sciences of the United States of America* (*PNAS*), neuroscientist Lauri Nummenmaa and colleagues tried to determine whether people feel that emotions are physically manifested in consistent parts of the body. They asked 773 people to tell them where in their body they felt different emotions with these steps:

1. **Participants sat alone in a dimly lit room in front of a computer screen that displayed a body outline.**

2. **A prompt asked them to reflect on where in their body they usually feel different emotions.**

   For example, the prompt asked, "Where do you feel fear?"

3. **Participants were asked to click on the computerized body outline in front of them to tell the researchers where they felt these different emotions.**

The results of Nummenmaa's experiment — which were the average of all clicks of all participants for each emotion — showed that the chest, throat, and head were the parts of the body that people mentioned most as seats of different emotions. On our path to find out how we can best craft our flow, we may want to understand more about who we are. For example, if we are anxious we may not necessarily be aware of that all the time, because that's just who we are. And that's fine. But because we know that anxiety is likely to extract us from flow, we need to be aware of that part of our personality if we have it. To investigate whether we have it, a first step is to identify where in the body we feel anxiety or fear. Once we've identified this, we can keep a mental eye on that body part and see if it pokes at us with emotion frequently. You can figure out where your body tells you how you feel.

Repetitive movements, such as those you do while practicing a craft (knitting, dancing, singing, and so on) can calm your nervous system. Building a flow practice can particularly soothe an anxiety-riddled mind, whether you're anxious because of a situation or as a personality trait. Flip to Parts 3 and 4 to find out more about how to tailor a flow practice to your life.

Anxiety can manifest in your body in many ways: It can feel like a stinging sensation or a very subtle numbing sensation. So, how can you tell whether you're anxious? Ask your body.

Take a look at Figure 3-2. It looks very similar to what people in the above study were asked to color. Now color the body parts where you feel the different emotions. Use red colors to indicate heat (good or bad), stinging, or pleasant arousing sensations, and blue colors for deactivation, coldness, or heaviness.

FIGURE 3-2: Mapping your anxiety in your body.

Figure 3-3 shows the average locations identified in Nummenmaa's study; where other people feel these emotions in their body. Basically, the researchers overlayed the clicks of many, many research participants on the body outlines into *one* body outline. Like this, they obtained these "heat maps." The darker the color on the body you see, the more research participants had clicked on that body part for the emotion in question.

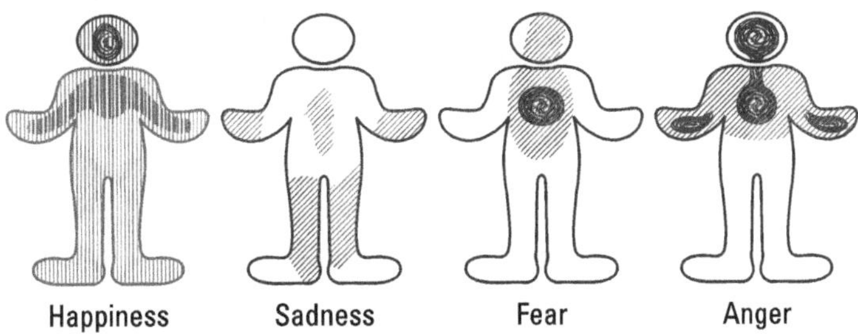

FIGURE 3-3: Average locations identified in Nummenmaa's study.

Credit: Adapted from: Nummenmaa, et al. Bodily maps of emotions. Proceedings of the National Academy of Science. 2014 Jan 14;111(2):646–51. doi: 10.1073/pnas.1321664111.

Compare with your drawing to see where you feel anxiety. You don't need to do anything in particular right now. Just take this information about yourself with you. Perhaps pay attention to what situations poke at that body part, making you feel fear or anxiety. Likely it is a good idea to stay away from such situations or people when you're seeking flow.

Figuring out why specific situations or people provoke these emotions in you may be important and useful for you, so you can change this for the better in your life. But for flow, your focus should be on positive affect (and who or what gives it to you), as this helps you generate flow.

Emotional intelligence

Emotional intelligence is the ability to understand and manage your own emotions and recognize and work with the emotions of others. Emotionally intelligent people:

>> Use their emotions like a compass (in interactions with others and alone), to guide their own thoughts and decisions.

>> Can perceive emotions in others and manage their own.

>> Lead empathically, which stimulates teams and leads to enhanced job performance in everyone.

Some research in a business context suggests that to predict success, this trait might be more important that traditional metrics such as IQ. Daniel Goleman's 2005 book *Emotional Intelligence: Why It Can Matter More Than IQ* (Bantam) discusses the importance of this trait. It can also help you build a flow habit. Emotionally intelligent people realize when things are uncertain around them; and when it all becomes a bit much for a predictability-loving brain, they have solutions:

>> They first get out of their head (where worries and ruminations reside) and take action, such as engaging in aerobic exercise, or a performative art (dancing, singing . . .).

>> They inject predictability into the situation by controlling the actions of their physical body, using repetitive movements (whether that's running or knitting). These actions help restabilize a brain on the edge because of unpredictability.

>> They proactively create environments that are flow-conducive by using cues that have previously been associated with positive affect, flow and energy.

Emotionally intelligent people ensure to focus on positive emotions:

>> They identify what emotions they like to feel and figure out what can give them those feelings. They reverse engineer the feeling that they like having through the actions that they take.

>> They count their blessings, focus on the good things that happened in their day, or in their life in general.

Positive affect (the tendency to experience positive emotions) is a significant flow trigger — it helps you maintain attention and find intrinsic motivation because your actions gain personal significance (all of which fall into the 10 Flow Elements discussed in Chapter 2). Emotionally intelligent people simply purposefully set out to feel good. For them, it's an easy calculation: Rumination activates negative topics within memory systems — so they introduce positive activations through positive thoughts to deactivate the negative ones.

WARNING

If you don't score high on emotional intelligence, consider actively trying to use some of the emotionally intelligent techniques discussed in this section. But remember that having emotional intelligence doesn't mean that you suppress your negative emotions. In my book *The Pathway to Flow* (Vintage), I talk about several emotion regulation strategies to manage your emotions — I also briefly explain them in Chapter 16 in this book.

Alexithymia

Alexithymia is a personality trait marked by difficulty labeling and experiencing (or making sense of) your own or others' emotions. If you score high on alexithymia, you likely don't really understand how to label emotions by using words. For example, an alexithymic person doesn't understand why someone would say, "I'm so excited," instead of describing the body's reaction, like "my heart's so overstimulated."

People who have alexithymia are sensitive to body signals; but they don't really understand those signals and probably try to avoid them. This avoidance can involve avoiding people, even people they love, just to avoid feeling the physical sensations those people trigger in them. This dysfunctional suppression habit harms people, relationships, and team work. Around 10 percent of the population have this personality trait. So, of ten people you know, one is likely to be noticeably alexithymic.

TECHNICAL STUFF

Alexithymia has some genetic predisposition. Heritability estimates are around 30 percent (meaning a moderate influence of genes). In systematic reviews, scientists found that the genetic predisposition for alexithymia may be caused by atypicalities in the different aspects of brain function (for instance in the dopamine D2 receptors, and in the genes that metabolize neurotransmitters). More research is needed to find out how exactly these factors contribute to alexithymia. Interestingly, around 50 percent of people who have *autism* (a neurodevelopmental disorder that affects how a person sees and interacts with the world and other people) also have alexithymia.

Alexithymia can also be acquired. Research shows that people suffering post-traumatic stress disorder (PTSD) may feel a certain depersonalization, also with regards to their emotions.

People who score high on alexithymia have less activity in the brain systems that are involved in emotion (around the insula and amygdala). At the same time, they have more activity in sensory areas of the brain. This disconnect between sensory processing and emotional processing can make it difficult to tap into the Flow Element that deals with perception-action fusion (see Chapter 2 for the details on this and the other Flow Elements), which usually helps you get absorbed in what you're doing.

To flow if you have alexithymia, use routines and repetitive movements to create a flow habit. These habits can pull you away from the physiological turmoil that you feel in response to the social world around you. The repetitiveness of the movements can soothe the physiological rhythms of your body, too.

Optimism

Optimism means that you generally expect that the future will bring good things. Here are some of the flow-appropriate elements of an optimistic personality:

>> Highly motivated to go the extra mile, which makes it easy for them to find intrinsic rewards in an activity (an important Flow Element — see Chapter 2).

>> Not discouraged by setbacks because they think they're headed toward a positive end result.

>> Generally have good physical and mental health, which helps them avoid worries and ruminations (which can negative impact flow).

>> Can regulate their emotions and cope with change or negative events.

>> Have better social connections than pessimists, not necessarily just because people like being around a positive thinker, but because optimists will work harder to maintain those connections. Pessimists may just disengage when interactions get difficult.

>> Not likely to ruminate.

>> Put more effort into high-priority goals but not into low-priority goals. This capacity to focus on one thing helps them tap into flow — especially because they tend to design tasks to have little rewards and feedback along the way. (Another important Flow Element — see Chapter 2.)

>> Simply prepared to work hard for something they care about, in all domains of their life.

Pessimists: Just keep at it, even if you don't feel like it. Repeating an action, rooting for it, going the extra mile *can* really help you develop a flow habit. For optimists, the motivation comes from the *doing*. Dopamine fuels motivation and dopamine is fueled by action. You cannot *will* this into being, these processes only happen in your brain from physical action outside, in the world. It's hard to imagine if you haven't experienced it. You'll feel it if you let it happen. So, for some portion of your day, every day, practice your flow activity and try to enact the optimist. Set a timer for 10 minutes and try it out.

Intrinsic motivation

Intrinsic motivation, as described in Chapter 2, is one of the ten elements of flow. Intrinsic motivation has something to do with feeling intense joy just by doing what you do and helps make an activity feel so effortless when you're in flow. It is not considered a personality trait in itself. Rather conscientiousness and openness to experience are personality traits that often result in someone being intrinsically motivated. It is a very stable driver of our behavior, so let's have another look at it, regardless of your personality traits.

Scientists battle about what exactly intrinsic motivation is and how a person can get it. Some people seem to just get it when they feel that an activity is particularly relevant to them. In that case, a person does what they do just because of the joy of doing that thing. Just the *doing* becomes a source for reward and satisfaction. They don't focus on the final product, nor on any prizes, praise, or payment. People who feel intrinsically motivated for their task generally feel better; are more productive; have a sense of achievement, passion, and purpose; and feel less fatigue during a task.

Intrinsic motivation fuels focus. Intrinsically motivated people focus on little steps and rewards along the way, pinging their reward system. They use these little hits as guide and the satisfaction that comes from them as fuel. If you're perhaps not naturally intrinsically motivated, see Chapters 6 to 9 where it's all about crafting movements step by step, and setting the right mindset *during* the activity.

Flowing with the Autotelic Personality

Mihaly Csikszentmihalyi, the psychologist who defined the elusive state of full engagement as *flow*, also proposed that a certain personality type is particularly flow-prone. This personality type, which he called *autotelic*, is characterized by a series of traits:

>> **Driven by intrinsic motivation and curiosity:** They're just insatiably curious about the world and constantly try to find out more. For instance, they have a cherished morning ritual of reading Wikipedia for an hour before getting up.

>> **Don't necessarily follow rules and conventions:** They feel comfortable ignoring the norms if they don't align with the task at hand. So, they care little about what others think about them or about what they do. Psychologists call this perspective *low self-centeredness.* This can potentially make someone seem selfish. They become so involved in their goals that they don't attend to the needs of the people around them.

>> **Feel compelled to excel:** Challenges don't dishearten them; on the contrary, challenges motivate them.

>> **See setbacks simply as part of the task itself:** Failure is just data that will help perform better *next time.*

Autotelic people are very flow-prone. Flow is part of their lifestyle: Practice, eat, sleep, repeat. They enjoy the routines and rituals that work for them (which may not fit into what society deems normal). If you suspect you're not autotelic — try to enact the behaviors I explain above and in Part 2 of the book. A lot of this is setting up the neural pathways that help us move through our day in an autotelic way.

Getting to Know Your Flow Potential

Personality traits are to a certain degree heritable — the heritability estimates range between 30% to 40%. But that doesn't mean that you are a victim of your genes.

At `Dummies.com`, you can do the below Big Five Personality Questionnaire by professors Christopher J. Soto and Oliver P. John to find out where you lie in terms of your mixing desk of personality traits. This can help you identify possible obstacles that you might need to overcome and habits that you might need to build, considering the current state of affairs that is *you*. Do you score high on openness to experience? Great. Do you score high on neuroticism? Then perhaps make sure to develop habits that calm your nervous system so you can tap into flow. This process of guided self-reflection can help you identify how you can tailor flow into your life.

It is important that you know that regardless of any questionnaire results you might get, you can't assume that one thing causes the other.

Now let's look at some other aspects of your personality that may make you flow-prone. What would your replies be to these two questions: Are you someone who finds it easy to submerge yourself in a task, regardless of whether other people will ever see and admire the result? Are you someone who easily loses track of time while you're submerged in a task, regardless of whether there is noise around you or other people may be judging how you look or what you do?

These two questions describe people who are very flow-prone. If you do not naturally have this autotelic personality (see the previous section, "Flowing with the Autotelic Personality"), at `Dummies.com` you can find the General Flow Proneness Scale by the scientists Magdalena Elnes and Hermundur Sigmundsson. This is a questionnaire that will tell you something about *your* flow-proneness. Again, this is to guide you in understanding more about *your* flow potential — how easy or hard you may find tapping into flow *right now*, considering your personality, routines and rituals, current skills set, and so on.

What this type of questionnaires help you with, is to identify possible obstacles that you might need to overcome, and habits that you might need to build, considering the current state of affairs that is you. This process of guided self-reflection can help you identify how you can tailor flow into your life. You do have to make them yours, and for that, they need to fit you.

Science doesn't know what came first: Brain differences that make people more flow-prone, personality traits, or flow. But science has shown that the brain is plastic (meaning, it has "neuro*plastic*ity" which is the ability to form new connections between neurons, in other words, *to learn*). Your brain never stops being able to learn throughout your life. You can train skills, increase and decrease receptors in your brain by performing and practicing actions and complex behaviors in your life.

If you want to get right to action, jump to Chapter 4, which talks about your body orchestra; or if you want to see the behaviors of people who are flow-prone (and whom you can try to copy), check out Chapters 5-10.

Chapter **4**
Your Brain-Body Connection

There is a remarkable relationship between your brain and your body. Although you might picture the brain as something tucked away inside your skull, it's constantly exchanging signals with everything that makes you, *you*. Long ganglia (nerve cells) travel from the brain through the spinal cord and down into the body, connecting with organs, muscles and all the way out into the skin on your tip toes. Sensations from the world travel inward, the brain responds, and the body answers back — information travels outward. This continuous dialogue shapes your emotions, your actions, your focus, and your sense of self.

In this chapter, you can look at the key parts of this network — the areas of the brain that help you sense, move, imagine, and make meaning — and how they stay in touch with the organs and systems of the body. Together, they form what I call your *body orchestra*: a dynamic, finely tuned system designed through evolution to help you navigate physical, social, and emotional challenges.

By understanding how this orchestra works, you can gain insight into how different environments and cues affect your inner state. This knowledge becomes especially powerful when it comes to accessing flow. Some experiences support your brain-body harmony, while others disrupt it. Knowing the difference between behaviors that direct one or the other symphony helps you guide your mind toward balance, clarity, and deep engagement.

Getting a Feel for Your Brain-Body Connection

The *cortex* is the external layer of your brain, called the *gray matter.* The cortex is *associative,* meaning that it has long connections that help information travel long distances. It connects the human brain so that people can do all those things that make them unique in the animal kingdom, such as thinking, memorizing, using language, having consciousness, and using imagination (see Chapter 7 for more information on how to use the imagination as a tool to find flow).

Different parts of the cortex are responsible for sensory processing:

>> **Motor cortex:** Responsible for movement; exists below where you'd place an Alice band on your head.

>> **Sensory cortex:** All about taking care of touch and other cues to your skin (soft, tear, hot, cold, pain); just in front of the motor cortex.

>> **Auditory cortices:** Enable you to hear; sit close to your temples, and a little toward the back of the head.

>> **Visual cortex:** Occupies, funny enough, a large part of the back of your head — and you thought you see with your eyes!

In pictures of the brain, the cortex looks wrinkled. That's because it's folded into ridges (*gyri*) and grooves (*sulci*) so that a large surface area can fit inside the small space of the skull. The sensory cortices receive information from the sense organs via relay stations inside the brain, where complex systems constantly work to keep you alive.

Many people forget that your brain is delicately connected with the rest of your body through the spinal column. Inside it, something like a tunnel that houses long *ganglia* (bundles of nerve cells) runs from your brain into all parts of your body and allowing information to flow back and forth — something that scientists call *bidirectional* channels of communication.

Every thought, movement, and sensation emerges from this intricate network, which I call your *body orchestra.* (Flip to the section "Playing Your Body Orchestra," later in this chapter, to get an idea of how the body orchestra works.)

Traveling to a Special Island of Cortex

Back in 1796, German anatomist Johann Christian Reil made an intriguing discovery. Beneath the outer layer of the cortex, he found a small, tucked-away piece of cortex that looked like a tiny island folded into the brain. He named it the *insula*, which is Latin for *island.*

The insula sits deep inside your brain, tucked toward the center (shown in Figure 4-1). It integrates and processes information from many parts of the body. While it's not a 'brain hub' for flow — it does play an important role for our ability to tap into flow, as we'll see later.

Unlike much of the rest of the cortex, the insula sits somewhat closer to the brain stem and has a lot of connections with the systems that keep you alive and ticking. It's like a busy little hub toward the center of your brain's survival network.

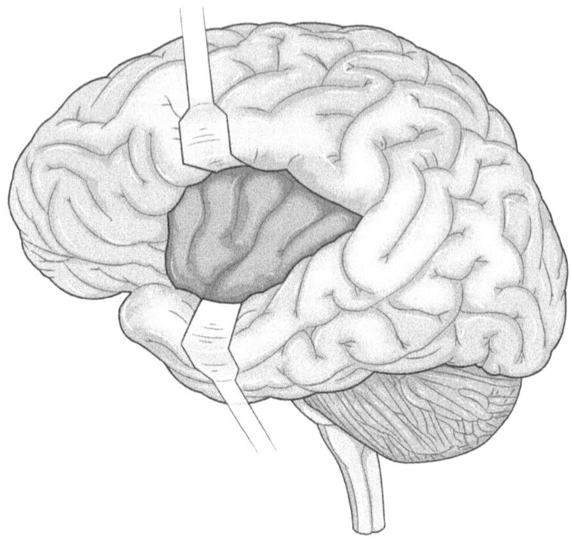

The insula plays an important part in many brain functions:

>> Integrating sensory and emotional information by using rules stored in parts of your *prefrontal cortex* (the part of your brain that uses executive functions to manage thinking, emotions, and behavior) to help guide your behavior.

>> Processing physical pain and emotions.

>> Processing social pain and other social emotions such as rejection, acceptance, shame, and embarrassment.

>> Integrating social information from your senses and the cortex to make decisions based on that information (for example, whether to approach or avoid):

- You see a smile through receptors in your eyes that funnel the visual information to the visual cortex.

- You hear a pleasant tone of voice through receptors in your ears that project to the auditory cortex.

- You feel a caress through the receptors in your skin that send the information to the sensory cortex.

Besides the social and emotional feelings that the insula helps your brain interpret, the insula also plays a role in your physical health:

>> **Maintaining homeostasis:** *Homeostasis* is balance within the body — biochemical agents, such as nutrients; water; temperature; and so on.

>> **Monitoring the body's internal state:** The insula keeps track of your internal state through the sense called *interoception* (for example, it can determine whether you're hot or cold, tired, have a pounding heart).

>> **Regulating your immune system:** The insula connects brain systems that keep the immune system tuned as it should.

>> **Undertaking immunoception:** *Immunoception* is the process by which the insula monitors and regulates the state of your body's immune system, also influencing immune responses.

Note how the insula is involved in both social and emotional processes that influence our psychological well-being, and in processes related to our physical health, like our immune response.

Playing Your Body Orchestra

You can't tense your insula (the brain region discussed in the previous section) in the way that you can tense muscles in your body (like your biceps or quads). So how do you stimulate your insula in a good way? Through the behaviors that you do with your body and the people and things that you surround yourself with in your environment.

Your environment influences the insula — and the many other systems in your brain. Information from your surroundings travels to your brain through your senses (seeing, hearing, touching, smelling, tasting, as well as interoception, proprioception and exteroception), via long nerve cell bundles (*ganglia*). (Check out the list of a person's eight senses in Chapter 2.) Via relay stations in the brain, the information then goes to where it's needed for action.

Healthy actions and surroundings can activate restoration processes in the body and make you feel calm and serene. For instance, by doing sports or by surrounding yourself with people you like and who like you, you keep your body orchestra finely tuned. (See Chapter 6 for information about how movement and social contact establish the settings for flow in your brain.) On the other hand, danger and risky environments and behaviors activate survival mechanisms in your brain and send your mind into jumpy excitement, or worse — spinning into ruminative loops and worries about the future. In such a state, flow is incredibly unlikely to come. (We'll see more about this type of mind-hooks that prevent us from finding flow in Chapter 9 and Bonus Chapter 1 at www.dummies.com/go/flowfd).

REMEMBER

You can have a say in what state is activated in your brain and body, and what you feel, via the choices that you make: what you do, who you're with, and what environments you put yourself into. If you feel that you don't have much control over these things in the day to day, but you would like to — this realization can perhaps be the start of a change. There is no need to think about this as a dogma. Small moments of making choices that give you little glimpses of a few minutes with a flow activity can help you manage what your insula (and you) is exposed to. We'll develop that in what follows.

Coordinating your brain, body, and environment

As discussed in Chapters 9 and Bonus Chapter 1, some cues and environments have real hooks on your mind because of their effect on super quick processes in your brain that you can't control. After you identify these factors, you can set boundaries and keep them from entering your brain. Sometimes you need to set literal boundaries for these cues as when you turn away, change the room, face a different direction, or go somewhere else (A dance class? A museum? For a walk? Horseback riding?). Or you develop a flow-practice so that you can engage in that activity when you need a break from such cues (Model trains? Knitting? Yoga? Bake a cake?). Like this you control what cues enter your senses and what effect they have on your brain. You can take a look at the clever choices of flow-prone people in Part 2.

The science that we have been looking at in this section, that studies how the brain, body, and environment affect each other has a somewhat intimidating name — *psychoneuroendocrinology.* It focuses on how the human brain and body have balance and connection. To a degree, you can have a say in what information travels along these connections, through choices, actions, rituals . . . See Figure 4-2.

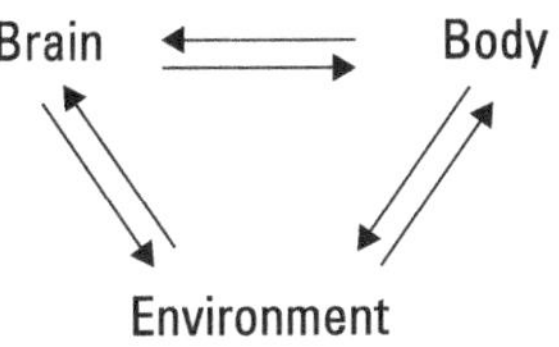

Recognizing small rituals

Every morning, I go to a small café, where I join a large group of usual suspects. We don't actually know each other; we just happen to come to the same spot to start the day. We greet each other, smile, and then simply share space: tables, the scent of good coffee, and a wonderful calm ambiance infused with café sounds, scents and the soft murmur of those who come in pairs.

One small ritual unites us all: the morning newspaper shuffle. This café offers a few different papers — some more conservative, some more liberal. The group has its favorites. Pages are shared, passed around, softly negotiated. That café ritual creates a very special sense-scape for all of us. Its cues travel to our brains as electric signals via our nerve cells. Besides the obvious soothing cues that enter through our eyes, ears, tongue, and nose, we also experience the soothing effect of cues that enter three senses that we often forget about:

>> **Our interoception:** The sense of what's happening inside your body, such as the heartbeat, breathing, or hunger. You feel it, even if you don't think about it.

- >> **Our proprioception:** Tells you where your body and limbs are in space. You know whether you're leaning back in your chair, tapping your foot, or reaching for your coffee.

- >> **Our exteroception:** Your sense of the world around you — the layout of the café, the distance to the tables, and how crowded it feels.

The café ritual is different from, say, sitting alone at home at the kitchen table. As you can explore in Chapter 6, even loose, low-commitment social rituals can prepare the mind for flow.

Their power lies in our ancient history: In prehistoric environments, small, predictable morning rituals performed within a larger social group were essential for survival. Being surrounded by others who were awake, alert, and engaged signaled safety. It meant predators were less likely to approach, that someone else might notice danger before you could, and that the group was functioning as a coordinated whole. These subtle cues allowed the nervous system to shift out of vigilance and into a state where curiosity, creativity, and problem-solving could flourish.

Today, rituals like my morning café experiences echo that ancient dynamic. The light social contact, the shared rhythm, the quiet negotiations over newspaper pages — all of it acts as a modern signal that we're among others, in a safe and predictable environment. And when the brain senses safety, it frees the body and mind to enter flow.

Appreciating Different Body and Mind Symphonies

You actually have a lot of agency in what happens inside you, if you know what cues trigger what processes inside your brain. (See the preceding section about how brain, body, and environment interact.)

For example, when it comes to newspapers, ask yourself, "Do I really need to read this gore?" Probably not first thing in the morning. What about e-mails? Do you really need to read them first thing when you arrive at work? You don't know what chores, requests, or challenges they contain. Is reading them going to make your mind creative and productive, helping to tip you into flow?

Identify what cues break your focus and stir up arousal and ruminative thoughts and worries in your brain and body — and quarantine those cues. Assign them slots in your diary (as when you only check e-mails from 12 to 1pm, only deal with admin between 2 and 3pm); don't let them invade other parts of the day. The symphonies that these cues play in your body, if you let them, have a negative impact on flow. If what surrounds you stresses or scares you, or suffocates you in boredom, these reactions have repercussions on your brain and body.

Our "body orchestra" can play tunes of horror and drama, or it can flow, like the bows of a violin. If you have a body and a brain, this applies to *you* too. Let's have a look at why this is the case and why there is no avoiding this.

Hearing the fear symphony

In what archaeologists call the Middle Paleolithic period (about 100,000 years ago), or the Stone Age, no civilization of the kind we modern humans know today existed. But we have a brain that is very similar to that of the Stone Age human. This means that we have danger detection mechanisms in place. For example, if we see a tiger with long, pointy fangs — how does our brain know that it is dangerous? It's all about the *cues* — and if our brain deems these cues to be dangerous, our body plays the fear symphony, preparing us for fight or flight, as illustrated in Figure 4-3. There is no avoiding this.

The symphony follows these general steps:

1. **The cue Tiger with Long Fangs enters your neural system via your eyes.**

2. **It travels as little electrical impulses through the optical nerve and into the brain.**

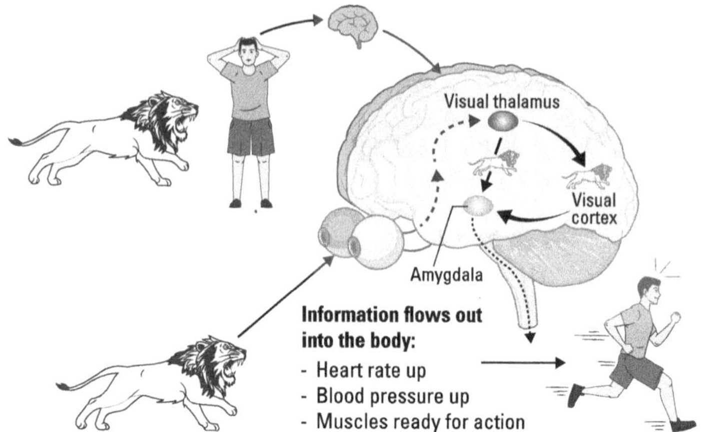

FIGURE 4-3: The fear response.

3. **These electrical impulses reach the visual thalamus.**

   Normally, the visual thalamus sends information on for further processing, to the visual cortex. That's approximately when we become aware of what we're seeing.

4. **If the visual thalamus deems the information in these electrical impulses dangerous based on past experience, on the size of the beast (larger than us), pointiness of the fangs (can sting us painfully), etc.**

   It operates a danger detection mechanism in no time to keep you safe. This operates outside of your awareness.

5. **The visual thalamus sends this information directly to the amygdala.**

6. **The amygdala sends the information along neurons to long ganglia (long nerve cells) that travel from the brain into the body's large muscles.**

   Because of this quick-moving information about danger, your body gets the signal before your mind's eye is even aware of that danger.

Fear is an emotion that keeps you safe because it quickly prepares the body to act. However, it feels terrible to your conscious mind, and you definitely can't find flow when you have the fear symphony ringing in your brain and body.

You probably know what it feels like to have this mechanism set off the fear symphony; for example, when a friend jumps out at you from behind a corner and you involuntarily startle. Your body reacted before you knew what was happening. This joke set off an evolutionarily very ancient mechanism: the fight-flight-freeze response, which helps us humans survive. Your brain uses the same neural mechanism of the fear response to keep you safe from an angry bear, the social embarrassment of getting out on the dance floor or a too large pile of e-mails. This connection between brain and body (which produces shaky knees and a pounding heart) explains why emotions such as anxiety or fear produce physical reactions.

This fear response causes loads of stress hormones to flood your body — it's a true symphony that engages many instruments. And if this symphony goes on for too long, these stress messenger substances actually contribute to deregulation of your wonderful insula (flip back to the section "Traveling to a Special Island of Cortex," earlier in this chapter, for more about this part of the brain), which can deregulate your immune system and increase the probability that you fall ill.

REMEMBER

Know when you're exposing your senses and their receptors to prolonged periods of danger or stress. Extract yourself from dangerous modern-world situations whenever you can so that you can create peace of mind without a loud fear symphony shouting "Alarm!"

Part 2 shows you how to create a flow practice that can help you regulate this fear symphony for when it does ring out inside you. In Part 3, you can see how to apply that flow practice to your life.

Embracing the social symphony

You can direct your body orchestra into a soothing rhythm of restoration and calm feelings by doing what you can to choose whom you spend time with. Social cues can play the fear symphony (see the preceding section), or they can soothe you with the social symphony:

>> **Smiles and friendly voices:** Human brains are hard-wired to react to a smile and a kind tone of voice with relaxation. Experiments show that humans often mimic the facial muscle movements of positive expressions in social

surroundings. This facial feedback activates restorative processes in our body like wound healing and immune regulation.

>> **A friendly look in the eyes:** Eye contact in a non-threatening environment has a similar effect as seeing a smile. Give and take a friendly glance if you feel comfortable with it.

>> **Caresses:** If you can start your morning ritual with loved ones, try to reserve some time for holding hands, giving a hug, and perhaps caressing. Special receptors in your skin called CT receptors respond only when stroked at a specific slow speed (1–10 centimeters per second) — caressing speed.

When the receptors in your senses fire after a soothing stimulus, little electrical impulses travel to the parts of the brain that regulate your immune system (such as the insula — see the section "Traveling to a Special Island of Cortex," earlier in this chapter). Some scientists recommend that you have at least eight hugs a day to keep healthy!

REMEMBER

What surrounds you (or who you choose to surround yourself with) reaches into our brain and body through the many sense receptors throughout your body. As much as you can, choose what you do, where you are, and who you're with wisely so that this body orchestra of yours can help play you into the flow state. Learn to identify helpful cues in Bonus Chapter 1 online.

A Functional Behavior Analysis

In the section "Appreciating Different Body and Mind Symphonies," earlier in this chapter, I talk about what scientists call *causality* — how something that you do or perceive with your body triggers various reactions within your body. This basic principle of psychology also applies to flow. When you can understand the causality — what cues trigger what reactions in your body and mind — you can use that information to reverse-engineer flow.

A great tool to help you understand causality is functional behavior analysis (FBA). This is a method that psychologists and their clients use to identify what in their surroundings and the people they interact with make bad (or good!) behaviors happen. A FBA involves examining the following components of a behavior:

>> **Situation:** what happens around you just before you do what you do?

>> **Organism:** what's the feeling inside your body right now? (Hungry, angry, sleepy?)

>> **Response:** the action you do

>> **Consequence:** what happens as a result? Do you get a reward, a punishment or nothing at all?

You can see an example of a FBA in Figure 4-4.

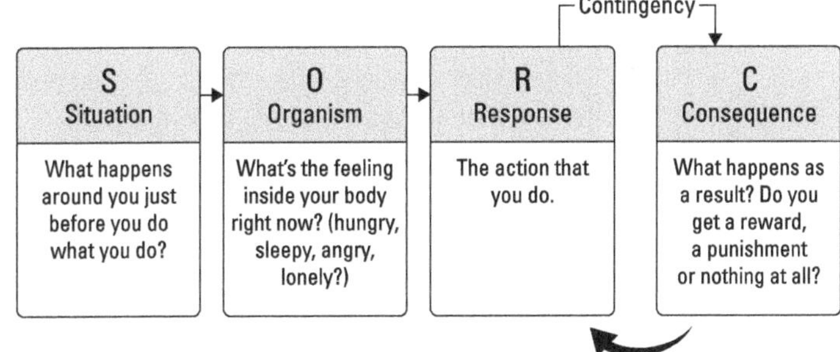

FIGURE 4-4: Functional analysis of behavior (FBA).

Credits: adapted from: Lincoln, et al. (2017). Using Functional Analysis as a Framework to Guide Individualized Treatment for Negative Symptoms. Frontiers in Psychology. 8:2108. doi: 10.3389/fpsyg.2017.02108

Doing a FBA with a behavior that bugs you can give you a sense of agency, the impression that you're in control (or at least working to get there). This helps to remove unpredictability in your life which you need to tap into flow (see Chapter 2 for more about this Flow Element).

After your brain has encoded the cues of the situation that preceded the action, those cues will be part of perception-action loops in your brain, so that you now execute the action that's usually connected to that cue each time you see the cue. For instance, smoke another cigarette each time you're in *that spot* or with *these people* (situation) and your body feels edgy (organism) — as a *consequence* you feel a rewarding feeling.

Or you always drink another drink when you're just home from work (situation) and feel tired (organism) — as a *consequence*, you feel relaxed. And so on. You do these things, even though you know they're not good for you, in part because of the habit loops that your brain has created, which is basically a link between cues and actions that have been rewarded in the past. I cover those loops in detail in Chapters 6 and 7.

The following sections unpack the two examples of FBA I gave in the preceding paragraph.

Smoking cigarettes

What is it that makes us smoke? If we do a FBA, we may find out that it's not just the nicotine.

- **Situation:** You're in a club that smells of cigarettes, hanging out with the people you usually smoke with.

- **Organism:** You feel a little edgy or stressed (exactly the feeling that always made you take a smoke).

- **Response:** You reach out and take a cigarette from your friend when they offer you one.

- **Consequence:** Positive reinforcement. Your brain gets the drug (nicotine) and calms down. You feel satiated. This positive consequence reinforces and maintains the response (grabbing the cigarette) the next time that the same cues present themselves in a situation.

Doing a FBA helps you identify what it is that may compel you to smoke. Is it the people? What if you were with other people, would you smoke then too? What if you found other ways to get a relief and feel relaxed? A flow practice could help filling that gap.

Being a couch potato

You have so many plans and things to get done when you get home after work — maybe you want to finish weeding your garden or go for a run. But you need to evaluate the draw of the couch:

- » **Situation:** You get home in the evening after work and see the couch and the TV.

- » **Organism:** You feel tired and hungry. You've had a long day, and you have fond memories of relaxation on that sofa stored in your memory systems.

- » **Response:** You let yourself drop onto the sofa and switch on the TV while you gobble down some simple food.

- » **Consequence:** Positive reinforcement. You feel satiated, satisfied, and sleepy. Your brain rings with endorphins, your plan to go for a run is forgotten. The positive feelings provide your brain with the association between the couch and a fast track to enjoyment. Tomorrow evening, you'll do the same.

Sometimes, just changing the outline of the room can help changing a problematic pattern. The cues have changed, you attach new actions to them. Perhaps avoiding the living room, close the door as you get home, so you literally don't *see* the couch at first, could be a way to set boundaries for your senses. Go straight to the kitchen or the garden.

Finding your FBA

Consider a problematic behavior that you know you have and which you think perhaps keeps you from engaging in what could give you flow; use the components outlined in the section "A Functional Behavior Analysis," earlier in this chapter.

Situation

What cues can you find in the situation or the environment that usually triggers you to leave the path that you want to be on? A specific room, people, temperature, activity . . .

Your situation could have this type of cue:

- » The presence of your smart phone in your visual field.

- » Your family speaking to you.

- » Chocolates and sweets.

Organism

What cues can you find inside your head and what feelings and sensations inside your body?

What about yourself (your sensations, feelings, and memories), makes you vulnerable to the cues you identified in the preceding section? Here are some ideas:

>> Current anxiety

>> A feeling of hunger

Response (your action)

How do you respond to the cue that you identify in the section "Situation," earlier in this chapter — the response that you want to change? Maybe your habitual behavior in response to the cues is that you:

>> Grab your phone and swipe.

>> Turn on the TV and sink onto the sofa.

>> Give in and chat with your loved ones.

>> Start cleaning (as procrastination).

>> Play with your pet (as procrastination).

Result (what happens?)

>> dopamine hit from likes on social media

>> reward through the appreciation by other people

>> other neurochemicals in your reward system, satisfying you

If you repeat this chain of events, outside and inside yourself (as outlined in the preceding sections), this behavior becomes a habit that you can find hard to break. Repetitions of actions on cue are the basic principle of *associative learning*, sometimes referred to as *Pavlovian learning* after the Russian scientist Ivan Pavlov, who set up an experiment that trained dogs to start salivating just by hearing a bell ring because previously the bell always rang when they received food.

REACTING BEFORE THINKING

People do like to tell themselves that they're rational beings who have good reasons to do what they do. Yet, plenty of science shows that's not always the case.

In the 1950s, Professor Leo Festinger coined the term *cognitive dissonance* to explain the tension between a person's beliefs about who they are (a reasonable person with logical reasons to do what they do) and conflicting or sabotaging actions. When actions and beliefs don't align, you start a process of self-justification that ends with a great reason for why you did what you did:

- "They had it coming" (after you lash out at someone)

- "I didn't plan to start my diet today anyway" (after eating another sweet)

Read more about this puzzling effect in the human mind, in the book *Mistakes Were Made (But Not By Me): Why We Justify Foolish Beliefs, Bad Decisions, and Hurtful Acts*, by Carol Tavris and Elliot Aronson (Harvest Books).

TIP

Some of the situational cues can be hard to change. Perhaps try to put the phone in another room while you engage in your activity, negotiate an hour of *you-time* where the family leaves you to your own devices, don't have palatable foods at home — simply don't buy them, which removes the cues.

Connecting Your Reward System

In Chapter 3, you can walk through the science that shows the neurotransmitter dopamine is an important messenger substance that humans need to learn new things and to find flow. However, dopamine over-indulgence can also become a problem if you fall into the dopamine trap, which happens easily with some cues. You can get hooked on that little feeling of achievement, however empty it may be. And you can form bad habits, forms of *learned contingencies* (the association of a stimulus with the likelihood of an outcome) between a cue, action, and reward (see the FBA above — this goes for good and bad habits!). Some activities can provide you with many dopamine hits in a very short time span and therefore form a habit loop very quickly (I talk about habit loops in Chapters 6 and 7):

>> Scrolling, liking, swiping on social media

>> Taking drugs

>> Playing games

>> Physically exerting yourself to excess

With these activities, your time becomes one big exhilarating cloud of cha-chings for your brain. After you experience this dopamine cloud, you start craving it. The reward system of your brain becomes dysregulated because of the unnatural amount of dopamine flowing through it. These states can sure feel very absorbing — however, they are far from healthy flow as you can see in Chapter 9 and Bonus Chapter 1 (`www.dummies.com/go/flowfd`).

Figuring out where free will fits in

Dopamine does play a part in what might seem like your loss of free will (see the preceding section). But the action that triggers the dopamine release is the real culprit: the activity that you choose to do and the cues in the environment while you do it. Also, how you do the action, whether in moderation or in abundance, determines the reward that you get from it. And the memory of the reward motivates you to do exactly the same action again.

In Chapter 9 and Bonus Chapter 1, you can find out how to identify and rid yourself (and your surroundings) of cues that prevent you from tapping into flow.

Going camping in ancient Greece

Ancient Greece had two main philosophical groups when it came to pleasure and meaning in life, and they lived in separate camps:

>> The **Hedonists:** Chased the quick and easy highs. They lived enthralled in pleasure — food, sex, and wine. A lot, whenever.

>> The **Eudemonists:** Believed that the highest aim of life is to achieve a state of true well-being or human flourishing (not just momentary pleasure). They preached that for real fulfilment in life, you must seek meaning.

Let's say, the story goes that the two camps in ancient Greece where these philosophers lived were connected via a road. Once a week (sometimes twice!), these two groups of philosophers met for a good philosophical discussion (and some wine and dance!). They mixed and matched pleasure and purpose, and everyone went back home happy afterwards. Funny enough, your brain's reward system works in a very similar way. It has two parts (like the philosophical camps) closely connected via a neural pathway (like the ancient Greeks' road):

>> **The hedonistic part of the brain:** Sits deep down in the reward system, close to the brain stem.

   This system is all about survival and reward maximization (food! sex! now! a lot!).

>> **The eudemonistic part of the brain:** Sits just on top of the hedonistic.

   This system has broader connections to the rest of the brain, including with the meaning-making systems, seeking purpose in life. It has an overview of the consequences of your behavior because of its connections to the memory- and decision-making systems. It also defers gratification (using impulse control) and applies rules to your behavior.

Really, these two parts of the reward system are just subdivisions of the same system, connected by a road of neural pathways. This probably sounds very harmonious, so you may ask, what's the problem? Well, you don't have a problem at all, as long as the behaviors that you choose to do *maintain* the road between the two camps (the hedonic and eudemonic strivings) well-connected.

Giving too much power to one camp

You can start to have problems if you give preferential treatment to one of the two parts of your reward system. Say that you pay attention to only the eudemonistic part (as when you're on a never-ending asquetic quest for purpose and meaning). You'll probably faint in boredom at some point. If you decide to only pay attention to the hedonists of your brain through your behaviors (such as indulging in social media, gaming, and so on for hours on end), you likely create a bad habit or even a behavioral addiction in your brain.

Professor Antoine Bechara and his colleagues at the University of Southern California study the addicted brain. They wanted to find out what happens when a person overstimulates the hedonistic part of the reward system. Their research showed that the hedonistic part of the reward system stopped communicating with the meaning-making portions of the brain. Basically, the neural pathway that connected the two parts of the research participants' reward system wasted away. In our ancient Greece analogy, the road that allowed the two camps of philosophers to visit each other was closed. In the addicted brain, the access to meaning-making, impulse-control, rule-following processes in the brain was severely reduced, which manifested in peoples' behavior and feelings (as illustrated in Figure 4-5).

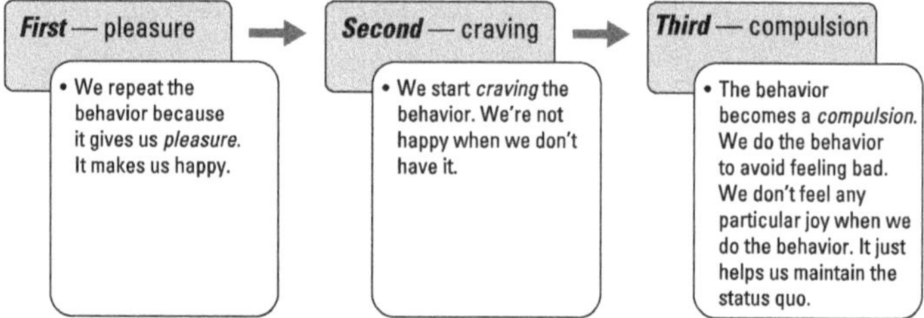

FIGURE 4-5: The way into addiction.

The journey from pleasure to compulsion follows these steps:

1. **You repeat a behavior because it gives you pleasure.**

   It makes you happy.

2. **You start to crave the pleasure that the behavior gets you.**

   You're not happy if you don't have that pleasure.

3. **You start doing the behavior compulsively.**

   You do the behavior to avoid feeling bad. You don't feel any particular pleasure; it just helps you maintain the status quo.

When you develop a compulsion, you're on the way to become addicted. You have a very strong habit loop in your brain (flip to Chapter 7 for more on habit loops), which you can't easily break out of without treatment. You can form these kinds of unhealthy habit loops when the cues are substances (like heroin or alcohol) or rewards that you get from certain behaviors (such as social media, gaming or gambling). Some cues deregulate your reward system, making the hedonists take over and seemingly depriving you of your free will. When the hedonistic brain regions have taken over, you can achieve almost none of the ten Flow Elements (Chapter 2). See more about these particularly bad behaviors and addiction in Chapter 9.

Finding behaviors that help flow

Some behaviors lend themselves particularly well to help you find flow because of the type of reward that they give you. I call them *pleasure-plus behaviors.* They entice both the hedonist and eudemonist parts of your brain (which you can read about in the section "Figuring out where free will fits in," earlier in this chapter), because these behaviors link easily to the 8 behaviors that we know are helpful for tapping into flow (flip to Part 2 of this book for more details about these 8). Dance is one example of such pleasure-plus behavior.

FLYING STEPS

In 2025, I had the opportunity to collaborate with the large hip-hop dance organization, Flying Steps Education gGmbH. A government mandate had thousands of children across Berlin's schools receive hip-hop classes as a way to introduce physical exercise into their lives. I witnessed how some of these children developed flow in their use of dance and exchanged dysfunctional behaviors with better ones. Some children said that when they used to get bored at home, they'd do something like watch TV or annoy their siblings. After starting dance classes, they'd turn on music and practice dance moves instead.

These children unwittingly used functional behavior analysis (FBA; discussed in the section "A Functional Behavior Analysis," earlier in

(continued)

(continued)

this chapter) to correctly identify the situation (being at home) and how they feel (organism: bored), and instead of responding by turning on the TV or bothering their siblings (response), they developed a new response, putting on some music and practicing their dance moves. They received a reward through dance (endorphins from the physical activity, sense of achievement, and expression of feelings through dance), which reinforced this response.

Understanding the Wanting-Liking Principle

Modern neuroscience distinguishes two states of mind in relation to reward that are important if we're attempting to tap into flow — either we *like* something or we *want* something. When we're *liking* something, we've already got it; we're enjoying it *now* in the present. When we're *wanting* something, we don't have it yet, but we're striving toward it, either in mind or in action (or both), to get it *in* the near or far *future*. For flow, it's important to differentiate the two mindsets. They trigger different sets of neurotransmitters to rain down on your neural connections, and this is very relevant for flow:

>> **Wanting:** Dopamine-infused brain soup that makes you strive, feel edgy in the present, and chase after some final reward (that may never come!).

>> **Liking:** This brain soup of the neurotransmitters endocannabinoids and endogenous opioids gives you a feeling of satisfaction, of placidly enjoying the now.

I refer to these two states of mind that constantly compete for our attention the Liking-Wanting principle throughout this book. For flow, we need to work on activating the Liking-mindset. Its special brain soup helps maintain our attention in the present moment and activate all the 10 Elements of Flow that you can check in detail in Chapter 2. In Part 2, you can find out how to activate this liking state in your brain and create the present so that your brain *likes* it.

2

Reverse-Engineering Flow

Chapter 5

Priming Your Brain for Flow

t's time to start building your pathway to flow. Let me ask you something about yourself. What fully absorbs you? What makes you lose track of time and forget everything around you?

Maybe it is something close to home? Helping a child with a school volcano project can unexpectedly pull you into a state of flow. You start out supervising, but before long you are shaping the cone, mixing the eruption, and debating the right color for the lava. The activity stirs memories of your own childhood—of making things by hand, concentrating deeply, and losing track of time. The clock fades into the background, your attention sharpens, and what began as helping becomes shared focus and quiet absorption.

If you can't think of a recent example of what gives *you* flow, reflect on your childhood: What activities could you do for hours on end without getting distracted or bored? Consider whether family or friends perhaps told you about times when you were so completely engrossed in something that they found it nearly impossible to get your attention because you were so focused.

In this chapter, you'll find out how to identify what gets you to flow. It also explores three behaviors that, while highly absorbing, can actually make finding flow difficult. And I introduce what I call the eight Guiding-Star Behaviors for flow, which get you flowing *now*.

Getting Ready for Flow

Take a moment to think about what generates flow in your mind; zoom into yourself and ask the below questions. Without any pressure, write what bubbles up in your mind on the following lines. You don't have to commit to anything you write down here, and you can change it later if you want. But give it a go.

» What absorbs you fully?

» What makes you forget everything around you?

» If you don't remember any recent example — think back to your childhood: what did you do for hours on end?

What have family and friends perhaps told you about your younger self, about when you were totally engrossed? It was completely impossible to catch your attention when you were . . .?

What was *that* for you?

____

____

____

In case you wrote something really highbrow on the above lines, let me briefly tell you about some of the loveliest examples I've heard of what gives some people flow: building model trains (or cars, or houses, or planes), gluing glitter stones on cups, organizing a stamp collection, putting pearls on strings, cutting paper clippings, building apartments for ladybirds in match boxes, gardening, editing spreadsheets, organizing cupboards, practicing calligraphy, figuring out how to write with the non-dominant hand, using *mirror writing* (writing letters and words in the reverse so that they read normally when held up to a mirror; like Leonardo da Vinci did).

TIP

Regular engagement with what brings you flow has a wonderful effect on your brain. After a while, the cues alone can take you away into the zone, even if you're far away from your comfort zone (as when you travel, immigrate or simply are not in the right head space as when you're stressed, angry of scared), and your senses are bushy-tailed and alert. Using your favorite cues and rituals attached to those cues can work wonders for dipping the mind into flow.

Singer Rod Stewart is known to have taken his model trains with him on tour, including the villages and the mountains! I know of at least one comedian who has a ping-pong table back stage. He knows that familiar and repetitive movements act as a washing machine for his mind, letting him step on stage clear and focused.

REMEMBER

The list of possible flow activities is endless; never feel ashamed for what gives you flow. Find what works for you and exploit it.

Now that you have that flow activity from childhood (or more recently) in your mind, I have another question: Why did (or do) you like it? What did you like about it? And, how did it make you feel? Jot down a couple of thoughts and feelings about this activity on the following lines. Don't think about grammar and punctuation. Just write down what's on top of your thoughts right now.

____

____

____

No need to overthink this. Here are some simple reasons that average people list for what they like about being in flow:

>> It's just me and the activity — I just need myself and it.

>> It feels so satisfying — and I somehow feel really *me* when I do it.

>> No one judges me, not even myself; it also stops my thoughts from spinning.

>> It's organized and something that I do in the outside world, something that I can touch, not just in my head.

>> I feel I can actually *do* something when everything else seems hopeless.

>> I have clear and manageable goals. I receive instant feedback on how it's going from the activity itself (see Flow Elements 2 and 3 which you can read about in Chapter 2: "clear goals" and "receiving reliable feedback from the activity itself").

>> It holds my attention, and I feel this glow keeping me going.

>> It gives me peace, feeling effortless, and I'm free to create.

>> It makes me feel *so me,* so authentically myself.

You now have an idea of what gives you flow and you've recalled to yourself what it feels like and what you like about this feeling. Let's now continue to explore this special state of absorption that flow is. Many states of mind are absorbing, yet not all of them are healthy. For example, rumination or gambling are absorbing states of mind, but not healthy — you can read more about this in online bonus Chapter 2: "Healthy and Unhealthy States of Absorption."

Recognizing Negative Mind-Hooks That Thwart Flow

Mind-hooks are behaviors, mindsets or cues that grab and hold your attention, but, importantly, *prevent* you from finding healthy flow.

My Danish publisher Svane & Bilgrav decided to give my book that has the English title *The Pathway to Flow* (Vintage) the Danish title *Opslugt.* This word means something between *eaten up, absorbed, engrossed, immersed, enchanted,* and *not in this world.* (I have a vivid image of myself being gulped up by a whale when I hear the word in Danish.) *Opslugt* can describe both positive and negative absorption. It can mean flow — but it can also mean being trapped by media, rumination, gambling, or other unhealthy mind-hooks.

In Greek mythology three Gods embody perfectly what the three worst mind-hooks are for flow:

>> **Nike:** Goddess of victory (encouraging your competitive feelings)

>> **Dionysius:** God of celebration and wine (getting you to chase pleasure, no holds barred)

>> **Tyche:** Goddess of fortune (making you take those risks)

Everyone gets competitive at some point in their lives, indulges in feasts and festivities, and takes risks that maybe they shouldn't have. That's a good thing — that's part of life. It's what makes you enjoy, build resilience, and grow.

But recent neuroscientific evidence cautions that these three gods — while incredibly *more*-ish — can hamper your flow. In Chapter 4, you can see how overindulgence in Dionysus's very hedonic activities kills the connection between the hedonistic and the eudemonistic parts of the brain's reward system. In Chapter 9, we take a closer look at the science about the behaviors competitiveness, pleasure seeking, and risk-taking, and why overindulging in three Gods of Mind-hooking can't help you reach flow.

Following the Stars as a Guide to Flow

To achieve flow regularly, it's so helpful to follow a guide — like stars can guide sailors through stormy seas. In the same way that the *Pleiades* (a cluster of stars in the sky) have helped guide sailors since humans started to travel in boats, long before there was GPS, *eight* key behaviors can act as your Guiding Stars of Flow. Together, these 8 completely analogue behaviors help your mind and body reach a state of flow more easily.

If you read the eight Guiding Star Behaviors in the following list vertically, you see AIR TIMES — think of the combination of these behaviors as times in which your body and brain are set for flow; you're in the air, your mind flowing, like on a space voyage. Besides, scientific data shows that people who find flow easily (see Chapter 3 for what makes some people more "flow-prone" than others), make sure to regularly . . .

Have	**A** esthetic Emotions
Use their	**I** magination
Have a	**R** outine
Never stop their	**T** echnique Practice
Set an	**I** ntention
Practice regular	**M** ovement
Use their activity for	**E** xpression
Seek a	**S** ocial Community

To find flow, aim for *Air Times*, meaning, include these Guiding Star Behaviors of Flow in your everyday life:

>> **Aesthetic emotions:** Feelings of awe, being moved and wonder are triggered by the activities that you do, things that you see, hear, touch . . . These emotions connect you back to yourself and induce a feeling of transformation of time and space. Leave time in your day to feel awed, moved, and expanded by aspects inside your flow activity — the moves, the colors, the space, the textures, the people. More on aesthetic emotions in Chapter 8.

>> **Imagination:** Use your imagination to power your movements. If your mind's eye remains shadowy, consider external sensory aids to spur your actions. Mental imagery assists the brain in optimizing the motor commands for your practice. Visualization exercises create good movement habits in your brain. The power and potential of the imagination to fuel your flow is explained in Chapter 8.

>> **Routine:** Carve a routine out of your day, or even just a small ritual for five minutes, to submerge yourself into the movements of your craft. Routines and rituals appease your regularity-loving brain. Those repetitive movements become a washing machine for your mind. The special flow-inducing effect of routines and rituals for your brain is developed further in Chapter 6.

>> **Technique practice:** Your routine also provides you daily technique practice, which can forge new neural connections in your brain's movement systems. With time and repetition, these movements pass from explicit and effortful behaviors (that you need to think about each time you do them) to implicit memory systems; they become your second nature. More on this special kind of magic between your ears in Chapter 7.

>> **Intention:** Set intentions *within* every practice session that allow you to remain in the moment, having clear, attainable goals within the activity that you are doing. If you're singing a favorite or new song, the attainable goal is the next bar of the song, not "singing the whole song." If you're drawing, don't think of the finished beautiful or horrifying landscape, but set your mind to the very next line you're drawing, and how it relates to the rest of the drawing. This personal, meaning-led goal aligns your neural activity to make it happen. See Chapter 8 for more on intention-setting that is conducive to flow instead of toward the Gods of Mind-Hooking (as when you compete, want to post your picture on insta).

>> **Movement:** Get 150 to 180 minutes of aerobic exercise per week. All systems in the brain are intertwined with

the brain's movement systems. For your brain, everything is movement, and without it, your brain goes stale and becomes edgy. See more about the science of movement and how important it is for flow in Chapter 6.

>> **Expression:** Equipped with the language of your craft, you can express what's on your mind and in your heart through the movements of that craft. You dance it out in a club, pour your heart into the pages of a diary or a song, or express the eeriness of existence through colors and lines on a canvas. This special antidote to distress and looping thoughts is described in detail in Chapter 7.

>> **Social community:** Connect with the people and groups that surround your hobby activity. Among like-minded people, their smiles and support, the parts of your brain in charge of immune regulation boost the processes of health and restoration. Even if you think you're better off alone, Chapter 6 might give you some science about why a little bit of it will fine-tune your mind for flow.

You can develop a flow tool that includes all of the eight behaviors in the preceding list, but you don't have to. Activities such as dancing can unite all eight (see Chapter 11); reading (see Chapter 15) can't. To set the settings for flow in your brain and body, you want all eight behaviors in your life (even if not necessarily all in your flow–activity). I tell you the science of what these behaviors do for you in Chapters 6, 7, and 8.

You might look at a musician and identify that, while they easily tap into flow, they certainly don't follow some of these stars in their life. And they definitely chase after the goddess Nike; they're very competitive. Perhaps they hardly ever exercise (so, they never follow the Guiding Flow Star of *Movement*). Einstein probably didn't either. How, then, can these people tap into flow so easily if they don't follow all the Guiding Stars of Flow? Chapters 1 and 3 talk about how some people are simply *flow–prone*, meaning they have flow predispositions. Besides, some creative people have an advantage in their brain: They have years of practicing the right habits for flow (you can read more about what this means in Chapter 6). The good news is, with time, you can build those habits, too.

You must set the right settings to flip your mind into the flow state. In Chapter 4, I discuss functional behavior analysis (FBA), a tool that you can use to figure out what can get you into flow, perhaps by using the 8 Guiding Star Behaviors for flow that you have seen in this chapter and which I continue to develop across Chapters 6, 7, and 8. But make sure that you stay clear of the Gods of Mind-Hooking (check out how to spot them lurking about your favorite activity in Chapter 9).

Chapter 6

Movement and Social Bonds

I n Chapter 4, I introduce what I call the *Guiding-Star Behaviors of flow* — the actions and ways of being that can help guide you to flow, in the same way that the stars used to guide sailors to their destination in the Middle Ages when there was still no GPS.

Even in the modern world, there is no digital device like GPS that could catapult your mind into flow. Instead, we can focus back on the analogue behaviors and ways of navigating life of the people before us — as their and our brains have a lot in common. Archeological and anthropological evidence suggests that humans have sought flow ever since. Flow doesn't fossilize. So, there isn't "*a flow state*" on exhibit that we could check for inspiration in a museum somewhere. But as I explain in detail at the end of Chapter 2, what we can do, is to look at traces from the past. That includes traces of things that people made, as much as trances *on* the things that people made.

Like ornamentation and decoration on pottery, coloring of garments — science shows today that *producing* these aesthetic traces on things (as when we draw, carve, knead or knit) is flow-inducing. Or we can look at *use wear* — like the regular marks, chips and dents on some animal teeth that are due to humans using them. Lines of teeth were sown onto garments by stone age people. If you wear this and move rhythmically, as when you dance, this generates a soothing regular rattle sound that eases your dancer mind into flow.

Modern neuroscience also shows *why* these activities are flow inducing. And science has identified 8 behaviors that are particularly helpful to create a pathway to flow in your mind — you can read what all eight of them are in the side bar "Going on A Star Voyage to Find Flow." Knowing what these behaviors are makes it possible for you to apply them to other activities than those that I mention above. You can choose your favorite activity that you'd like to find flow with, and then *reverse-engineer* flow.

In this chapter, I describe two of these eight Guiding Star Behaviors of Flow: movement and social bonds. You can read about the other behaviors in Chapters 7 and 8. Here I dive into the neuroscience behind why you need regular movement and social bonds to access flow; they're not just nice-to-haves. These activities help adjust the settings in your brain and body, clearing mental space for flow.

Guiding Flow Star 1: Everything Is Movement

The marine mammal known as a sea squirt moves a lot while it's a larva. It dances in the currents of the oceans. But when it develops, nature tells it to find a rock, a dock, or some other immobile surface, and settle down. The larvae have a kind of forever superglue inside their *papillae* (small fleshy projections) that they use to glue themselves to the spot that they find. Then, they eat their brain — and they move no more. For the rest of their lives, sea squirts just sit there, filter-feeding plankton that happens to flow their way.

"Much like professors once they've found their tenured position," jokes movement neuroscientist Professor Daniel Wolpert in his 2011 TED-Talk "The Real Reason for Brains."

Neurophysiologists — scientists who study the live brain in action, sometimes at the level of single neurons by using tiny electrodes — are discovering many remarkable things about the human brain: It has fascinating systems for perception, memory, language, emotion, immune and hormone regulation, and reasoning. Yet, despite these diverse abilities, a common thread might surprise you: Every brain system is intertwined with the brain's *movement systems* — the networks in the brain and nervous system that plan, coordinate, and execute physical actions.

So, for your brain, *everything* is movement. The only process that doesn't rely on movement is secretion, like sweating. Every other process relies on connections to your body. Without movement, your brain becomes restless. If you glue yourself to a sofa, binge watching the latest TV series, your brain sees this lack of movement as an alarm signal, telling it something is wrong. In an evolutionary sense, immobility indicates danger — if you aren't moving, your brain thinks you're trapped, injured, ill, or otherwise unable to move. Your brain's survival systems scream in agony if you do this to yourself.

Because of your body's need for activity, movement is the first Guiding Star Behavior for flow (see Chapters 5, 7 and 8 for more on Guiding Star Behaviors for flow — and you can see in the side bar).

GOING ON A STAR VOYAGE TO FIND FLOW

These are the eight Guiding Stars of Flow explained in detail in Chapters 5, 7 and 8. You'll find the first two, Movement and Social Bonds, in this chapter.

1. **Movement**. Collect 150-180 minutes of aerobic exercise per week. All systems in the brain are intertwined with the

(continued)

(continued)

movement systems. For our brain, everything is movement, and without it, our brain goes stale. You must move.

2. **Social Bonds**. Connect with the social community surrounding your hobby activity. Among like-minded, their smiles and support, the parts of your brain in charge of immune regulation boost processes of health and well-being.

3. **Routines and Rituals**. Carve a routine out of your day, even just for 5 minutes, to submerge yourself into the movements of your craft, on repeat. This appeases your regularity-loving brain. Those repetitive movements become a washing machine for your mind.

4. **Technique Practice**. They will also be your daily technique practice, that will forge new neural connections in your brain's movement systems. With time, and repetition, these movements pass from explicit, effortful, to implicit memory systems; they become your second nature.

5. **Expression**. Equipped with this new language of your craft, you will be able to express what's on your mind and heart, through the movements of your craft. As when you dance it out in a disco, purr your heart into the pages of a diary or a song, or express the eeriness of existence through colors and lines on a canvas.

6. **The Imagination**. Use your imagination to power the movements. If your mind's eye remains shadowy, consider external sensory aids to spur your actions. Mental imagery assists the motor planner of the brain in optimizing the motor commands for your practice. All this creates good movement habits in your brain.

7. **Aesthetic Emotions**. Aesthetic emotions triggered by the activities you do connect you back to yourself, induce feelings of transformation. Leave space in your day to be awed, moved and expanded by aspects inside your hobby — the moves, the colors, the space, the textures, the people.

8. **Intention**. Set a soft, playful intention at every practice session. Aim for an attainable goal; singing a favorite or a new song, draw that beautiful or horrifying landscape, dance a cherished dance step, etc. This personal, meaning-led aim will align the neural activity to make it happen.

Here are some ways your brain will respond to prolonged inactivity:

- » **Fight or flight:** You experience a primal arousal to threats, real or imagined.

- » **Cognitive disruption:** You have difficulty thinking clearly and solving problems.

- » **Rumination:** The brain activates all sorts of negative memories, just to make you move. As a result, these memories rise to your inner eye as *thought loops* (cycles of negative or unproductive thinking).

- » **Physiological arousal:** Your heart rate, breathing rate, and level of stress hormones all rise.

- » **Emotional agitation:** You become anxious or stressed, feel generally low.

REMEMBER

The human brain doesn't really distinguish the kind of danger a person's in. It can't tell the difference between you sitting too much, being ostracized by your peers, or sensing a dangerous animal outside in the dark. It just activates the fight-or-flight system. See Chapter 4 for how stress plays your body orchestra and blocks flow.

Movement itself calms the mind because your body stops sending signals about needing to move to the brain. This calms your nervous system, gets rid of the excess arousal and prevents ruminations and worries. Once freed of these distracting loops of thoughts, this helps you reach or continue your flow state.

TECHNICAL STUFF

According to many studies, sitting excessively during the day is linked to an increase in ruminative thought loops. And scientists agree that it causes all sorts of physical problems. The act of sitting bends your hips unnaturally forward, straining the lower back. You probably have your head thrust forward, leaving your neck looking like a humpback whale, straining your upper back. Most chairs cut off circulation in the legs. As you can read about in Chapter 4, your body and brain work together in a carefully directed body orchestra. Your inner body contains specialized receptors that send signals to the brain about how the body is doing (Chapter 2 talks about the senses, including those internal ones).

Getting out of your head and into your body

You probably know the to-do-list loop: "First, I'll do this, then that, then that, and then I'll be done!" — and over it starts again. Despite having not completed a single task on the list, creating it still feels rewarding because the very act of outlining what you want to do feels like progress. Each time that you complete the to-do list in your thoughts, you think, "All done!" For a brief moment, your brain savors the satisfaction of having completed a task — and your reward system explodes in a short jubilation.

That sense of satisfaction motivates your primal brain — the one that wants a quick dopamine hit. For me, this type of merry-go-round of a mental to-do-list happens when I'm working on a scientific article. When I cycle off to yoga on my bike, I have different sections of the article I need to write hovering in my mind. I think: "First, I'll write that paragraph, then that other; then, I'll deal with that section that doesn't work quite yet. Ah, and I need to redo the analyses for that little bit to complete that section. Oh and that graph needs another tweak. But when I finish that, I can submit the article. Yaaaay!" And then I start again at, "First I'll . . . "

These thoughts aren't negative (at least, I hope not!). It's just part of what happens when you plan future actions. It activates your neural systems for memory, recall, planning, and rules, as well as triggering the reward system and its shot of dopamine to motivate you toward your goal. Humans are fairly unique in the animal kingdom because they can simulate the future and plan ahead.

Comparative psychologists — scientists who compare cognition across species — research whether birds (such as crows and ravens) and great apes (such as chimpanzees and gorillas) can do similar mental time travel. Science doesn't have a clear consensus on whether other animals can think ahead, but if they can, studies suggest they can do so in only a very rudimentary way.

Humans are unique in their ability to plan ahead — but because of that ability, they need to avoid getting stuck in loops. Circular thoughts are normal, even remarkable — but they're poison for flow. Research shows that people can't effectively redirect these thoughts, especially when each loop ends with a small reward.

To avoid getting stuck in thought loops, get out of your head and into your body. Movement helps you with this, big time. Your movement activity should absorb as many of your senses as possible. (And you can read more about how to make that activity interesting and filled with joy in the section "Guiding Flow Star 2: Social Bonds and Flow," later this chapter.)

Especially if you have a flow activity that doesn't give you a lot of movement (such as writing, reading, knitting, working on spreadsheets, and so on), you may find it challenging to shift gears into flow and get those thought loops to stop. But if you make sure that you have enough movement in your life, in general (more on that in the section "Movement throughout your life," later in this chapter), then you can find flow more easily. You need to get out of your head and into your body to find flow. You must fuse actions with awareness. (More on that connection in Chapter 7.)

Taking a yoga class can help you get back into your body. At first, when you sit down, the looping lists still swirl through your mind. But while the class gets going and becomes more challenging, you need all your mind power to focus — and the to-do lists are silenced. A dance or a run can have the same effect. Figure out what works for you: Maybe a good run gets you back into your body.

You don't have to be a hardcore athlete, dancer or artist to increase your movement enough to find flow. Plenty of not-very-sporty geniuses make a habit of moving every day. British author Charles Dickens said that "walking restores the soul." The Japanese author Haruki Murakami says that he writes for six hours each day and then goes for a long run or swim. Movement makes the brain go round.

Movement throughout your life

So, how much movement in your life do you need to set the settings for flow in your brain, to help your brain rid itself from all that unhelpful arousal that inactivity produces inside us?

The World Health Organization (WHO) has access to enormous amounts of data about the current world population's health. They can run large statistical models and look at how different variables — such as how much people exercise in a week — influence risk of developing different diseases or even dying. What does that have to do with flow? Well, it's all about preventing negative things to happen to your body which could derail your ability to find flow — like unhelpful thought loops for example. Exercise is such a simple first step to take on your pathway to flow. Step by step, literally, you'll be getting closer to the flow zone.

According to WHO recommendations, the amount of *aerobic exercise* (activity that makes your heart rate rise above 140 beats per minute) that you need per week depends on your age:

>> **Age 5 to 17:** At least 60 minutes of moderate- to vigorous-intensity physical activity daily

>> **Age 18 to 64:** At least 150 minutes, up to 300 minutes, per week of moderate physical activity or at least 75 minutes of vigorous-intensity activity per week

>> **Age 65 and over:** At least 150 minutes, up to 300 minutes, per week of moderate physical activity or at least 75 minutes of vigorous-intensity activity per week

Depending on your age, you should also do specific training for the large muscle groups of your body:

>> **Age 5 to 17:** Activities to strengthen muscle and bone three times per week

>> **Age 18 to 64:** Muscle strengthening of major muscle groups two or more days per week

>> **Age 65 and over:** Physical activity three or more days per week (to enhance mobility and prevent falls) and muscle strengthening of major muscle groups two or more days per week

The data shows that if you don't exercise regularly, you have about 20 to 30 percent increased risk of death. Other risks depend on your age group.

Children and adolescents who move insufficiently have

>> A high risk for obesity

>> Poor heart-health and fitness

>> Behavioral problems and less pro-social behavior

>> Reduced quality sleep

Adults who move insufficiently have increased risk of

>> Death

>> Cardiovascular disease

>> Cancer

>> Type 2 diabetes

Young children and elderly people particularly benefit from regular movement practices that also involve coordination:

>> **The young:** Children benefit from movement coordination exercises for their cognitive development. For example, one study showed that dance-coordination exercises that included geometrical concepts helped children improve in their written geometry exams.

>> **The not-so-young:** Elderly adults benefit from movement coordination exercises to prevent both physical and cognitive decline (keeping both the body and brain healthy). Movement exercises also provide a work-out for cognitive functions. Elderly adults who don't move daily not only have more frequent falls, find it harder to avoid obstacles, and have more injuries — they also have more memory problems, have more difficulty finding words, and struggle to solve logical problems.

So how to get started with getting this much-needed movement into your body? Do you need to go for a run? Dance? I recommend to start with something much more feasible. Walking!

Maybe where to start is with what my friend did. He had a different motivation than flow at first: Miguel had always been over weight his whole life. After the pandemic he had what his doctor called "clinical levels of overweight" (a BMI of 40). One day he just got up one morning and walked. He started walking each day, in the mornings, just 30 minutes. Everyone can get off the sofa and walk for 30 minutes.

Morning lunch time or evening — whatever works for you. Differently abled people also have plenty of opportunities to get the heart rate up over the 140 beats per minute. Miguel increased exercise and today, 3 years later, his weight is "normal" from a medical point of view (BMI of 20). He is the happiest person on earth, and without aiming for it, he noticed that his mind space freed up too. He is currently finding flow with renovating his first own home. We *must* move each day. It sets stuff in motion. The difficulty is, of course, to get that routine into our daily life. We'll speak more about that when we arrive at Guiding Flow Star Behavior 3 in Chapter 7.

TAKING ADVANTAGE OF CREATIVE MOVEMENT TO POWER YOUR FLOW

TIP

There is something about moving creatively as when you dance, make music, knit or craft that connects our brain in new ways and helps us tap into flow too. Besides, moving creatively creates intrinsic motivation — you want to do the activity because it feels good to do the action itself, not because you're expecting some ulterior reward. The movement itself starts to matter to you personally, which activates both parts of your reward system — the more immediate-pleasure-based one and the meaning-based one introduced in Chapter 4 — making flow easier to achieve. (You can read about how intrinsic motivation is one of the 10 Flow Element in Chapter 2.)

For more about movement-based habits that can encourage creativity and flow, where they come from and how to make them, check out Chapter 7.

Guiding Flow Star 2: Social Bonds and Flow

People who tap into flow regularly make sure to have social bonds in their lives. Even famous lone-wolf creators made sure to have social rituals woven into their everyday lives. Jane Austen, Pablo Picasso, Victor Hugo, and Leo Tolstoy — they all had families and social lives, but also clear boundaries for their work.

Family life and friendship groups can certainly become a full-time fixture, but many highly successful and productive people who use flow to boost their success say that they factor the social stuff into their day's plan, just as much as they plan for their work. Maybe you have a morning routine of hugs with your partner before having breakfast together, or you schedule a coffee in the afternoon with your best friend. For finding flow, rituals of social bonds — laughs and physical contact — help you reach flow in the times that you set aside for those flow activities.

Social isolation

According to data from the WHO, social isolation and loneliness significantly increase risks for our physical health — for stroke, heart disease, diabetes, cognitive decline, and early death. For our mental health — loneliness doubles the risk for depression, heightens our anxiety levels, and can lead to suicidal thoughts.

Unless you have a very strong flow practice anchored in your brain, it will be impossible for you to find flow when you're feeling lonely or socially excluded. For how to prepare yourself for times of isolation, see Part 4 of this book (meet with people socially distanced, even with strangers, make sure to smile at each other, look each other in the eyes, listen to the radio — the radio hosts become part of your everyday, they are your pandemic family, and so on. Get "social nuggets" into your system). It's not because you're not strong-willed enough that you won't be able to flow if you're lonely. It's simply because your physical body will detect the threat, and switch on the stress symphony (see Chapter 4).

REMEMBER

Research shows that loneliness and other social stress is one big possible reason for autoimmune diseases. When the body is unhappy, again, as in the case of lacking movement opportunities, signals raise to our brain that become cues in terrible merry-go-rounds of ruminations and worries — making Flow Elements 9 and 10 impossible (= breaking those loops; see Chapter 2).

Social exclusion

Emma (not her real name) was having a great time. She was playing ball with the two cool girls in class. It was the first sunny day of the season, and the ball game went back and forth and back and forth over the lawn. They were having fun, their naked feet feeling the grass for the first time this year.

After the initial good moments, however, Emma noticed that the two girls only cheered at each other's "*good catch!*," never at hers. Plus, she had somehow slowly ended up on the shadowy part of the lawn. Here, the grass was still quite chilly and her feet were getting cold. First it was just a feeling, but then it became clear: the two cool girls were gradually "forgetting" to toss the ball her way. Their cold shoulder stung her chest.

This "game" that many people play in the real world, ostracizing other people in work-places, friendship groups, families, etc., has been taken to the lab many times. Researchers place

participants in front of computers and make them play the
"cyber ball game" (that's the name of the game Emma was
playing, but in the lab). They are told that they are playing with
two other research participants in different rooms. In reality,
it's just an algorithm designed to ostracize people. Before and
after the session, the scientists take saliva samples of the
participants — this is to check for the levels of stress hormones
in blood. Can you guess what social exclusion does?

Rejection and social exclusion impacts physiology — it switches
on our fight or flight response, as if we were a caveman being
chased by a sable tooth tiger. Social exclusion and loneliness
feelings can happen in the real world, as much as online. As a
result, stress hormone increase in the body, as does inflammation. This arousal raises to our conscious mind, from our
body, activating negative memories and other ruminative loops
in our brain, like worries and fears. It is poison for our body, and
for flow.

Research shows that even the simple fact that someone averts
their gaze or turns away from you in the real world, ignores or
ghosts your messages online makes stress hormones spike in
your body.

TECHNICAL
STUFF

If you struggle for social connection in your present life, try to
connect with others through a flow practice, such a hobby community (fitness, crafting, or dancing). You can have more luck
finding your people if they already share your hobby-interest
that you can connect over. Non-committal social connection,
such as sitting together in a café engrossed in your mutual
hobby, can give you a good place to start looking for connection.
See the end of this chapter or Part 4 for some examples.

TIP

Wandering with the vagus nerve

Nerves are communication channels throughout your body. If
you look through medical history books, many of them mention
one particular nerve time and time again: the *vagus nerve,* a key
nerve of the parasympathetic nervous system that supports
calm, recovery, and balance after stress.

We owe our initial knowledge of this nerve, which gets its name from its vagabonding nature (*vagus* means *wandering* in Latin), to medieval medical doctors who risked their lives by dissecting dead bodies in secret — an illegal practice. While doing their detective work, the vagus nerve kept catching their attention. It wasn't a single thread, but a branching network — one that seemed to wander everywhere. No matter where in the body the doctors worked, there it was:

>> **All the vital bits:** Emerges from the brain, runs through the spinal cord, and connects with the heart; from there, it branches off to the lungs and to the gut

>> **The face and voice:** Connects the brain with the body's facial muscles, as well as the *vocal tract* (the parts of the throat that enable a person to speak)

>> **Hearing:** Connects the muscles and nerves in the ears, which enable a person to hear, with the brain

The vagus nerve connects a body entirely. This nerve is so important to flow because it links how safe and balanced you feel within your body with how you feel in the world. Through the vagus nerve, signals travel constantly between the brain and the body, shaping heart rate, breathing, facial expression, vocalizing, and listening. When this system is working well, the body settles, attention opens, and interaction — whether with other people or with a task — feels more natural and fluid. When your inner balance is disrupted, you're more likely to tense up, disconnect, or become self-protective, making sustained focus harder to maintain.

TECHNICAL
STUFF

Nerves transport information from one part of the body to another, via a mix of tiny electrical impulses and biochemical processes. Electrical impulses (called *action potentials*) travel along the neuron thanks to the flow of ions along the nerve. When the electrical impulse reaches the end of a neuron, it triggers a biochemical process in which the neuron releases neurotransmitters into the tiny space between that neuron and its neighbor neuron. That neighbor neuron reacts to the neurotransmitters, and the piece of information travels on as an electrical impulse through that nerve until it reaches its end, triggering the release of neurotransmitters. And so on.

But the vagus nerve wanders through your whole body. The information travels directly, no need to "jump" between nerves. From face to heart, from voice to gut, from ear to lungs, and so on. It provides a direct connection between the inside of your body and what American neuroscientist Steven Porges calls the *social engagement system*, which includes the muscles of your face, your hearing, and your voice — and which *engages* with the social world outside you.

In Chapter 4, I talk more about the special connection between your body and brain and the environment via bidirectional channels of communication — information flows from one to the other and back.

GIVING THE VAGUS NERVE A COLD SHOWER

If you want to briefly see the vagus nerve in action, take a cold shower. Afterwards, you feel so relieved and satisfied because of the neurotransmitters, such as endorphins and dopamine, that your body releases. Your nervous system passes from sympathetic activation to parasympathetic activation:

- **Sympathetic:** Rouses you for action. Think, "the cheerful sympathetic one!" This is the system that makes you ready to fight-or-flight, but it is also a system that is useful for action in general, like your work and when you're having fun.

- **Parasympathetic:** A relax-and-restore system that slows your breathing and heart rate, and switches on restorative processes in the body. It functions a bit like a break to the action of the sympathetic activation.

A cold shower can switch off the fight-or-flight sympathetic nervous system. The vagus nerve takes care of the *diving reflex,* which switches on the parasympathetic nervous system when receptors in your skin by cold water and holding your breath. When you submerge your body — especially your face — in cold water, although it does give you a great feeling, evolutionarily speaking, it's actually to protect your body from the shock of the cold. And the vagus nerve supports this reflex.

Soothing cues: Faces, voices, touch

When you connect with people in whose company you feel safe, a special system in your body — the social engagement system — becomes very active. Steven Porges, a neuroscientist from the University of North Carolina, and his team work to raise awareness about this system, and especially about the face-heart connection that is at the core of the special power that social bonds have on our mental and physical health.

Through senses such as vision, social information from the people around you help regulate your nervous system. This information can include a smile, a caring voice speaking to you, or the sound of kind laughter. When you receive this information, your breathing slows down, as does your heart rate. Stress hormones are eliminated from the blood, and inflammatory processes in the body are reduced. Other people can trick your brain into a restorative state just by being present in a kind way.

Metaphorically speaking, hands seem to have channels to the heart. In one study, a team of researchers from Yale University played a trick on their participants' social engagement system. They gave them either a cold or a hot drink to hold in their hands. Then they asked them questions about another person that also took part in the experiment. Those participants holding a warm drink described the other person as more caring than did those holding a cold drink.

Another team of researchers recreated the experiment, with participants simply holding a cold or a warm therapeutic pad — and got the same results. Humans' sense of touch is easily tricked into social bonding. In another experiment, a group of Japanese researchers had two groups of overseas university students text their loved ones abroad — either just using their smartphone or while also holding a furry toy. Compared with the smartphone-only students, the students who clutched a toy while texting had less stress hormones in their blood after only 15 minutes of texting.

Channels from the social world around you funnel information via your senses to the brain and then to your heart, gut, and other organs. When these surroundings are good — for instance, in a non-judgmental and non-competitive hobby community — these lovely others switch your body to restoration. Your brain regulates your immune system, preventing or reversing inflammation in the body and signaling to your conscious mind that a fight-or-flight situation is over. This mind-and-body state provides a wonderful foundation to finding flow. The social symphony rings out in your body — see Chapter 4 for more about this body symphony.

Understanding how a person bonds

Connecting with other people and feeling that you belong somewhere is important for your physical and mental health — and therefore, for your flow potential. But for many reasons, you may find making social connections difficult. Perhaps you're an introvert, or perhaps you're just not surrounded by the people who tick like you, so you can't find much to talk about. What to do?

Neuroscience has uncovered four fascinating mechanisms by which your brain tricks you into feeling connected to people around you. You just need to find opportunities to attend the same event, such as a concert, a play, or a movie night — or, even better, do synchronous movements together, such as singing, dancing, or knitting. When people walk in lockstep, dance to the same groove, or otherwise sync their movements together, these four exciting neural mechanisms in the human brain are triggered:

>> **Co-representation**: When you move, your brain generally knows that you're the one moving. Likewise, when you see others move, your brain represents that movement as the movement of another person. However, when you and another person are doing synchronous movements, your brain gets confused in the most wonderful of ways. The neural activation of my and your movements suddenly overlaps in the motor system — so the brain now represents somehow both you and the other person as one.

Neuroscientists call this process in your brain co-representation. Research suggests that people who move in sync feel friendly toward each other afterwards, help each other more readily, and more efficiently solve a problem together.

>> **Synchronization of your body's rhythms**: Whether you're moving together or just attending to the same cue, your brain responds by syncing your body rhythms with those of the other people around you. Suddenly, you all feel closer to each other.

>> **Release of bonding hormones**: Moving together in synchrony directs your body orchestra into a bonding symphony (see Chapter 4), making bonding hormones such as oxytocin and prolactin stream down onto your neural connections.

>> **Arousal misattribution**: If what you do or attend to is a little more exciting — such as watching a scary movie or trying to figure out an escape room situation — you can experience a funny process called arousal misattribution. (Read more about this in the section "Arousal misattribution," later in this chapter.)

You've probably experienced a situation in which you feel closer to someone, even if you haven't known them for long, after you solve a difficult problem together because your brain attaches an arousal sticker for that person in your memory system because of that bonding experience.

TIP

All creative activities that you can practice socially can eventually help you synchronize your brain's systems with those of others and give you the dose of social contact that your brain needs so that you can perhaps find flow more easily in other domains of your life, where you might not have as much positive social connection. See Chapter 12 for some examples of group flow.

TIP

If you want more guidance on making the best of the social connections you already have and perhaps forging new ones, I recommend the book *The Laws of Connection: 13 Social Strategies That Will Transform Your Life* (Pegasus), along with the social media feed of its self-diagnosed introvert author, David Robson.

Conforming as a survival strategy

The modern human brain looks very much like a homo sapiens brain 300,000 years ago. It hasn't really been updated. Prehistoric humans had to belong to a group to survive. And the human baby needs years of care. Even after reaching adulthood, a human body's strength is far less than most similar-sized animals. But humans have the remarkable ability to live in large social groups without killing each other. No other mammals can live in such large groups as we do — there are no mega-cities of dogs, cats; not even of elephants.

Evolutionary pressures have therefore made sure that humans feel great when they're conforming to the status quo. This helps with being able to live together in large groups. Neuroscientific studies have actually shown that research participants' reward systems light up when they conform to a group norm. So, people even have neural systems that react with pleasure when they conform to the status quo. This may seem counter intuitive as we're often taught that we shouldn't be conformists. Especially in individualistic societies we like to think of ourselves as not very conformist at all.

Yet, that doesn't mean that our brains don't have the hardware to do it. This information is important to set the settings for flow in your brain. Our mammal brain craves this "fitting in" and reacts with great distress to the lack of it, and to social exclusion. So, we need to feed it social nuggets to appease it. Sometimes this means that we need to conform to a social norm we may not agree with. Be careful with conformism too. Your brain may work to make you fit in, even if you don't. Notice when you're putting up with abuse, just to fit in.

I'm sending you out into the wild here, to connect with other people for *positive* health effects and to boost your flow potential in other parts of your life. For example, I encourage you to seek social bonds in hobby communities. This doesn't mean that these communities are somehow holy goodness and always healthy. Absolutely not. Look out for signs of abuse and social exclusion wherever you are. Guard your social brain fiercely. See more about the risks of social connection and how to avoid them in Chapter 9 and online bonus Chapter 1: "Selecting Cues and Setting Boundaries."

AROUSAL MISATTRIBUTION

In 1974, scientists Donald G. Dutton and Arthur P. Aron from the University of British Columbia conducted an experiment to determine whether environmental factors influence how people perceive others:

- **A stressful situation:** The researchers had a young lady stand on a scary, high-altitude bridge while people walked by her. Because of the anxiety caused by the instability of the bridge, the people's hearts pounded and hands were sweaty while they crossed. At the end of the bridge, a couple of researchers asked each bridge crosser how attractive they found the young lady they passed on the bridge.

- **A normal day:** On another day, the young woman stood in a crowded shopping mall. A couple of scientists stopped random people who had just walked past the young woman to ask them how attractive they found her.

On average, people found the same woman more attractive if they encountered her on a scary high-altitude bridge. Dutton and Aron called this phenomenon *arousal misattribution* — your brain attributes the arousal that you feel because of the situation to the person. As much as this confusion can provide a great mechanism to connect with someone, it can also be dangerous to feel so close to someone you don't really know.

Arousal misattribution plays its own special kind of symphony in our body, which can play a trick on you. You can mistake the physical connection with someone — orchestrated by your brain after an arousing situation — as genuine connection. Please remember that you can only really know someone after spending meaningful time together.

Trusting your social instincts

Research shows that often people surround themselves with others who don't have their best interests at heart. Rather than trying to avoid all of it altogether (social isolation), practice ways to notice harmful others and put up boundaries to protect yourself.

Look out for what psychologists call your *social emotions* — feelings that you get through your interactions (in the real world, online, or even in your thoughts). These sensations that come from social connection include positive emotions (such as gratitude, pride, love, sympathy and affection), as well as negative emotions (such as guilt, shame, embarrassment, jealousy, envy, and contempt).

If you're not very good at labeling your and others' emotions (see Chapter 3), look out for physical sensations (such as heat, stinging, sinking, etc.) that usually accompany these emotions.

Interoception, the sense of your body from within, includes information about what you feel inside yourself, such as your heart beat, breathing, whether you feel hot, cold, or hungry — and your emotions. (Find a full discussion of the body's senses in Chapter 2.)

So, when you're around people, pay attention to your body. What is it telling you? Friend or foe? Follow these steps to find out:

1. **Take the emotion test in Figure 6-1 in relation to different important people you're surrounded by daily. (You can read more about this test in Chapter 3.)**

    You may have to surround yourself with these people, not by choice (such as coworkers).

FIGURE 6-1: Mapping how you feel in our body when surrounded by people you see daily.

2. **Identify what emotions you feel and how they feel in your body.**

3. **When you detect a negative feeling, acknowledge it.**

   Don't suppress it simply because you perhaps have to interact with that person.

4. **Try to understand where the feeling comes from by using the functional behavior analysis (FBA) tool.**

   You can read about this tool in Chapter 4.

   For example: Is the person ostracizing you? Ridiculing you?

5. **After analyzing your interactions, you have identified the triggers.**

   Now you know what the triggers of your bad feelings are.

   Ideally, find a community of people where you don't feel these negative emotions. Choosing loneliness can sometimes provide an initial solution, giving you time to withdraw from the situation. But then seek connection again — with people who elicit positive emotions in you.

If you don't choose wisely between friends and foes when you have the choice, you may find that flow remains elusive. With your body's fight-or-flight system on high alert when you're surrounded by foes, you can never achieve *sensory decoupling* (where your internal thoughts are separated from the input of your environment), one of the ten Elements of Flow discussed in Chapter 2.

STUDYING HAPPINESS

Scientists have collected data for more than 80 years now — for the world's longest study of happiness. What did they find so far? Besides regular exercise that keeps the body healthy (movement, which you can read about in the section "Guiding Flow Star 1: Everything Is Movement," in this chapter), what made people lead the happiest lives wasn't money, job security, or academic achievement — it were the social bonds they had.

Lack of movement and social isolation in your life can prevent you from finding flow. For evolutionary reasons, lacking these life elements makes a very unrestful mind, which makes keeping your attention on a task long enough to tap into flow really difficult. On the other hand, research shows that regular movement and social connection protects people, lowering inflammation in the body and the risk for serious illnesses, as well as extending life and stimulating mental health. They also help you build the foundation of your flow practice. Movement and social bonds set the settings for positive affect in your brain — precisely what you need for flow.

Chapter **7**

Rituals, Technique, and Expression

Everyone wants to have productivity in life and business. Researchers from a famous consulting firm say they have data to show that you can get up to 500 percent more productive if you can access flow. Some trends present productivity and flow as necessarily related, and some people say that you use flow to become productive.

But that connection doesn't actually exist: As soon as you start aiming for *extrinsic motivation* (external rewards that motivate your actions) such as productivity (answering ten e-mails, getting praise from the boss, finishing a draft, solving a formula, writing functioning code, and so on), you sabotage your access to flow.

In Chapter 2, I explain the ten Flow Elements that describe what it feels like when you're in flow, one of which is *intrinsic motivation* (Flow Element 5; when you do something for the joy of doing it). For an example of extrinsic motivation, you probably don't sit and move your thumb vertically over a screen because you find that motion itself fun — you do it on your smartphone, perhaps for hours per day, because of the extrinsic rewards that you garner if you do that motion within a social media app (likes, insights, beauty, funny stuff, and so on).

Conversely, you can find movements rewarding and fun to do for the *doing* itself. Examples of movements you may feel intrinsically motivated to do include moving your hands across clay as you spin your pottery wheel, or through the air in a beautiful dance motion. For this wonderful feeling of Flow Element 5 (intrinsic motivation) to take hold in your chest and make your mind tap into flow, you also need to keep an eye on Flow Element 7, the skills-challenge balance. You should find the activity you're doing neither too hard nor too easy. How can you achieve this balance — and keep it? The magical word is *mastery*. Now don't let the word mastery demotivate you. It all begins with the first step.

In this chapter, you can explore how body movements can shape brain function and carry you through the day — and into flow. (I talk more about the movement systems in your brain in Chapter 6. Here, we'll take this knowledge a step further.) Routines, rituals, and supportive habits provide the most reliable antidote to procrastination, lay the groundwork for clarity and presence, and offer the balance between skill and challenge that flow requires.

Also, I talk about technique practice and the surprising ways that it reshapes the brain. Far from being mechanical or restrictive, it fuels many of the same qualities that make flow possible.

Expressivity, an elusive concept that's often hard to define, gets the *For Dummies* treatment in this chapter to make it tangible and practical and to show you how it supports your flow practice by giving you mental calm and effortless action.

Aiming for Flow

If you want to follow a science-based pathway to flow, focus on your flow practice, whether that's at work or in your personal life. When you can focus consistently on that practice, productivity tends to follow — but as a side effect, rather than a target.

Instead of working harder on being productive, you work harder on creating the conditions in which flow can arise by engaging deeply with the thing that you do (or want to love) and by shaping your behavior around three foundational practices: routines or rituals, technique practice, and expression.

These words can sound prescriptive, even a little like schoolteacher instructions. But when you look at them through the lens of neuroscience, they become something else entirely. They're not rules, but rather ways of working with the brain and body, instead of against them. I call these behaviors three of the Guiding Stars of Flow because they can help you tap into flow (I introduce all eight Guiding Stars of Flow in Chapter 5; in this chapter we'll see Guiding Stars of Flow 3, 4, and 5.)

If you take a look at Chapter 2, where I explain what it feels like to be in flow by summarizing what I call the ten Flow Elements, you can see how the Guiding Stars can help you get there:

>> **Guiding Star of Flow 3:** Routines and rituals help you create good habits and can enable Flow Elements 2, 3, 6, 7, and 8. In the following section ("Guiding Star of Flow 3: Routines and Rituals"), I go into detail about this Guiding Star.

>> **Guiding Star of Flow 4:** Technique practice builds mastery in your brain and can stoke the same 5 Flow Elements as routines and rituals. Check out the section "Guiding Star of Flow 4: Technique Practice," later in this chapter, for further discussion.

>> **Guiding Star of Flow 5:** Expressivity can be a difficult concept to grasp. But in the section "Guiding Star of Flow 5: Expression," later in this chapter, I try to make it totally touchable and practical — and explain how it can get you Flow Elements 1, 6, 9, and 10.

Neurophysiologists (scientists who directly examine the electrical activity inside the live brain to determine normal and abnormal functioning) have found that the brain has fascinating systems for perception, memory, language, emotion, immune- and hormone regulation, following rules, reasoning, and more. And all of these different brain systems are intertwined with the brain's movement systems. So, for your brain, really, everything is movement. Besides, your brain is connected through the spinal cord to the rest of the body. Long *ganglia* (clusters of nerve cells) run through your spine and into muscles, organs, and so on. You have a constant flow of information between the two. The movements that you do with your body can literally change what's going on in your brain. It's all about choosing the right moves.

Guiding Star of Flow 3: Routines and Rituals

People who tap into flow regularly make sure they have routines or rituals in their daily life — actions on repeat that feel rewarding and familiar to them. Plus, routines and rituals have some very useful effects for flow on your brain. Importantly, you don't have to make a routine complex or overly disciplined.

Maybe you have a morning routine; something as simple as starting the day with a cup of coffee, watering your plants, or walking your dog. Think about what's always around you when you do that routine. What do your eight senses perceive? (I discuss the eight senses in Chapter 4.) Psychologists call everything that enters your senses *cues.* For example, you smell the coffee brewing (cue) or feel dewy grass under your shoes (cue). Recognizing the cues that impact your senses during your routines and rituals can help you understand the conditions that, every day, lead you to the ritual or routine. And this understanding can help you create rituals and routines that best support achieving flow.

REMEMBER

In this section, I use the word *routine* a lot. If you can more easily identify with the term *rituals*, rather than *routines*, please feel free to use that term. The word *routines* can sound prescriptive and like you have to do a lot of work, discipline, and drilling. This perception can stop you in your tracks, especially if you have *demand avoidance*. That's a behavior profile to resist demands, requests and expectations. It can be caused by emotional exhaustion or sensory overload (such as in people who are very stressed or at risk of burn out). It also often occurs in people who have ADHD or autism, where it is likely an anxiety-driven need to resist such demands, often referred to as pathological demand avoidance, or PDA (check out Bonus Chapter 5 at www. dummies.com/go/flowfd). To avoid that your brain resists the suggestion of a "routine," I invite you to think about the science that I talk about in this section as the movements of a ritual that you really like.

You probably have routines throughout your day. Perhaps you always put a specific hat on when you write. Or maybe you put on a specific outfit so that your skin feels that particular fabric when you do yoga. Maybe you burn incense while you draw; or you sit in a café, surrounded by the scent of coffee and freshly baked croissants, while you code. Do you put on a candle each time you practice the piano? Or do you listen to a specific song that gets your mind flowy while you wing those spreadsheets?

The French Enlightenment philosopher Voltaire (1694–1778) wrote and dictated his works in bed as part of his morning rituals. If you do an Internet search for "Castle of Voltaire in Ferney," you can take a look at the gold-adorned bedroom that constituted the *cue-scape* of flow for Voltaire. I use *cue-scape* playfully here. Just like "landscape" is a view of the lands and "moon-scape" is the view of the moon, "cue-scape" is what type of cues are around you — not just to your eyes, but to all eight of your senses.

TIP

Look out for the cue-scapes around you, and for which cues are conducive to flow and which are not.

In your evening routine, maybe you get home, feeling exhausted, grab some chips from the cupboard, throw yourself on the sofa, switch on the TV, and let your mind drift away — which is possibly *not* an example of healthy flow (see Bonus Chapter 2 at `www.dummies.com/go/flowfd` for the difference). You can have routines that benefit you, but some routines can have a negative impact on your life and productivity. And your brain establishes the good and bad routines in the very same way.

Developing routines (rituals!) through habit loops

Routines and rituals are actually made of movements (actions) that you execute after receiving a cue in a given situation and then feel a reward from doing that movement. You see the sofa (cue), and you lower yourself onto it (action), then you feel relieved (reward). You see the remote control (cue), and you switch on the television to your favorite program (action), which provides the dopamine hit that follows (reward). You often do these things without thinking. But how do these movements get so hard-wired into your brain that they become second nature and you seem powerless to change these habits that force you to live a life with not enough movement, even though you know better? (See Chapter 6 for discussion of Guiding Star of Flow 1, movement.)

Neuroscientists call this succession of cue-action-reward *habit loops*. Each time your senses take in the cue, the promise of reward logged in your memory systems pulls you forward to do the action and garner the reward again (a process called *positive reinforcement*).

When you repeat actions over and over again, your brain initiates an energy-saving process. It's much too costly in terms of energy expenditure for your brain to do every movement consciously and with intention. At the start of learning a skill, you need to think about the process very effortfully. With time and repetition (with routines or rituals), these actions get encoded from explicit, effortful memory systems into implicit, procedural memory systems. You can read more about this transition in the section "Guiding Star of Flow 4: Technique Practice," later in this chapter.

You don't have one brain for good habits and another for bad habits. The same neural systems make both. That's a blessing and a curse at the same time. You can work to control the cues that you expose your senses to, and you can identify these cues (and make a conscious choice to change them!).

Of course, you never deal with just one cue — you face many cues and many small and large actions of your body. For that reason, you can find it difficult to manage your responses consciously. So, first consciously create the conditions (meaning a good cue-scape) that can guide you to good flow-bringing habits, and then, second, expose yourself regularly and strategically to these cues and actions for them to pass from explicit to implicit memory systems. The following section takes a closer look at how your brain makes movement, how it learns and optimizes movement, and how that movement becomes second nature, so you stop thinking and start to use that movement functionally or for expression.

Learning through habit loops

Any skill that you have — whether blinking, breathing, walking, or speaking — is constructed from many habit loops in your brain. The *habit loop* is the basic unit of learning in the form of special neural connections coded into the movement systems of your brain. Many habit loops make up routines; actions that form a whole ritual and that you execute on cue. With time and repetition of ritual or routine, the perception-action gaps become smaller in your brain (this reduction of the perception-action gap is Flow Element 8, discussed in Chapter 2), so you don't think consciously about this action anymore — it passes into your brain's implicit memory systems. You just see the sofa, and your brain does the action of lowering yourself onto it. Figure 7-1 shows the three elements of a habit loop.

As illustrated in Figure 7-1, after you establish this loop and repeat the action (like you do when you repeat routines and rituals), your brain works tirelessly to reduce the perception-action gap. While the gap between the cue (what your senses perceive) and the action (what you do) diminishes, the cue-action association becomes more automatic and you need to give less and less attention to the whole process for it to happen. It just happens. For good and for bad habits alike.

FIGURE 7-1: The three elements of a habit loop.

REMEMBER

As you can read about in Chapter 2, Flow Element 8 is that wonderful feeling that you get in flow when you experience a fusion between your actions and your awareness. That feeling occurs after you reduce the perception-action gap. So, you need to craft good habit loops to achieve flow.

THE EGYPTIAN GOD OF MOTION AND THE SOLAR SCARABAEUS

Every morning, over and again, the sun rises, and you have a persistently beautiful gift at the tips of your fingers and toes, ready to be unwrapped: 24 new hours to fill with tiny and huge steps toward your dreams — and to build a flow practice.

Like the little scarabaeus beetle that rolls its little dung-ball on and on, every day anew, the ancient Egyptians believed that the God Khepri rolls the round ball of the rising sun up over the horizon every day. The dung-ball-rolling scarabaeus is Khepri's symbol, and he's also often depicted as a scarab-headed man (see the figure in this sidebar). He brings the morning sunlight and invites humanity to be reborn for a new day, full of actions.

Step into that new wonderland every morning, and make it yours! Of course, that's the catch: While you step into the day, your brain steps with you (and it's full of habits — good and bad ones alike).

Khepri symbolizes all the opportunities of rebirth, new beginnings and transformations that you can undertake every morning afresh. However, when discussing neuroscience, he also symbolizes the loop — in brain terms, the habit loop. Many people's brains contain dung-ball habits that roll them through their days. More often than not, people find these habits quite difficult to separate from, even if they don't like those habits. Why can't you just snap out of it? The section "Turning cues into drivers of actions," in this chapter, looks at a complex behavior (or ritual) that can help unwind those loops, and how that all relates to flow.

Turning cues into drivers of actions

You can develop any kind of habit, whether positive or negative, by going through the cue-action-reward series discussed in the section "Developing routines (rituals!) through habit loops," earlier in this chapter.

For example, if you want to figure out how to drive a manual-transmission car, you need to develop a shifting habit:

>> **Cue:** Accelerate until the car starts making a whining sound. That sound provides the cue that you need to change gears.

>> **Action:** You change gears (hopefully, smoothly!).

>> **Reward:** After you change gears, the whining stops, which makes you relax because dopamine rains down on your neural connections.

>> **A habit loop starts building:** This dopamine reward makes those connections stronger, which starts to form a habit loop. Dopamine acts as a learning signal for your brain, telling you to do that action again for more reward.

The next time that you hear that whining from your car, you do the same action. You repeat this behavior in part because your brain knows that it'll get the reward of dopamine. With time and repetition, this habit loop gets stored in implicit memory systems. This frees up resources in your brain. That's how you can now both drive while shifting gears, singing along with the song in the radio, or have a conversation.

You go through the same process if you develop a habit such as eating cupcakes every day. Say that you have a box of cupcakes at home (maybe someone gave them to you). With those cupcakes at home, you can develop a bad cupcake habit (as shown in Figure 7-2):

>> **Cue:** You see the box that contains the cupcakes (it stares at you!). That's the *cue.*

>> **Action:** You grab a cupcake, put it in your mouth, and chew and swallow it.

>> **Reward:** The tons of sugar in the cupcake triggers your brain's reward system, releasing dopamine.

>> **A habit loop starts building:** With time and repetition, eating cupcakes becomes a bad habit via positive reinforcement. It's a routine that you do when your eyes see the cupcake box.

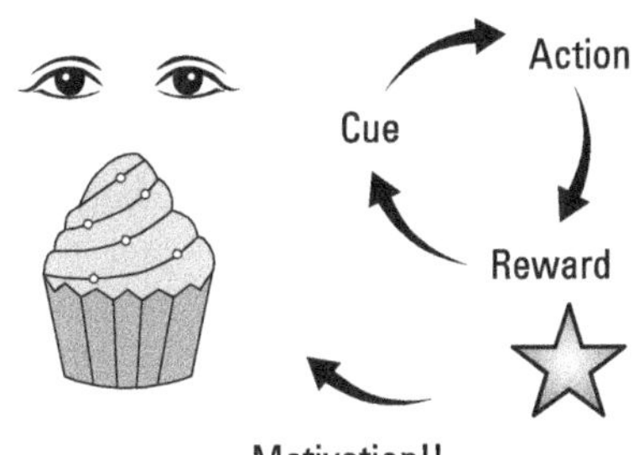

FIGURE 7-2: The making of a bad cupcake habit.

Turning motor plans into complex moves

You might assume that it's your muscles that make your body move. However, the truth is that the command to move comes from your brain. The way your brain makes movements is complex, but let's break it down a little. For the purposes of developing a flow habit, know that your brain encodes habits in huge numbers into *motor plans* (detailed plans for how your brain executes complex movements). By executing movements repeatedly, complex skills (such as driving a car, dancing, drawing, or knitting) become engrained in your implicit memory systems, that you execute when your senses perceive the right group of cues (never only a single cue).

Motor plans consist of many motor commands. *Motor commands* are the actual neural signals from the brain that travel via long *ganglia* (groups of neurons) in the spinal cord to execute particular movements of your body. The motor plans get shaped by practicing the movements. A motor plan never involves just a single movement; instead, it includes movement sequences. Everything — from your habitual daily routines and rituals, to the movements of a sport, craft, or profession — involve complex movement sequences that you execute on cue.

REMEMBER

Daily habits, the behaviors that you routinely do, consist of many motor commands that form motor plans for specific movement sequences which always execute when your senses perceive specific cues. These habit loops mostly happen outside of your awareness.

People usually think of habits as complex movements, such as brushing your teeth (a good habit) or doom-scrolling before bed (a bad habit). However, from a neuroscientific perspective, habit loops are dopamine-infused loops of cue-action-reward at a very tiny level. To change the bigger habits, you need to straighten out some of these habit loops and fortify others.

Understanding how your brain forms habits can help you change those habits. The first step to change your habitual movements (for instance, to bring a new movement routine (ritual!) into your life) involves detecting your cues that spin you into your habitual actions (see the following section).

Recognizing your cues

You can find cues that trigger behaviors everywhere — they constantly engage your eight senses (which I talk about in Chapter 4) if you let them. They spin you into your habitual actions and thoughts, preventing you from changing the track of your best laid plans. Cues can come from:

>> **Inside your head and body:** Engaging the senses of interoception and proprioception

>> **Your habitual surroundings:** Engaging the senses of sight, hearing, touch, smell, taste, and exteroception

>> **Your friendship groups:** Engaging all your senses!

Of course, the three cue groups in the preceding list are inter-related. Those from the environment and from other people enter your brain via the external senses and add on to the cues that your senses of interoception and proprioception already provide.

Bonus Chapter 1 goes over these groups of cues in detail and provides examples. But when it comes to routines, what you let into your senses — the cues in your surroundings (for example, the news, social media, or events) or from people around you — enters your brain and can become cues that trigger negative habit loops. The more you repeat these habit loops, the smaller the perception-action gap becomes, and the less conscious control you have over how you feel. Choose wisely. To build a flow habit, you might sometimes have to turn your back on some cues (either figuratively or literally) to prevent them from entering your system and disrupting your focus.

Putting the right habit loops in place for flow

"Habit is the bed of creativity. Tuck yourself in," says Steve Rushing in his article "25 Daily Rituals Of History's Most Successful . . . And What You Can Learn From Them" on Medium. And in terms of habits being the core of flow, it's right on.

Because habit loops shape your daily actions, reactions, and even thoughts, guard yourself against habit loops that work against your plans and goals. Some loops help you focus, create, or solve problems; others pull your attention away, often without you noticing. If you know how to arrange these loops, you can protect your focus and flow.

Here's an example: Tim, a stock market trader in Frankfurt am Main, Germany, shared with me his ideas about habit loops. In his brain, he has a ton of habit loops that he uses to detect good and bad patterns in numbers; he sees bull and bear market trends; he knows when to hold a stock (in trade jargon, to hold on for dear life [HODL] — meaning don't sell!), rather than sell it and invest heavily (you only live once [YOLO] — which means invest heavily!), and he can do a DD (meaning a *due diligence analysis* to determine all the factors potentially affecting a stock) in his sleep.

But he refuses to read a newspaper because he doesn't want that information in his *thought landscape* (the term is a very literal translation of a German expression, *Gedankenlandschaft*); you can clutter up your thought landscape when unrelated cues enter your mind's eye while you try to focus on something. For Tim, all that information becomes cues for other thoughts, it's like a domino effect. One thought leads to another, and he says, "Then it all spins together, and distracts and disturbs me from what I'm doing. If I read a newspaper, my productivity drops that day."

Of course, I'm not suggesting that you shouldn't read the news. However, like Tim, you may want to wisely choose when you expose your senses to certain cues (such as newspapers, social media, people who trigger you, and so on) because of the effect that you know they have on you. Simply acknowledge that you have a special relationship, a habit loop, with that cue; then put the cue into your day where it fits (if you can't avoid it altogether), such as reading the news at a specific time of day because you don't want the world to go to shreds without you knowing about it but also don't want it to interfere with your life. Make sure you engage with cues that are likely to disturb your thought landscape outside of your flow practice.

Letting helpful cues into your thought landscape

To see flow in action, look closely at the cues and routines that shape your day. To stick with the example of Tim (introduced in the preceding section), who operates in a high-performance environment and knows flow well, he has clear ideas about what prevents him from finding flow. But knowing what stops flow isn't the same as knowing what gives you flow.

Tim, like many flow-prone people, generally doesn't really know what makes him tap into flow so easily, and he can't offer much advice about how to achieve it. Such people may suggest you focus on routines and rituals, and offer vague advice. "I just do it," Tim said when I asked. However, we can examine Tim's behaviors to see how he strings together cues and actions for "Guiding Star of Flow 3: Routine and Rituals."

Tim's morning starts with an alarm clock that catapults him out of bed at 5 a.m. He runs for 3 miles (5 kilometers), eats a healthy breakfast, and meticulously grooms before starting his 12- to 16-hour work day.

REMEMBER

Just to be clear, you don't need to become a health guru (or work such long hours as Tim) to find flow. I use him as an example to illustrate how he strings cues and actions together in his life. Like with many flow-prone people, without knowing it, Tim has placed strategic cues in his surroundings that benefit him big time.

Take a look at Tim's cues, particularly scents, sounds, how he feels in his body (proprioception/interoception; flip to Chapter 4 for more about these senses), and cues from other people:

» **Scents:** He uses specific scents throughout his day — wood-like scents in workspaces, lavender in the bedroom, and the cologne he's used for years that signals the start of his day.

» **Sound:** He prefers absolute silence in the mornings to set the tone for the day. At work, he listens to electronic music on headphones (such as music by the duo Tube & Berger) or rhythms that mimic movement (for example, music that sounds like a train in motion) to maintain focus and momentum.

Adding a rhythm to your flow practice, perhaps always the same music, can help you pace the movements and acts of your flow activity, acting as cues from the environment that tip your brain into action. Rhythm has a special *gating effect* (meaning it helps the brain to filter out redundant, repetitive, or irrelevant sensory stimuli), which you can read about in Chapter 10.

» **Cues from the body:** He starts each day with a run, creating a distinctive bodily feeling — active and engaged, taking action — that his brain now associates with starting the day, helping him get set up, physically and mentally. That feeling in itself has become a cue for action. The mind is ready to flow. He also schedules his meetings, travels, and engagements by taking into account his energy levels, considering the work load in specific weeks, and so on. The calm serenity that he needs for tapping into flow at work is always present, and he's not distracted by factors such as sleepiness or pains from too much traveling.

» **Cues from other people:** He manages interactions with clients and coworkers very carefully — by checking his work e-mails at set times (usually around lunch), avoiding morning meetings during his most productive hours, and limiting social media to once a week or special occasions.

I don't have a clear answer for where flow-prone people get the drive to include such cues in their lives. For some flow-prone people, their parents or siblings made sure that they had positive associations between the feeling of flow and specific cues in their environment while growing up. In other cases, the individuals themselves realized that they already had positive associations with specific cues, and so they expanded the cue-scape that helps them tap into flow, building on those early cues of their life.

So, look out for cues that you like and find ways to combine them with actions that you need to do every day. For example, What scent to you really like? Does a particular scent relax you? Does a particular scent get you energized? Experiment with scents to see what can provide you a positive cue.

Tailor your movement routine to your personality. Some very flow-prone people aren't like Tim; they don't move regularly. Einstein wasn't known for his physical prowess. Flow works for the flow-prone who aren't big movers because they have:

>> Other flow-proneness traits (see Chapter 3)

>> The good luck that their families brought the right flow-supporting habits into their brains early on

You can use the power of habit loops in your brain to make your actions in the day less effortful — and leave space for flow to come. And you can use such habit loops to reduce the perception-action gap in your brain for your flow activity (which opens up possibilities for tapping into many of the Flow Elements that I discuss in Chapter 2).

If you want to know everything about habits, where they come from, and how to make them, read *The Power of Habit*, by Charles Duhigg (Random House).

In the following section, you can look to sports neuroscience for advice on how to craft the right habits in your brain, why you need the right loops of cue-action-reward, and how to avoid creating sloppy loops in your brain.

Being aware of lurking bad habits

For the human brain, everything is movement, which I talk about in the section "Developing routines (rituals!) through habit loops," earlier in this chapter. So, even if you're not an Olympic athlete, you can take what people who move for a living know about how the brain makes and optimizes movement because you move all day, too, even if you just use movements of your mind that you execute on cue. The human brain doesn't have systems for Olympic sport and systems for working at desks. It's all one brain with *one* movement system, which you can optimize.

Sports neuroscientists working with Olympic athletes are obsessed with perfection. It's all about the right serve, the right grip on the racket, the right position of feet, hands, head, and torso. The tiniest amounts can make the whole difference. Athletes need to get the move right from the outset because if they don't, they create the wrong habit loops in their brains. Your brain can't distinguish a good angle of the wrist during a serve from a bad one. As long as the ball goes in the approximate direction that you want it to, your brain gets that dopamine reward. Your brain creates a habit loop with the action that you just performed.

For an athlete, that habit loop creation can cause a problem because it makes their actions imprecise and also makes their performance vulnerable to interference from the outside. In sports neuroscience, this interference is called *choking under pressure.* When the athlete is under stress (for example, playing in front of a roaring crowd, being behind an opponent in points, or being emotionally wound up), they fall back onto bad habits and often lose the competition.

Sports scientists see in the data that — no matter how much the training focuses on eradicating the wrong positioning of the wrist — when under pressure, the bad habits (which are usually the simpler, less elaborate actions) return.

Read a powerful account by Scott Boswell about what it feels like for a cricket star to choke under pressure in *The Guardian* newspaper article from 2020 "Under pressure: why athletes choke" (www.theguardian.com/sport/2020/nov/05/under-pressure-why-athletes-choke).

Non-athletes can gain two important lessons from why a pro athlete can choke under pressure:

>> **Changing already established habit loops is hard.** It takes time, and especially in moments of stress, anxiety, and other emotional turmoil, you likely fall back into old patterns. To counteract those bad habit loops, look out for your cues, change the bad ones, and introduce new ones. Resist your brain's tendency to go with the familiar. Do less, but do it well.

>> **Listen when someone who has experience warns you away from bad habits.** Whether in your work, flow practice, or sports practice, slow down and make sure you learn the movements well from the outset. For example, in an Argentine tango dance class, teachers often start by showing you how to step from the inside of your foot toward the outside of your foot while you roll off during a step. In this dance style, you need to walk (and later dance) consciously and delicately for stability.

>> Every type of work and practice has plenty of little technical subtleties that you may not know, and you therefore inadvertently introduce a bad habit loop into your brain that can later make finding flow difficult because you keep making little mistakes in complex movements without realizing it. Ask the experts of the craft what bad habits (and the cues for those habits) you should look out for.

REMEMBER

Sloppiness, stress, and exhaustion make bad habit loops, whether for life, work, or specific habit actions. Especially under stress, people fall back on those bad movement habits (just think of the sofa, how it's a cue that attracts you, especially when you're stressed and want to escape).

If you create strong and efficient habit loops in your brain, they can make you resistant to interference from the outside and inside of your mind. Set your mind to create some routines/rituals that work for you in your everyday life. Become a detective for cues, and never underestimate the power of an alluring cue such as sofas, sweets, and TVs to drag you into a dung-ball habit (which you can read about in the sidebar "The Egyptian god of motion and the solar scarabaeus," in this chapter).

In this section, I want to encourage you to give your life a flow practice space, until those movements on repeat craft your own flow habit in your brain. If you tailor your pathway to flow to your needs, you can step into flow when you need it. You need to find the very small difference between being pulled about by cues like a marionette by the strings and having agency over your life by performing beautiful skillful actions.

You have technique practice (Guiding Star of Flow 5, discussed in the following section) to aid your routines and rituals of everyday life, turning the dung-balls of your brain into beautiful pearls on a string that light the way through your days, making you flow and feel great.

Guiding Star of Flow 4: Technique Practice

People who experience flow regularly make sure to give their flow tool regular technique practice, even if they have only five to ten minutes between all the to-do's, e-mails, and meetings.

Did you know that Einstein failed his university entrance exams in language and history? That he was broke and unemployed at some point? The myth of the genius is that they woke up one morning and excelled. As a result, too many people think that either you have the ability to create, have success, and find flow, or you don't.

The secret of the genius, if done right, involves technique practice because of the powerful effect that repeated intentional movements of your body have on your brain. (Flip back to the section "Putting the right habit loops in place for flow," earlier in this chapter, for more on the role of repeated movement in establishing a flow practice.) As we said in the previous section: *Habit is the bed of creativity. Tuck yourself in* — and we may add: and flow will follow.

Studying the brains of musicians and gamers

Jazz players can play themselves and their audience into a trance-like state — they find group flow together, especially when they improvise. *Improvisation* is that moment where the musicians take all the rules they know about playing music and use them to express something that's not in their notes, not pre-arranged, and not agreed on beforehand. They jam.

In 2016, a team of researchers (probably huge jazz enthusiasts) from Drexel University, in Philadelphia, Pennsylvania, designed an experiment to help jazz musicians get even more creative during improvisation. Or, so they thought.

In the mid-2010s, researchers hyped *transcranial magnetic stimulation* (TMS), in which scientists use magnetic fields to introduce electric energy into the brain, in an attempt to boost cognitive functions. In this case, the researchers wanted to zap musicians' brains to boost their jazz improv.

Jazz musicians show incredible skill during improvisation. So, the scientists' logical assumption was that introducing more electric energy into the prefrontal systems of the musicians' brains via TMS would boost their performance because the prefrontal systems hold on to all the rules. So, they hypothesized that introducing more energy into these systems would lead to more improv skill.

The experiment enlisted two groups of jazz musicians; a group of beginners and a group of professionals. While they played, the researchers applied TMS to the musicians' prefrontal cortices.

The results showed that the novices got slightly better at improvising, but the professionals got worse. Other research in the past years had similar results when looking at professional musicians' brains while they improvise. As soon as the pro plays themself into the flow state, their brain seems to let go of the activity in those rule-loving prefrontal systems. So, when musicians are improvising, they don't have more activity in these systems of rules, they have less. Instead, deeper structures of their brains take control — systems that are about intuition and letting go of the self, which perhaps explains why musicians (and other people who reemerge from experiencing flow) feel as if they've been part of something greater than themselves after a session.

To answer why professionals get worse when their prefrontal cortices receive a boost in energy, professional gamers' brains may offer insight. A team of researchers from the University of Tübingen in Germany invited 40 participants to have their brains scanned by using an electroencephalogram (EEG; a machine that monitors electrical activity in the brain through electrodes placed on the scalp) and their heart rate recorded while they played the video game Thumper. Half of them were advanced and regular videogame players, half had never played this particular game before.

A special connection exists between the heart and the brain. When your heart beats, the brain notices it; each beat makes your brain's electrical activity spike a tiny bit — your brain saying, "Hello, heart. You're still there, great!" You can measure each beat, in fact, as electrical activity inside your brain. So, by using an EEG, you can not only measure what your brain is doing, but also the so-called *heartbeat-evoked-potential* (HEP), electrical activity in your brain that reflects a signal from your heart (in this term, *potential* just means spike in activity); basically, the cross talk between your brain and heart.

In the gamer experiment, the more absorbed the players were during the game, the lower their HEP spike, meaning that players' brains were less attuned to their hearts. They let go of what scientists call *self-referential-thinking,* meaning the brain's awareness and monitoring of the body. However, the hearts and brains of the absorbed did communicate. The whole crosstalk between body and brain just became more efficient. The data showed that the more absorbed a player was, the better their performance in the game — and the higher the (very low!) HEP spike in their brain. The players' brains had simply cut away all unnecessary hubbub and relied on efficient communication only in neural networks needed for intuitive, fast, and efficient action.

Saving energy through training

So, why is technique practice a Guiding Star of Flow if the professionals stop using the parts of the brain that hold on to the technique and all its rules (as discussed in the preceding section)? And why do Olympic athletes have their perfectionist training routines (as discussed in the section "Being aware of lurking bad habits," earlier in this chapter)?

The jazz musicians, gamers, and athletes don't stop using the rules that they learned; very much the contrary. Their brains had passed the skill from the explicit memory systems that cross-talk with the prefrontal cortex to another level, the implicit memory systems that connect with the intuitive part of their brains.

Consider your first driving classes. At first, you didn't think that you could ever do all those actions at the same time. Different movement sequences for head, eyes, hands, arms, legs, and feet to deal with and coordinate:

>> The gas and brake pedals

>> The gear stick to shift the gears if you have a manual transmission car

>> Levers for turn signals and windshield wipers

>> Rearview and sideview mirrors

>> The other cars in the street

>> Bicycles, motorcycles, and pedestrians

But today, you navigate the busy morning traffic while singing along to the radio, having breakfast, talking to someone, or just thinking your own private thoughts. All while your body executes the motor sequences of driving.

A movement sequence can become your second nature. You suddenly have enough resources to do other stuff, perhaps listening intently to an audiobook, while your body executes all these complex coordinating movements on cue, as if on autopilot.

The trader Tim (whom I talk about in the section "Putting the right habit loops in place for flow," earlier in this chapter), athletes (discussed in the section "Being aware of lurking bad habits," earlier in this chapter), and jazz players and gamers (see the preceding section) — not to mention you learning to drive a car — all take advantage of a mechanism that the human brain has developed to perfection over millennia of evolution, which allows you to learn very complex things (such as driving a car, performing athletic movements, speaking languages, playing jazz, and so on). This energy-saving mechanism, discussed in the following section, is unique in its complexity and astounding in its simplicity.

Passing a skill from explicit to implicit memory systems

When you keep repeating a movement, your brain recognizes this repetition. In terms of energy efficiency, you need to expend too much effort to have full awareness each time you do movements. It burns too many calories to be so conscious! Therefore, conscious repetition of an action — whether performing a serve, making a dance move, typing on a keyboard, or singing a song — causes your brain to initiate a transition from *explicit memory* (the effortful, conscious sort of memory) to *implicit memory* (unconscious memory, which takes less effort). Scientists also call implicit memory *procedural memory.* You might call it *autopilot.* See Figure 7-3.

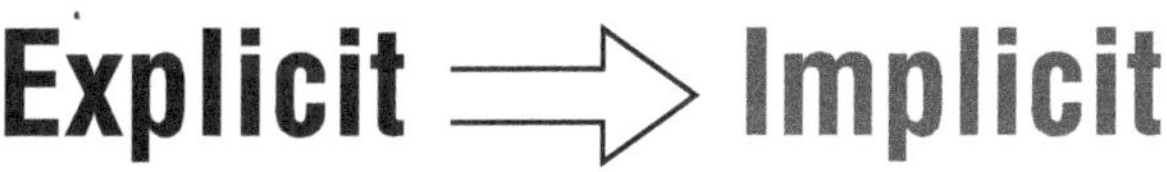

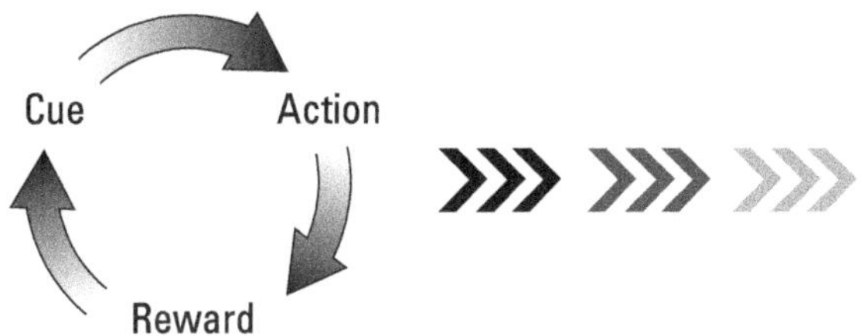

The implicit memory system helps explain why sports scientists want to prevent their Olympic athletes from scooping up bad habits (which I talk about in the section "Being aware of lurking bad habits," earlier in this chapter). After you transition these bad habits to the implicit memory systems, you really have to work to break out of that autopilot.

TECHNICAL STUFF

Parts of your memory systems sit in the *temporal poles* of your brain (the area from your temples and back toward your ears). The entire network of our memory system spans more systems, such as the *hippocampus* (which supports memory, learning, navigation and perception of space), the *dorsolateral striatum* (involved in transmitting sensory information), the *amygdala* (which handles emotional processing and memory), and the *neocortex* (the source of higher-level functioning).

To influence your memory systems, to trick them into helping you build mastery (as when they store a skill in the implicit system), choose the movements that you repeat with your body *wisely*.

REMEMBER

Your brain links all the habit loops needed for a motor sequence into motor plans (which you can read about in the section "Turning motor plans into complex moves," earlier in this chapter). Then it shifts it all to the next level — to the implicit memory systems — so that the brain can execute the motor plan all in one go, without needing conscious awareness of every single step. This transition helps with Flow Elements 6 (feeling effortless) and 8 (reducing the perception-action gap), and you feel that you become the movement — see Chapter 2 for what that's all about. And you can read more about how to work your flow practice so that it becomes second nature in Chapter 10.

To hold Flow Element 7, the skill-challenge balance, you must keep working your skill. And remember: *Habit is the bed of creativity. Tuck yourself in.* Flow happens inside actions that require skill. And you get skill from technique practice. After you practice intentionally for a while, your brain switches on energy-saving mode, which initiates the passing of this set of actions into the implicit memory systems. When this switch happens, your flow practice becomes second nature.

Looking at how technique training changes the brain

Your brain changes in a use-dependent way. Although changes in muscles and tendons can take two to three months of training to become visible, changes in the brain actually occur much faster. When you practice a skill, the neural pathways involved in that skill get strengthened.

Think of that neural pathway strengthening like how a simple muddy path in the woods can slowly become a small road because people repeatedly travel on it. Then it becomes a street, and then a motorway. Although you may find traveling on a muddy path difficult, you can travel fast along a motorway. The same transport principle applies for information in your brain. Training creates motorways for information to flow in your brain. It reduces perception-action gaps and increases the density of habit loops that compose motor plans for complex movements within your implicit memory systems. Therefore, you can focus on creating and flowing away, instead of on the movements, having to focus on the skill itself.

REMEMBER

Habit is the bed of creativity, tuck yourself in – and flow will follow. Habit is the bed of . . . [say it out loud!]

Neuroscientists show these training-dependent changes in the brain's neural pathways with neuroimaging scans. For example, in a study where a group of adults learned to juggle, researchers visualized changes in the participants' grey and white matter by using neuroimaging scans. Here's a breakdown of these parts of the brain:

>> **Gray matter:** The cell bodies of the neurons, their *dendrites* (branching impulse-reception cites), and their *terminals* (where the impulses originate)

>> **White matter:** The neuron's *axons* (the long bits), covered in *myelin,* a white insulating fatty substance that protects the axons

After just one week of training, the neuroimaging scans showed changes in the jugglers' visual motion area (called *V5/MT*) and in the *posterior intraparietal sulcus* (which sits between the brain's two hemispheres toward the back).

The V5/MT area plays an important part in your brain's processing of visual motion, and the posterior intraparietal sulcus helps coordinate your hands and eyes. You need those parts of the brain in good working order if you want to follow and catch multiple objects flying through the air while you juggle.

Those jugglers' brains had changed in a use-dependent way — specifically, in a juggle-dependent way. The human brain can fine-tune neural pathways so specifically and delicately by following a very peculiar little map, which I talk about in the following section.

Meeting the tiny human in your brain

In 1937, the neurosurgeons Wilder Penfield and Edwin Boldrey shared an incredible discovery that they had made during their surgeries: what they called the *sensorimotor homunculus* of the human brain. During their surgeries, they used tiny electrodes to stimulate different bits of both the motor cortex and the sensory cortex in their patients' brains.

The motor cortex and sensory cortex stretch over the center of your brain, lying right beneath where you would put on an Alice headband, with the sensory cortex just in front of the motor cortex. In Chapter 4, I talk about how your brain looks wrinkled because it has a much too huge surface to fit into your skull if laid flat. So, a lot of brain matter exists within the *sulci* (the grooves and folds of your brain). In particular, the *intraparietal sulcus* looks like a dividing line of your brain from front to back — like a very straight parting of your hair.

With their electrodes, Penfield and Boldrey detected a sort of map of the human body inside these two strips of cortex. Along that Alice band of your brain, different areas manage different parts of your body. Take a look at Figure 7-4 to see the sensorimotor homunculus of the human brain. Some parts of the body, such as hands, lips, and tongue, appear very large in this representation, while areas such as the knee and head have proportionally much smaller representation.

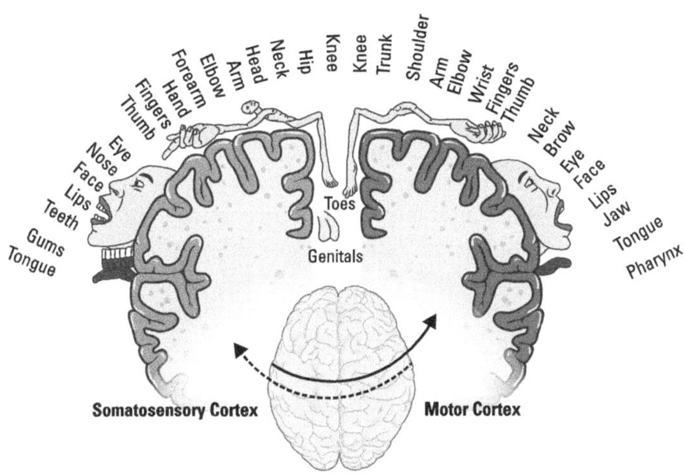

Think about the many subtly different moves that you can make with your lips, tongue, and fingers: much more complex movements than what you commonly do with your head and knees. The more complex the moves you need the body part to do, the more space that body part occupies in the sensorimotor cortices of your brain. That's why the tiny human in your brain has such different proportions than a real human.

Thanking your neuroplasticity

Neuroplasticity is your brain's capacity to form new connections (many habit loops, discussed in the section "Developing routines (rituals!) through habit loops," earlier in this chapter) and rework existing ones — basically what you revise when you practice a technique (as discussed in the section "Looking at how technique training changes the brain," earlier in this chapter). While you practice your technique, your brain's neuroplasticity changes an unknown, mysterious sequence of movements into a skill that you master, becoming your second nature.

REMEMBER

The sensorimotor homunculus (discussed in the preceding section) gives you a map of the different parts of your sensorimotor cortices that you stimulate based on which skill you're practicing. Little by little, connections strengthen and become more efficient and flowable.

If one part of the sensorimotor cortices gets damaged — for instance, by stroke or accidents — other parts of these cortices can potentially stretch out their connections, sprout some new axons, and help the part that can't function to its full potential. Neuroplasticity works from birth till you leave this world. While you engage in the repetitive movements of your fingers tapping on the keyboard or writing words in longhand, this neuroplasticity can help you develop your pathway to flow because your senses decouple and your mind becomes more able to tap into flow.

When people go into flow-like states, the activity over prefrontal parts of the brain diminishes, and instead activity increases in systems deep down in your brain, including the limbic and those that are about intuition, and that help you connect with your authentic you. In the following section, you can dig deep into that newly found second nature with your skill, going one step further on your pathway to flow, by following "Guiding Star of Flow 5: Expression."

Guiding Star of Flow 5: Expression

People who are flow-prone make sure to express themselves, their authentic self, regularly. They may practice this self-expression through their flow practice itself, their work, or a separate activity that they do, outside of the practice that they want to give them flow. Expression plays a role in finding Flow Elements 9 and 10 — ridding yourself of worries and ruminations, and giving yourself a feeling of control (see Chapter 2). Self-expression loosens up the mind so that flow can happen.

Getting it out of your system

Professor James Pennebaker and his colleagues have spent decades researching the effects of self-expression through writing. In their many experiments, they have people without any writing expertise practice a very simple task. The participants write, by hand, for about 20 minutes two to three times per week what they feel. The researchers give the writers simple instructions: "Focus on writing what you feel, less on the facts and the logistics of what has happened. Download onto the page what you feel like." They also instruct participants to not show this writing to anyone, but throw it away after they complete the exercise. The objective of these writing sessions involves getting their feelings out of their system without falling victim to the risk of disclosure while they do.

Risk of disclosure is a concept from clinical psychology that basically says don't share your drama with anyone who can't help you out of it, and who may judge you, ostracize you, or ridicule you as a result of your sharing. People who use social media often assume that somehow disclosing their trauma can help them in some way. It can't. It can only make the situation worse.

Researchers in the writing studies keep in touch with the participants over long periods of time, getting additional information from them. Besides asking whether they continue to do their two to three writing sessions per week, the researchers also look at factors such as the participant's wound healing capacity, their immune markers, and how often they visit a doctor over a six-month period. The researchers find, over and over again, that compared to a group of people who practiced a different kind of writing (just logging systematically what they do in their lives), the expressive writers tend to have better wound healing, better immune markers, and fewer doctor visits.

The fascinating effects of expression have also been researched within the field of *dance/movement therapy* (DMT), a special type of dance practice used for people who struggle with psychological issues including anxiety or depression. This very structured practice includes treatment factors such as exercise, social contact, and expression. In a large meta-analysis (a statistical method used to analyze results from many independent studies systematically, to determine an overall effect of an intervention like DMT), Professor Sabine Koch and her team from Alanus University and SRH University, both in Germany, find that the treatment factor most linked to improvements in anxiety levels and depressive symptoms is *expression.*

In clinical therapeutic settings, therapists strongly encourage that patients do verbal, written, or other types of signal-based expression about what's going on. This expression decreases arousal in the body, and the person can relax, making them more attuned to find flow because they set their mind free through spoken, sung or written words, symbols (by drawing for example), or symbolic gestures (as when they dance or play music).

Even if you don't see yourself as either a writer or a dancer, I assure you that you don't have to create objectively great work to experience the glorious effects of expression. To dig a little deeper into how you can take advantage of the power of expression within your own practice, the following section examines a memorable space that everyone can relate to: learning a language, whether verbal, sign, or written.

Speaking the language of your flow tool

If you have, or have had, a partner who comes from a different language community than your own, you know firsthand how unfair it feels when you have an argument in their language. They stride ahead with amazing arguments, while the emotion of the situation makes you choke under pressure and stumble over your own words — even if you know their language well.

This situation happened on a global stage when Ukraine's President Zelenskyy had an uncomfortable public conversation with U.S. President Trump in the Oval Office (https://www.bbc.com/news/articles/c2019j0w9glo). President Zelenskyy has a very good command of English and has improved his English skills admirably fast since the start of the war, so what happened here? Well, the emotionally charged situation happened. In the same way that Olympic athletes can fall back on previous levels of skill when under pressure (which I talk about in the section "Being aware of lurking bad habits," earlier in this chapter), a language skill that we have recently acquired or improved can fail. The habit loops for this language are simply not yet strong enough to function under emotional pressure. Intentional repetition of the movements of your skill will help you grow those neural connections into the implicit memory systems of your brain, where they will be available to you, also under pressure.

Think about the process of learning the right habits for your life, work, and flow practice like the process by which the human brain learns a language. Language is movement. The smallest cue of language is the sounds, shapes, or written words. Then comes the action; your vocal apparatus needs to learn to vocalize the words (that's movement!) or your hands need to learn to form the shapes of the new language and associate meaning with those sounds or shapes.

Your tongue, mouth, and facial muscles (as well as your hands and arms if you're learning a sign or written language) create many movement habits. The reward comes when it sounds or looks right, and when your teacher or the person in front of you finally understands the word you want to communicate. That's your habit loop full circle. (To be clear, saying or signing one word involves many habit loops that cluster into motor plans, which I talk about in the section "Turning motor plans into complex moves," earlier in this chapter — but for the purposes of this example, just think of them as one loop.)

First, you only string words together, then you start to form real sentences. Then you communicate longer sentences, and you stop back-translating into your own language. This language skill — a type of motor sequence for your brain — starts to pass from effortful, explicit memory systems to procedural, implicit memory systems.

REMEMBER

Besides beginner's luck, where you might get a word or a sentence right the first day (or score a goal your first time in a game, make a big win on the stock market on your first day trading, and so on), building a flow habit in the brain involves technique practice (flip back to the section "Guiding Star of Flow 4: Technique Practice," earlier in this chapter). After the brain passes the skill to the implicit systems, mastery keeps pushing you to remain on the fine balance between skill and challenge (Flow Element 7, see Chapter 2).

With time and practice of a new language, you can learn to combine ever more complicated sentences, going from simple interactions to meaningful conversations in that language; and eventually, you can read whole stories, perhaps classical literature and poetry, in that language. And you start expressing yourself — maybe even expressing poetry if you're in love with someone from that language community!

Identifying expression

People (including myself) have a hard time grasping what expression really is, objectively. Outside of obvious verbal expression, what is expression, *really*?

When I was a professional ballet dancer, expression was something that I just did: the moment when I stopped thinking (and worrying!) about the steps and positions, when I stopped thinking about what others may think and how perfect I looked (or not); when I'd just dance it out. I didn't usually experience it much in training or on stage. Rather, it happened during stolen moments, during escapes to the city's underground discos, that I became me again, expressing myself, far from the harsh conventions of daily rehearsals and the shouting ballet masters. It was then that I became the movement, lost myself, and flowed away into the night, becoming part of something greater than myself.

For me as a scientist, I understood what expressivity might be for the human brain when I read the article "Evolution of vocal learning and spoken language," by Professor Erich Jarvis, in the magazine *Science*.

You can watch Professor Jarvis explain the concepts from this article on YouTube by searching for the title "Erich Jarvis (Duke/ HHMI) Part 1 (and 2!): Convergent behavior and brain pathways."

Comparative neuroscientists (researchers who compare the brains of different living species in terms of function and structure), such as Professor Jarvis, have discovered that humans and other animals have some similar and some quite different neural connections. For instance, humans have special neural connections between the parts of the brain that process sounds and the large muscles of the body.

Some special *ganglia* (long clusters of nerve cells) in humans transmit rhythmic sounds from your ears to large muscles of your body in the form of little electrical beats, which drive your muscles to sync to that beat. This connection is *innate*, meaning that humans are born with it (wonderfully illustrated by a toddler if you play them a groovy song). And chimpanzees, mammals that have the scientific classification of order Primates, family Hominidae (the same as humans), don't have that special neural connection. So, they can't (and won't) groove along to a beat.

Neuroscientists like Professor Jarvis look at behaviors of humans and ask, "What parts of the brain 'make' this function?" In particular, Jarvis had observed that humans, a few other mammals (like Dolphins, Bats, Seals), and some groups of birds (such as parrots, hummingbirds and songbirds) — but not other primates (such as chimpanzees and gorillas) nor non-songbirds (such as pigeons, ducks, and flamingos) — can do the following:

>> Synchronize their body movements to an external beat.

>> Imitate each other's gestures and sounds.

>> Develop a vocal language that includes complex vocalizations, syntax, and meaning.

And these skills in the preceding list are present from birth. A few hours after birth, human babies' brains simulate rhythmic sounds if you play them some — which doesn't happen if you play them language or random sounds. Besides, babies imitate compulsively; they can't help but copy everyone around them — and with this imitation, they learn. And humans, as a species, are vocal learners.

The rhythm capacity that humans use to dance comes to good use when children learn to speak. Speech involves rhythmic sounds, strung together, which you imitate from those around you. If you're surrounded by English, then your brain spins the rhythmic sounds of the English language into habit loops. If you're surrounded by Danish, well, Danish habit loops it is. And so on. Songbirds have a very similar vocal language development.

Some comparative neuroscientists like Erich Jarvis propose that the neural pathway that controls these three skills in the above list has for some reason been duplicated in present-day humans and in some groups of birds. It's stronger; more information can flow. Erich Jarvis calls this "The Motor Theory of Vocal Learning Origin."

Birds and humans are two very different species whose likely common ancestor lived about 300 million years ago. It obviously must have looked quite different from humans or songbirds today. Yet, for some reason, those individuals who got the reduplication of that neural pathway had an advantage. Science probably can never know why and how this reduplication happened. Brain matter doesn't fossilize, and scientists can't tell from skeletons whether Neanderthals danced, imitated, and spoke.

After the neuroscientists identified the neural pathway that controls all these skills — the grooving, the imitating, and the talking — they wanted to know what else it controls. The neural pathway controls the *larynx* (the part of your vocal apparatus in your throat that you use when you speak). And this same pathway also controls the movements of your arms! So, it controls your gestures. When you express through your arms, such as when you gesture during a dance, play music, write, draw, or code, your brain sees that movement as a language, a body language.

So, for your brain, body language is just another register of expressive communication, a language that's not a verbal one. For "Guiding Star of Flow 5: Expression," you communicate through any movement of the body. That's why expression through movement can feel so liberating, the same as when you say something out loud.

For expression to work, you have to have enough skill and mastery of the language with which you want to express. You can't expect to express yourself through ballet moves if you haven't yet formed habit loops for those moves in your implicit memory systems. Repeated routines (rituals!) of daily ballet technique (or any expressive activity) can help you get to the point where you can express. (You can read all about rituals in the section

"Guiding Star of Flow 3: Routines and Rituals," earlier in this chapter.) But you definitely *can* just "dance it out" with your very own dance moves if you just put on that groove you love.

Being authentically you

What does it mean to be real? How and when are you very truly you? The Danish existentialist philosopher Søren Kierkegaard (1813–1855) wrote about defining the self well before neuroscience discovered that when humans conform to a social standard, their brain shows reward activity: Your brain loves to fit in. We're all conformists, more or less, very likely because in an evolutionary sense, the isolated individual didn't survive long. Humans needed group cohesion and to fit into the group to survive. So, the brain changed during evolution to reward fitting in. Free thinkers like Kierkegaard never tire of reminding everyone about the dangers of conformism and of not speaking up when the group may not be on the right track.

Many political debates occur around the matter of *groupthink* (when individuals accept a viewpoint or conclusion because they think the group supports it, whether the individual believes it to be valid or not; for example, whether you have a culture that allows for constructive criticism). But what does it do to the individual when they add so much social coating to their outside that they don't even know anymore who they really are? Who have they modeled themselves on?

In my 2021 *Aeon* online magazine article "To the core: A devastating loss can shatter the façade we put up for others, exposing our deepest, rawest self. A work of art can do the same," I examined the science of authenticity. When looking at people who make sure to express their authentic self from time to time — for instance, through a hobby practice such as expressive writing, dancing, singing, or music making — seem to

>> Have fewer depressive and anxious symptoms

>> Worry and ruminate less

>> Have better physical health

>> Experience flow more easily

>> Are more pleasant people to be around (not teetering on the edge like many people who keep it all inside)

>> Have better emotional awareness (perhaps because they suppress less and therefore have a calmer mind to recognize the emotions that they feel without worrying about them)

>> Are more attuned to their bodily signals, helping them to detect their own and others' emotions better

Although you need to be a team-player to survive (whether in life or business), and social contact is important for flow (as discussed in Chapter 6), you also need to be aware of the social coating that you add onto your authentic self. As you can see in Chapter 6, with the Porcupine Dilemma, other people most frequently cause ruminations and worries that may pull you out of flow, including because of the roles and models that they force upon you (or that you try to live up to). Taking moments away from that social coating and expressing yourself authentically, is a very healthy thing to do, and it helps with finding your flow.

TIP

If you want to try finding that authentic you, perhaps you can try what Professor Yona Kifer and her colleagues from Tel Aviv University asked from their research participants: Recall moments in your past where you felt authentically you. Doing that exercise made research participants feel happier, and they rated their wellbeing as higher than people who had recalled moments in which they had felt inauthentic. (By "authentic" and "inauthentic," the researchers meant a situation in which the participant had been [or, hadn't been] true to themself and experienced themself as behaving [or, not behaving] in accordance with their true thoughts, beliefs, personality, or values.)

If you do this exercise, perhaps try to remember what cues surrounded you when you had that *authentic you* feeling. Use these cues now, in other parts of your life. For example, many people say that the fragrance (cue) of freshly mowed grass brings back good childhood memories, or the sound (cue) of a specific song brings them back to a formative life experience. These cues can both pull you back to an earlier time and into actions. Use this mechanism now, for feeling *authentically you*, so that cues pull you into flow, instead of somewhere else.

When you hook on to this special feeling of you, or recall what it feels like to be yourself, you also do something else that's incredibly important for flow: You stoke Flow Element 5, intrinsic motivation. When you tap into what makes you feel like yourself with the activity that you do, that activity gains in importance to your brain and propels you forward because of the self-relevance of that activity.

Building a routine or ritual around a flow activity, making space for it in your everyday (such as when you practice its technique), can activate a very special energy-saving mechanism in your brain. The habit loops that you create through repeated conscious movements log this skill into implicit memory systems. It becomes your second nature. After this conversion to implicit memory, this language of your body provides a communication channel by which you can express things into the world that weigh on you, or otherwise occupy your mind. The repetiveness of the activity provides a washing machine for your mind, while your mind becomes more receptive to flow. People who experience flow regularly also tend to follow three Guiding Stars of Flow: imagination, aesthetic emotions, and setting specific intentions, which I talk about in Chapter 8.

You don't have to follow all the Guiding Stars of Flow through one single flow practice. As long as you make sure to collect all stars in your life, even if that's through different activities or in different areas of your life, flow will follow and you can collect all the health benefits of flow that we discuss in Chapters 1 and 4.

Chapter **8**

Imagination, Aesthetic Emotions, and the Right Intentions

Flow doesn't happen by accident. People who experience it regularly aren't simply lucky, and they don't passively wait for the right conditions to appear. They may not be aware of it, but observational studies show that by what they *choose to do* they actively shape their mind to focus their attention to move away from stress to a state of flowy engagement. Three powerful tools help you to do exactly that: the imagination, aesthetic emotions, and the right intentions.

In this chapter, you can stroll through the science that identifies why people who experience flow regularly make sure to use these three movements of their minds very purposefully. They use their imagination like an instrument that fine-tunes the actions of their body. They seek experiences that arouse *aesthetic emotions* inside them (feelings that you have in response to beauty, art, and other meaningful sensory experiences) — that make them feel awed, transformed, and expanded. The imagination and those special feelings move you forward and help your mind take flight. And, they help with the third tool we'll see in this chapter — setting an intention for flow. Setting the right intention makes your brain and everything around you conspire to help your mind tap into flow.

Letting the Stars Guide You to Flow

In Chapter 5, I introduce eight Guiding Stars of Flow. The eight refer to 8 behaviors that, when assembled within our life's puzzling meanderings are incredibly helpful to get our mind to flow. We'll talk about three of them in-depth in this chapter. I call them stars because you can use them as a navigation aid for flow — like sailors navigate the Seven Seas, following star clusters in the sky. You don't need to adopt each Guiding Flow Star to perfection; think of them as behaviors that, when cultivated, guide your path to flow.

This chapter focuses on these three Guiding Stars of Flow:

>> **Guiding Flow Star 6: *The Imagination*:** Many modern cultures dismiss the imagination as childlike, something nice to have but not essential for serious work or adult life. Neuroscience tells a very different story. The imagination is one of the brain's most efficient tools. It allows you to rehearse, recover, and feel motivated without force or effort. You can read about the imagination in the next section, "Guiding Star of Flow 6: The Imagination."

>> **Guiding Flow Star 7: *Aesthetic Emotions*:** Closely intertwined with imagination, you have aesthetic emotions,

those moments of awe and wonder. Far from being indulgent extras, these emotions tune your nervous system, loosen rigid patterns of thought, and create ideal conditions for flow to happen. You can read about these emotions in the section "Guiding Star of Flow 7: Aesthetic Emotions," later in this chapter.

>> **Guiding Flow Star 8: *Setting the Right Intention*:** I don't mean the distant, abstract kind of intentions that point vaguely toward future success, but short-term, embodied intentions that anchor you firmly in the present moment. When you set intentions within the action itself, not to the final goal, these "micro-intentions" align attention, perception, and action, allowing the brain to anticipate what comes next, instead of constantly reacting to what's already happened. Check out the section "Guiding Star of Flow 8: Setting the Right Intention," later in this chapter, for more.

Together, imagination, aesthetic emotions, and well-placed intentions form a quiet but powerful triad. They help you rest, recover, and keep going, while making the experience itself deeply rewarding.

Guiding Star of Flow 6: The Imagination

Many of the people who experience flow regularly make sure to use their imagination as a tool for developing their flow habit. The imagination, Guiding Star of Flow 6, doesn't involve just daydreaming — it's a tool that engages the brain in ways that optimize learning and performance — and surprisingly for many, sets the settings for flow.

Don't feel discouraged if you don't have a sense of imagination in the form of vivid mental imagery. People differ in how their imagination looks and feels.

According to the psychologist and neuroscientist Professor Anna Abraham, Director of the Torrance Center for Creativity at the

University of Georgia, humans have roughly five different types of imagination — or, ways in which they use their imagination:

>> **Perceptual or motor imagery:** Imagining sights, sounds, or movements

>> **Recollection and intention:** Remembering past experiences or planning future actions

>> **Creative combination:** Generating new ideas by mixing concepts in novel ways, finding unusual uses for objects, processes, thoughts, innovate the way things work

>> **Aesthetic experience:** Imagination triggered by art, music, dance or other sensory experiences that make us remember things from our past, conjure up new thoughts and images

>> **Altered mental states:** Shifts in consciousness that range from daydreams to more extreme or unusual experiences, such as when we dance ourselves into trance in a ritual or a techno disco

Humans vary widely in terms of how imaginative their minds are. You can use your imagination for flow, even if you don't think that you have any imagination at all. It's all about tailoring your pathway to flow to who you are and what works for you. Perhaps you use your imagination a little less — or you might discover a new way of using it that works for you.

REMEMBER

Sometimes, a mix of imagery types works best. You might also need external aids to boost your imagination. Perhaps you excel at auditory imagery but struggle with visual imagery — fine! Work with what you have.

The imagination is also a way to leverage your brain's natural love of learning and optimizing movement through sensory feedback. As a dance student, we were taught to use visual imagery for some movements. For example, think, "Make arm movements like a swan," (big movements) as opposed to "Make arm movements like a sparrow" (small movements). You automatically make different arm movements that would have needed a lot of words to describe without that mental imagery.

IMPROVING MOVEMENT THROUGH THE IMAGINATION

You can also use it for movement correction. Sarah, a dance student, couldn't figure out how to put her ribcage in the right position during a specific type of pirouette, so she kept spinning out of balance. It wasn't enough that she was seeing how others did it, and no verbal instruction solved the conundrum for her. But when her teacher put the hand on her ribcage and gave her a tactile trail of how her ribs should move during the turn, she suddenly could do the turn without falling over, by recreating the tactile sensation on her ribcage as she turned.

Scientists distinguish between the two extremes of imagination:

>> **Aphantasia:** Difficulty with or the inability to create mental imagery. Aphantasic people don't (or can't) use their imagination.

>> **Hyperphantasia:** The ability to create very vivid mental imagery. Hyperphantasic people can conjure up literally anything in their imagination.

And most people have imaginations that fall somewhere in between aphantasia and hyperphantasia. At `dummies.com/flow` you can test the vividness of your imagination.

REMEMBER

Having aphantasia doesn't mean that people are unimaginative. Notable minds that don't have a mind's eye include Pixar co-founder and Turing Award winner Ed Catmull, fantasy author Mark Lawrence, sci-fi author Yoon Ha Lee, biologist J. Craig Venter (the scientist who led the team that sequenced the human genome), and the video game designer Jonathan Blow. Just to mention a few.

People who have aphantasia do use their imagination — they just get some support. They use reference images, prompts, photographs, sensory stimuli that work to clarify — like the example that I gave in the preceding section about my pirouette dilemma. You can find Facebook pages for aphants that include loads of tips for how to tailor your imagination to your needs.

According to an article titled "Life without a mind's eye," by the journalist Christabel Lobo on Brainwise (`https://brainwisemedia.com/life-without-visual-imagination`), about three to four percent of the world's population are complete aphants.

Some birds have something similar to human imagination, even though it's probably quite rudimentary. These birds (such as crows and parrots) can use tools and manipulate them in ways that serve a goal — for that, they need to be able to represent the steps to get to that goal and know how to behave with the tool to produce a certain effect. Because we can't ask the birds why they're doing what they do, the behavior provides only anecdotal evidence. So what humans do when they imagine might be quite unique in the animal kingdom. Evolutionary pressures usually eradicate any superfluous cognitive capacities to optimize energy saving. Everyone better find ways to use this ability, then — if humans still have it, it perhaps serves an important purpose?

Diving into the neuroscience of the imagination

The imagination doesn't occupy a particular part of the brain. It's a mechanism that unites many different systems into a shared activation pattern. That may explain why your imagination can help you get absorbed in what you're doing — Flow Element 1 (See Chapter 2 for what all 10 Elements of Flow are). Your cerebral cortex, the wrinkly surface that covers your brain, contains the *associative cortex*, which integrates and distributes information to promote higher-level functioning. While you imagine things, a huge web of neural pathways activate throughout this associative cortex surface and connects with systems deep down within the brain, including also your memory systems.

Your brain's memory systems store previous perceptions, ideas, and memories, and the associative cortex enables us to combine this information in the most interesting and strange ways. You can imagine your most dreaded teacher turning into a clown, dragons flying through your living room — wonderful things that you can only see with your imagination.

Mathematicians and dancers often describe deep states of absorption (Flow Element 1 — see Chapter 2 for all 10 Elements of Flow), of time and space disappearing around them (Flow Element 4), of being the movement (Flow Element 6), and so on. For flow, mathematicians and dancers have much in common (whether they believe that or not) — they use their imagination in purposeful ways, to improve their performance and stay engaged.

Neuroimaging experiments show that doing an arithmetic task and using the imagination activates similar neural systems. Your brain hardly ever uses just one part for something. You have overlap in brain activation for activities that may not logically seem related but that your brain processes in similar ways. You might well use your imagination while you play with the numbers in your head so that you can determine how to calculate them.

You don't need to know all the neural systems engaged by dancing and by doing math, and the ways in which the imagination overlaps it all. After all, you can't activate parts of your brain at will, so knowing these areas can't help you achieve flow. But you can help your brain tap into flow by doing activities with your body (such as math or dance) and using your imagination while you do.

Many current schooling systems in the West don't take advantage of the benefit of movement-based curiosity and inquisitiveness, nor do they promote targeted use the imagination to make sense of concepts and ideas. Children are taught to sit still, to inhibit, control, and systematize — to a much larger extent than to use their imagination.

TIP

Of course there are important initiatives that promote the use of the imagination in the educational context. For example, check out the **Torrance Center for Creativity,** led by Professor Anna Abraham at the University of Georgia. Perhaps check out their substack In Pursuit of Creativity, that is devoted to cultivating creativity and serves as a resource to the educational professional specifically and the wider community more broadly: `https://thecreativepursuit.substack.com/`

In reality, the imagination is a *task-optimization tool,* meaning that it helps you complete tasks accurately and efficiently — and the imagination makes it *fun.* Plus, it helps you to set your mind for flow. The following sections give you two examples of people using their imagination to optimize their learning or performance on a task.

Dancing through geometry

It seems that in some cases, you can purposely enhance your learning of complex material by using your body movements — aided by your imagination.

Different teams from the University of Melbourne in Australia and the University of Vermont in the U.S. have researched this fascinating topic with similar experiments. They divided a large group of children into two groups. One group of children received a classical geometry lesson, and the other group received a specially designed dance class.

The researchers worked with a dancer to choreograph a dance routine that used movements that looked like the geometrical shapes the children were supposed to learn. The children learned the dance moves by referring to these shapes in space and using their imagination to figure out how to make a circle with their arms, a 90-degree angle with their body, and so on. So, for example, you can help children learn these geometrical shapes through their body. Imagining a triangle and then 'doing' a triangle helps the brain encode the information in an *embodied way.* You can even go a step further and lead the children to make a triangle with their arms *like a dragon's head* and a circle *like holding a large beach ball,* or telling them they should bend at a 90-degree angle *like a table.* And they got to groove to the music while laughing, giving and receiving smiles, and offering supportive glances.

The children in the dance class had a higher score on the geometry task that followed class when compared to the children who had the traditional math class.

Combining the introduction of complex materials with movement and imagination draws on many of your brain's neural networks and optimizes the learning process, while also making that process fun and interesting. And according to much scientific research, your brain more effectively remembers what it learns in a fun context and that's thanks to neurotransmitters like dopamine. Dopamine plays an important role in memory processes like information encoding. And when a situation is fun, it attaches little dopamine stickers to these memories which makes memory retrieval even easier.

Training your brain

Alpine skiers waiting for their next run often pretend to go down the slopes while in fact remaining firmly rooted to the spot. Bent forwards, leaning onto their ski poles, they move from side to side, their butt sticking out behind them. This kind of pretend play can look a little funny, but it's not a joke at all. They're firing up their neural pathways for the ski run in their imagination — and sports science research shows, by imagining and moving like on a ski slope, they improve their future performance.

From a neuroscientific perspective, imagining the slopes powers up activity in the imaginer's brain: specifically, in the movement and memory systems, powering up the recall of sensations in the body — how this type of slope, this type of curve, and this type of snow feel — preparing for *the real thing.*

The associative cortex, which spans the brain (I talk about this cortex in the section "Diving into the neuroscience of the imagination," earlier in this chapter), contributes to connecting all these movements, memories, and sensations together. By going through this imagined routine, the athletes already boost blood flow in the right pathways in their brain, even before their skis actually hit the slopes. In a business where the space between winning and losing can be in milliseconds, any additional activation boost can make all the difference.

Scientists that study athletic performance like sports and dance call this visualizing exercise that many athletes use, *mental training.* Dancers also use the imagination to optimize movements. Often, dancers rely extensively on what they see of themselves in the mirror for feedback. However, the visual information that the dancer sees in the mirror takes much too long to reach the brain to help change a movement while it happens. It takes ¼ of a second — an eternity in the super-speedy execution of motor commands in your brain while you move. Verbal feedback, like that of a teacher's advice, goes from your ears to your brain a little faster (⅕ of a second) — but still too slow to allow you to do anything about a movement that's already happening.

But the imagination provides you immediate information because it happens inside the brain's motor plans (which you can read about in Chapter 6). Expert dance teachers use imagination prompts in their instructions. And movement neuroscience confirms that's a really good idea, not just for dance training, but for optimizing any movement skill.

THE SEA AS A RESET BUTTON

When Pedro speaks about his hobby, fishing, you can almost see the time and space disappearing around him. His eyes lose focus and his facial muscles relax. "And I really don't need to catch any fish," he says. "Just me being there, on my boat, sets me immediately at ease, and I forget everything else around me." At the word *fishing*, his imagination pulls up the cue-scape in front of his inner eye of those placid, flowy hours spent fishing on his boat that his brain has logged in his memory systems, webbed into neural connections of positive affect. "What cues are around you when you're out there?" I ask. And with a smile, he describes it all to me. When Pedro talks about his fishing adventures, his imagination condenses around the scene on the boat and takes his mind away from the here and now.

The imagery includes the spicy smell of the Mediterranean Sea, the sight of the rugged coastal cliffs of the island at the shore that rise up over the turquoise blue color of the sea, the feeling of the sun on his skin and the rocking of the slim motor boat beneath him. (The rocking of the boat provides a repetitive movement, Guiding Flow Star 3, see Chapter 7, acting as a washing machine for the mind). "Sometimes, just the thought of those flow-filled moments can give my mind a break," he adds.

Pedro is the CEO of a large café chain, and his life is very stressful. Fifteen years ago, he got himself a motorboat license; and since then, whenever he can, he escapes for some flowy moments on his little cruiser. This small irregular ritual that Pedro has with himself unites several of the Guiding Stars of Flow that I explain throughout Chapters 6, 7 and 8, and they help him collect several of the Elements of Flow that I explain in Chapter 2. Other Guiding Stars, he makes sure to collect elsewhere in his life — he doesn't need to unite them all with the fishing hobby. For example, he's an avid runner, which means that he's fit and doesn't need to worry about getting enough movement into the system (Guiding Flow Star 1 — see Chapter 6). In his daily life, he's always surrounded by his employees and he has a wonderful wife and a large family — so he's not missing positive social contact (Guiding Flow Star 2 — also explained in Chapter 6). And he has strong routines that propel him through the day (Guiding Flow Star 3 — see Chapter 7).

"The day only has 24 hours, and more often than not, that's not enough." He laughs. He knows that he's as productive as he can get, yet, as he says, "The mind has limits."

That's when his imagination throws the memory of these blissful moments on his fishing boat in and out of his awareness, as if inviting him to take a break. He loves that these moments in nature make him feel awed, transformed, and expanded (which you can read about in the section "Guiding Star of Flow 7: Aesthetic Emotions," in this chapter) — and more often than not, make him feel small and part of something that is larger than himself. When he's out there he says, he's entirely focused on the here and now (absorption, Flow Element 1 — see Chapter 2), and he has very simple and concrete to-do's that provide him with intention (discussed in the section "Guiding Star of Flow 8: Setting the Right Intention," in this chapter), and those goals give him immediate feedback (Flow Element 3 — see Chapter 2).

And as I mentioned above, Pedro says that he doesn't need to catch any fish to get his flow feeling — ignoring any potential extrinsic rewards, doing the activity for the intrinsic rewards only (Flow Element 5 — see Chapter 2).

Using your imagination can also backfire. Sports science calls this problem *the ironic mistake*. Athletes under pressure can crack at crucial moments, and thus not perform optimally. Imagination can strengthen the right habit loops and prime the brain for action, but it can also cause you to commit the very mistakes that you want to avoid. For example, telling yourself "Don't hit it wide" in a tennis match actually activates the neural pathways for hitting it wide. Instead of focusing on what you don't want to do, focus your imagery on the action that you do want: Visualize the ball going straight, hugging the sideline, out of your opponent's reach. That's how your brain fires up the pathways to execute the perfect shot.

Power your flow with the imagination

When you go through the motions of a task in your imagination, you use the ten Flow Elements that I explain in detail in Chapter 2:

- >> **Flow Element 1:** Focuses you entirely on the task at hand. You're mapping your whole self onto the imagining in your mind.

- >> **Flow Element 2:** Gives you a very clear goal. It hovers before your inner eye while you imagine it.

- >> **Flow Element 3:** Provides you with immediate feedback signals from the activity when it feels right in the body (in the imagination — it all goes to plan).

- >> **Flow Elements 4 and 6:** Messes wonderfully with your inner clock. While you repeat the mental rehearsal and the story in your mind becomes more flowy, you also experience effortlessness and the feeling of time zipping by.

- >> **Flow Element 5:** Boosts intrinsic motivation. The imagination reaches into the neural systems of your sense of self and your experiences in the world and conjures up personal memories, making the activity incredibly intrinsically rewarding.

- >> **Flow Element 7:** Fires up your neuroplasticity. You challenge yourself just a little beyond your skill level. You start hovering where the demands of the task and your skill level meet.

>> **Flow Element 8:** Reduces the perception-action link. When you imagine, you boost activity in your brain's sensory and movement systems, getting you the feeling of being the movement.

>> **Flow Elements 9 and 10:** Removes rumination and unpredictability. You're focused on the multisensory experience of mapping your body movements onto what's in your mind.

REMEMBER Using the imagination is not only a way to optimize movement for performance, it can also help your mind stay in the moment and to set the settings in your brain to flow. (Flip to Chapter 6 for more about setting your flow settings.)

Guiding Star of Flow 7: Aesthetic Emotions

People who experience flow regularly collect aesthetic emotions in their life like vitamins. These emotions are Guiding Star of Flow 7.

Make sure to stop and admire a beautiful landscape and let the feeling of awe make you feel small and insignificant. Watch a movie or read a book that takes you out of your comfort zone, challenge your schemas and what you expect to see — receiving the goosebumps and the chills when realization and insight strike. Listen to music, give yourself a night at the ballet, or stroll through a museum to let these special sensory cues *move* you emotionally.

TIP You don't have to get aesthetic emotions from the activity that you want to give you flow. But very often, they go hand in hand. The important take-home-message is: to find flow, you need to have aesthetic emotions in your life. Very likely, with time and repetition, while you stoke the skills-challenge element of flow with that activity (Flow Element 7), you experience aesthetic emotions while doing that activity. (In Chapter 2, you can read about all the ten Flow Elements.)

The last time you walked out of the cinema feeling awed, expanded, or otherwise strangely different, ready to change your life, finding a whole new way to see the world, you were experiencing aesthetic emotions. Or maybe when watching a documentary about the history of Peru, you felt knowledge-based aesthetic emotions such as challenge, interest, and wonder as you realized how rich the cultural heritage of this nation is.

Aesthetic emotions introduce a certain flexibility into your neural systems, and your schemas (way you think about things/the way you do things) remain flexible, open to new experiences, ideas, and ways to do things and think about the world. You often feel part of something bigger than yourself.

Aesthetic emotions can help you achieve flow because they:

>> Are very absorbing (Flow Elements 1 and 2)

>> Help prevent ruminative thoughts (Flow Element 9)

>> Stop your worries about the future (Flow Element 10)

Aesthetic emotions pull you firmly into the present, making you aware of yourself in the moment and enjoy that awareness. In the Liking–Wanting principle (which I talk about at the end of Chapter 4) when you can activate the liking part of the principle, you have the right 'brain soup' flowing around in your brain: endogenous opioids and endocannabinoids. You feel so good, content, and optimistic about life, which primes the flow machine in your brain.

Triggering aesthetic emotions

The arts can elicit aesthetic emotions for many people. Say you're reading a book, and it's written in a way that makes you curious, so it captivates your attention. And then the story evolves, surprising you and pulling you in directions that you hadn't anticipated. Then the characters' actions make you feel sadness and nostalgia, and you're totally moved when the situation resolves completely against all expectations. And all that in a single page's reading.

You can also feel these emotions by looking at a painting, watching a movie, or performing a dance, as well as working on your bow and arrow, using your knitting needles, or spinning clay on a pottery wheel.

Your brain has no clear boundaries between what is and isn't art. So you also don't need to look for any boundaries between activities and objects — what works, works. You can feel aesthetic emotions about many things and it's about finding out what does it for you, and we'll see more about how to find out a little later this chapter.

Perhaps you think that your work can't cause you to feel aesthetic emotions. But you're probably wrong about that. Sometimes, it's about unlocking them first. Mathematician friends have sent me selfies with their awed faces in front of enormous formulas displayed on huge blackboards behind them, with the accompanying text, "This is extreme beauty!" Whatever inspires you to feel aesthetic emotions, you need engagement with the activity so that you develop a habit that triggers them reliably for you.

WALKING IN AWE

Several studies show that people who have regular awe-experiences in their life have better health and a higher life satisfaction. Also, people who have recently been awed help others more and are generally more prosocial than people who haven't. It somehow also shrinks the ego, something that can feel cathartic as when we find emotional release. Awe just makes you glow. These are good reasons for seeking to feel awed. Check out the book *Awe*, by Dacher Keltner (Penguin Press), for a lot of information about the science related to awe.

Consider taking an awe-walk in nature to get familiar with feeling aesthetic emotions. In one experiment, two groups of elderly people went through carefully crafted walks in nature. One walk included passing by incredible landscape landmarks — likely awe triggers. The other walk was just a pleasant walk but nothing special. The researchers gave the participants one task during the walk: Take selfies when they felt like it.

(continued)

(continued)

The researchers then analyzed the selfies:

- **Awe-walk:** The group of participants on the awe-triggering walk had taken selfies from angles that made themselves look really small and the landscape enormous.

- **Normal walk:** The group on the simple nice walk had taken selfies where they themselves looked bigger and the landscape was just the background scenery.

The researchers theorized that the selfies reflected how the walks had made the selfie-takers feel — small, in the case of the awe-walkers. Feeling-wise, both groups felt happy and healthy; however, the awe-walkers smiled more and were much more likely to help each other after their walk. And the photos suggested that they felt smaller — something that the researchers interpreted as a shrinking of the ego, which can help you remain open to new things.

Tracking your aesthetic emotions with the AESTHEMOS

Psychology researcher Dr. Ines Schindler has devoted much of her scientific career to studying aesthetic emotions. Together with colleagues across institutions, she has developed the Aesthetic Emotions Scale (AESTHEMOS), a validated instrument that captures the range of emotions people experience in response to art, activities, and other meaningful experiences. It was published in the scientific journal *PLOS One* in 2017 (`doi.org/10.1371/journal.pone.0178899`).

You can use a reworked version of it here, to figure out what type of aesthetic emotions you feel in relation to different experiences, activities, works of art, and so on. In addition, I provide a guide here to how this information in turn can help you figure out how to find the ten Flow Elements (discussed in Chapter 2).

The AESTHEMOS groups aesthetic emotions into four factors:

>> **Affection:** For a good flow activity, look for something that gives you the highest scores for the Affection factor. Such

activity has the highest probability to appeal to your intrinsic motivation (Flow Element 5).

>> **Pleasedness:** Overall subjective satisfaction. Whether pleasedness contributes to flow depends partly on your sensation-seeking needs (see Chapter 9). Pleasedness serves two distinct roles:

  - *A surface-level reward:* It provides immediate enjoyment and positive affect. This kind of pleasedness can motivate you, but it often lacks depth and fades quickly.

  - *Emotional regulation:* Activities that score high on pleasedness may gently capture attention (Flow Element 1) and soothe your emotions (Flow Elements 9 and 10), especially if you're experiencing stress or emotional turbulence in your life. In this way, pleasedness supports flow by stabilizing your emotional state, making it easier for you to engage deeply in the activity.

>> **Captivation:** Very captivating activities can really absorb your attention (Flow Elements 1, 9, and 10); however, when the novelty wears off, after the activity becomes familiar, you may find it less captivating. But if you can find something that keeps you captivated, this activity likely feeds into your skills-challenge balance (Flow Element 7).

>> **Aversion:** The aversion factor is a funny one. We humans go to the cinema, read books, and consume art that angers, scares, or even terrifies us. Many people enjoy a story that moves them to tears, making them very sad, indeed. People can find flow through activities that score high on the aversion factor, depending on their sensation-seeker needs (discussed in Chapter 9); but the aversion factor can negatively impact your quest for flow if it hooks your mind too much — as when it scares you. This makes your body go into an alert state which may also be very absorbing, but nothing like healthy flow for your mind and body.

The idea we want to develop now is to give you the tools to tailor the activity that you want to give you flow by paying attention to how you can stoke your aesthetic emotions. They are some funny companions, those feelings of awe, feeling moved, beauty, chills, goosebumps!

Let us now look at the AESTHEMOS in detail.

REMEMBER

You can apply the AESTHEMOS to anything that you do or experience. Use the AESTHEMOS to identify what activities, objects, and people make *you* experience these emotions most frequently.

Use the table found on at www.dummies.com/go/flowfd. The Aesthetic Emotions Scale (AESTHEMOS) to explore which activities give you aesthetic emotions. I've modified the original of the scale to fit our objective here to develop a flow tool. Follow these steps:

1. **Download The Aesthetic Emotions Scale (AESTHEMOS) to fill in from** www.dummies.com/go/flowfd

2. **Think of the most recent time that you felt the first aesthetic emotion that appears in the Affection factor section of the table.**

    The emotion description says, "It touched me."

3. **Write that experience in the Most Recent Example column for that emotion.**

    Like, nature walk. Reading the book called "....". Cooking dinner with "....".

4. **Repeat Steps 1 and 2 for all of the aesthetic emotions in this table.**

    You can record the same experience for multiple emotions if it applies.

5. **Examining all the experiences that you recorded in the Affection factor of the table, determine whether you referenced a particular experience more than any others and circle that experience in the table.**

    Based on your results, you'll have discovered what experiences give you the aesthetic emotions of the Affection factor.

6. **Repeat Step 4 for the other three aesthetic emotion factors in online Table.**

    Circle the experience that appears most in the Pleasedness, Captivation, and Aversion sections of the table.

7. **If you have different experiences that occur most often for the four different factors of the AESTHEMOS, you can refer to the bullet list above about the four factors to learn more about what this means for your flow possibilities with that activity.**

   Activities that stoke your Affection factor may be more durable activities to find flow with than those that trigger the pleasedness or captivation factors. But this can also depend on how much sensation seeker need your nervous system has. Take a look at Chapter 3 where I explain what makes us more or less likely to tap into flow in terms of our sensation seeker need. I also unpack this further in Chapter 8.

8. **Think of one experience that you can rate in relation to all of these factors.**

   If you can, have an experience immediately before completing this table. For example, rewatch your favorite movie, read a chapter of a book that you love, go for a walk or run, go to a museum, work on your latest code, solve a formula, create that spreadsheet you want to do, bake that cake, or go to the new coffee shop and have a latte.

9. **Rate how much this experience gave you the first aesthetic emotion.**

   Using a scale from 1 to 5, determine where that aesthetic emotion falls for that particular experience. In this scale, 1 means that you didn't feel that emotion at all and 5 means that you felt it very much.

10. **Write that number in the Rating of a Single Experience column.**

11. **Repeat Steps 5 and 6 for all the aesthetic emotions in the table.**

12. **Calculate the sum of all the numbers in this column for the Affection factor portion of the table and write that number in the Total line.**

    So you add all six numbers for the aesthetic emotions that appear in the Affection portion of the table.

13. **Repeat Step 11 for the other factor sections in the table.**

For the experience you choose in Step 7, which of the factors has the highest score? This tells you about the flow possibilities that this activity may have for you. It is important that you don't think of the factors as good or bad. They are all equally good. Whether they will give you flow depends more on you and your current circumstances (for example, also see Part 4 where I speak about adapting flow to different lives).

You can find the complete table and a blank version in this book's Cheat Sheet at www.dummies.com/go/flowfd, which you can download or print out.

You've probably noticed that there are some prompts every so often as you go through the rows of the AESTHEMOS. One says "*Experience you most frequently mentioned*" and the other says "*Sum.*" Take a look at the rows immediately above the prompts for each factor and insert the information, either the experience you've mentioned most frequently, or the sum of your ratings for that factor regarding the artwork or experience you've written at the top of column 4.

Completing this table helps you to consider:

>> What are the experiences that give you aesthetic emotions?

>> Do you have different experiences noted for the four different factors of the AESTHEMOS?

>> For a given experience, which of the factor has the highest score?

DIFFERENCES IN WHAT AESTHETIC EMOTIONS EACH PERSON FEELS

People react differently to different experiences for many reasons. What gives your friend aesthetic emotions doesn't have to trigger them in you, too. For your flow, focus on finding out what aesthetic emotions you like and do it for you. For flow the best ones are often those that make you feel absorbed and a bit different afterwards (different in a good way).

During the COVID-19 pandemic, Dr. Ines Schindler (the researcher who developed the AESTHEMOS — see this section) and I joined a team of researchers who were interested in understanding more about how children in Tehran experience fairy tales. Over a period of four months, Professor Khatereh Borhani and her student Zahra Agharkarimi invited 6- to 9-year-old children to participate in a fairy tale experiment online. In an online setting, we used a questionnaire to determine each child's attachment level to their caregivers. Then the children heard an audiobook version of a beloved fairy tale. After the experience, the children filled in the Aesthetic Emotions Scale (discussed in the section "Tracking your aesthetic emotions with the AESTHEMOS," in this chapter) in child-version: circling the appropriate drawing of a character, Tima, who was feeling different emotions.

The children generally liked the experience very much. But the AESTHEMOS results showed differences in reactions to negative emotions based on the children's caregiver attachment level. The more securely attached children:

- Didn't express discomfort with experiencing negative emotions during fairy tale listening (some fairy tales can be quite sad, scary, or infuriating!).

- Didn't like the stories less because of these negative emotions; but liked them as much as stories that just triggered positive emotions.

Feeling alive with aesthetic emotions

Aesthetic emotions in your life can facilitate flow for a variety of reasons. Aesthetic emotions trigger a number of Flow Elements (the full list of which you can find in Chapter 2):

>> **Intrinsic motivation (Flow Element 5):** Aesthetic emotions connect the activity the you're doing with your sense of self and what you love, which stokes your intrinsic motivation.

>> **Fusion of action and awareness (Flow Element 8):** Rewarding feelings help reduce the perception-action gap — we perhaps feel like we *are* the movement.

>> **Effortlessness (Flow Element 6):** They trigger dopamine showers on your neural connections, making the activities that you do within their glow effortless and pleasant.

>> **Absorption (Flow Element 1):** Aesthetic emotions completely connect your attention to the activity because these emotions draw on different systems in the brain, funneling activity into a cohesive whole that requires the mental space to focus on it.

You must like what you're doing to find flow. Engage in activities that give you positive aesthetic emotions. If you're not sure what your flow activity is, I make some suggestions in Part 3.

Guiding Star of Flow 8: Setting the Right Intention

People who experience flow regularly make sure to set short-term, reachable intentions throughout their day and for their flow activity. Intention is the Guiding Star of Flow 8. (See Chapter 5 for the full set of eight Guiding Stars of Flow. Their combined first letters unscrambled give us the word Air Times. So here we will now see how to set your intention to *Air Times*.)

You might feel tempted to look to professional athletes for inspiration. They're masters of intention-setting for success. However, as I describe in Chapter 9, if you focus on successes, such as scoring points, winning trophies, and getting other rewards, you're focusing on what psychologists call *extrinsic rewards* (like the final win, money, admiration from others, the finished excel sheet) — which are flow-breakers for most people. Instead, for flow, focus on *intrinsic rewards* (things that give us pleasure in doing them, without concerns for any external rewards we may garner; Flow Element 5, discussed in Chapter 2).

As soon as you focus on these long-term or final goals in your activity, your flow can fall victim to external interference. Too much can happen between now and then — such as external evaluation and judgment that can make you choke under pressure (see Chapter 7). Besides, the competitiveness of striving to win releases stress hormones into your bloodstream (which I talk about in Chapter 9), perhaps absorbing your attention, yet not helping your mind to tap into healthy flow.

REMEMBER

Flow happens in the now, so you have to fill *the now* with intentions that keep your mind flowing — now. When you *like* what you're experiencing *at the moment*, your body releases endogenous opioids and endocannabinoids that make you feel calm and serene (as opposed to the dopamine showers that your brain gets when you strive and *want* something). Flip back to Chapter 4 for more about the different effects of *liking* and *wanting* something — I call this the Liking-Wanting principle. Both parts of that principle fulfil important tasks in our life, but for flow, it's important to be aware of the difference, and choose *liking* what you do *as you do it*.

Crafting meaningful intentions

You have to be really concrete and clear in your intention setting; make it something that you can really grasp with your hands and aim for. Phrases like "The more you dream, the farther you get" don't work because they're not very concrete.

In the following sections, I offer some tricks for how to do this intention-setting so that it becomes concrete and meaningful, using neuroscience to unpack how to do that. What I suggest is that we undertake a little bit of a journey from the big picture intentions we may set, to the more concrete and hands-on intentions.

Peeling the Onion is an autobiographical book by Günter Grass (1927–2015), the German, Nobel Prize–winning writer, in which he unpeels his self, layer by layer, like an onion. He inspects his childhood, youth, and adulthood, examining all the events and feelings that motivated his actions and set goals to aim for. The book ends in 1959 — with the publication of his first book.

In this view, each person is an onion, grown, layer by layer, around the intentions that they set for themselves, one on top of the other, to become, well, an onion. If you separate the layers of the onion on the table, it's no longer an onion. This is definitely an existentialist idea about our self — *existentialism* being that philosophy that preaches that we are individuals and responsible agents with free will. We can set our intentions well, or badly. The intentions we set matter for how we feel. For flow, it's all about learning to set intentions that will give you positive affect — because, positive affect attracts flow. If you set intentions that are too general or too hard to ever reach, you'll feel emotions like frustration and your self-esteem may take a hit. Such too big intentions hook your mind firmly to the ground, making you feel small — you never make it beyond the take-off, you never fly. Such intentions are self-sabotage. To set the right type of intention for flowing into the air, we need to do a little bit of digging into our self. We need to see what it is that we really want — and how we can perhaps softly channel this *wanting* so that it doesn't become self-sabotage (as when we get ahead of ourselves or formulate too general intentions), but self-enabling instead.

To figure out how to set your intentions, start at the outer layers of your onion — the layers into which abstract phrases like "The more you dream, the farther you get" fit in. While you go, layer by layer, you pass through the middle layers, which might be more specific, but are often also more about extrinsic rewards like "making it" or gaining recognition or money. At the inner layers of the onion, you can find concrete intention-setting and that's where you want to look for what it really is that you *want* and whether there might be some self-sabotage ongoing.

The reason why it is so helpful to look at the inner layers of the onion, for the more specific *actions* that you want *to do*, is that, simply put, our neurons align along clear action intentions. So we better know which intentions we're setting! It's not always that straight forward to know your real reasons for acting as you do, but for flow it can be really helpful if you allow yourself to spy a little on these actions. You can help give your neurons the right intentions so that they support you on your pathway to flow.

Creating meaning

Ask yourself why you're doing a particular action, *"for what purpose?"*, every time that you take an action. Make that question your mantra.

Viktor Frankl (1905–1997), an Austrian psychiatrist, neurologist, and Holocaust survivor, thought a lot about the meaning of life and proposed using this question to guide your intentions. You can read more about this existentialist's thought processes in his book *Man's Search for Meaning* (Beacon Press). His book deals searching for the meaning of life. That's a very "outer onion level" question of course, as "the meaning of life" is very difficult to boil down to individual actions. But we can borrow this question (*"for what purpose?"*) to seek the intentions behind the different actions that we do. And then carefully reworking them if needed.

The following exercise helps you identify possible intentions behind some of your actions:

>> For what purpose did you go to the café this morning?

- To have a coffee

- To see the gorgeous barista

- To avoid doing a task I didn't want to do

- To write

- To read the newspaper

>> For what purpose did you pick up the newspaper?

- To read the news about a particular subject

- To appear busy and intellectual to people who look at me

- Because I don't know what to do with my hands

- In hopes of someone chatting me up because I'm lonely

>> For what purpose did you go running this morning?

- Because it makes me feel better afterwards and sets my mind for the day

- Because I love the feeling of the fresh morning air

- Because I want to lose weight to find a partner

- Because the doctor told me I need to

- To flirt with the other runners

>> For what purpose did you dance to this song?

- Because I love the song and wanted to enjoy it

- To get moving a little because I sat for too long and felt stiff

- Because everyone was doing it

- Because I wanted a particular person to see me

You may find facing the real intentions of your actions uncomfortable. At this mid-level of the onion, you can, in principle, identify your real intentions — the purposes, the *why* of what you do — if you can be honest with yourself. After this examination, you can work on changing your intentions.

When you want to find flow, you need to make sure that you're not setting your intention on external rewards for your actions because you need to tap into Flow Element 5, intrinsic rewards, not anything outside yourself. You want to identify which intentions can help catapult you into flow. So, in keeping with the Liking-Wanting principle explained in Chapter 4, you want to set your intention to an action that you like doing for the *doing* itself.

The Danish painter Kasper Købke says: "it is not important *what* you draw, but *that* you draw." It is all about *process* over progress. That's what sets your intention to the action itself, not to the outcome.

Flow Element 3 involves getting reliable feedback from your flow activity about how it's going — you know and feel that it's going well because of your perceptions. So you need to get down to a much smaller level of intention-setting, *within* the activity, to unpack the step-by-step of where to place the beam of your intention.

Getting down to the neurons

In the 1980s, a series of experiments conducted by the neuroscientist Prof. Benjamin Libet made the headlines because of what it showed about the human mind: Before you know it consciously, your brain already knows whether you'll perform an action.

Libet had asked his participants to perform actions — simple keypresses — while they were connected to an *electroencephalogram* (EEG; a testing device in which a cap of electrodes is placed on a person's head to measure the electrical activity in their brain). When a participant performed an action, the EEG showed a spike in the electrical activity over their motor cortices about 550 milliseconds before the actual movement. But when Libet asked his participants when they felt the intention to move, that feeling of intention occurred only 150 milliseconds before the action, 400 milliseconds *after* the brain's motor cortices had already fired.

These experiments immediately fed into the philosophical free-will debate, which breaks down into these general factions:

>> **Determinists:** Argue that humans have no free will, that what people do is determined by previous events that spin them through their days. Stanford University Professor Robert Sapolsky falls into this camp.

>> **Libertarians:** On the other extreme of the debate, philosophers such as Thomas Hobbes (1588–1679) and David Hume (1711–1776) lectured that individuals do have free will and are fully responsible for their actions.

>> **Compatibilists:** Think that past experiences, practices, and events can determine some aspects of human actions, but that people have complete control over some actions within their conscious free will. Professor Daniel Dennett (1942–2024), a professor at Tufts University, argued this philosophy.

By setting an intention to a concrete action that you can actually *do*, you align your neural activity with that goal. However, don't expect setting an intention alone to get you to that goal. The athletes who have the motto "The more you dream, the farther you get" have rigorous exercise regimes in their life ("Guiding Star of Flow 1: Everything is movement") and a strong social community around them (Guiding Star of Flow 2), and they consciously or subconsciously aim for the other Guiding Stars of Flow that I talk about in Chapters 6 and 7. These athletes have strong habit loops in place in their brains, which helps them align all the small, daily actions to the final goal.

REMEMBER

Set the right habits in your brain from the start — using the Guiding Stars of Flow — so that these neural loops can push you toward intentions for behaviors and thoughts that can get you to flow. Habit beats all talent. As I talk about in Chapter 6, when a skill passes into the implicit memory systems, it becomes second nature and becomes Flow Element 6, feeling effortless.

Sending an arrow ahead into time, pointing at the next concrete action that you want to *do*, straightens out your thoughts — and it aligns your actions and behaviors toward that goal. The famous Canadian hockey star Wayne Gretzky once said, "I skate to where the puck is going to be, not where it's been." Focus on that type of immediate next action (and what comes with it, including cues and sensations) to find flow.

Chapter 9

Avoiding Mind-Hooks While Seeking Flow

How many medals did your country win at the last Olympics? How many new clothes did you buy in your last shopping expedition? What did people think about your last carefully crafted social media post where you shared your new ideas? Competitive sports, shopping and social media are examples of activities that are very fun, exciting and *totally* absorbing.

It is important that we're able to be competitive, to outperform others and ourselves – that's key for any progress. If our ancestors hadn't bothered with competing for the best resources – we wouldn't be here. If our brains didn't have a reward system that keeps going towards pleasure options, even when it's hard to obtain them, our ancestors hadn't bothered with eating, drinking, having sex, finding shelter, etc. And if they hadn't taken any risks, they had never innovated, found pastures new to live on, nor risked it all for a better tomorrow. It's a good thing that there are systems in our brain that can deal with some uncertainty, even find it quite alluring (just think of the last suspenseful movie you saw, or book you read).

The systems in our ancestors' brains that allowed for all this to happen in well-crafted symphonies, involving hormones and neurotransmitters that played their body orchestra with both beautiful harmonious tunes (as when things went well) and discordant Stravinsky creations (as when things were *very* complicated) — are still there! You have the same systems. Current educational practices, however, don't really educate you in terms of how to manage this Ferrari of a brain. So, you're driving it, at times, without breaks and steering wheel. For flow, this is a problem.

This chapter examines these three powerful behaviors that I call *mind-hooks* because of the fact that they can prevent you from finding flow — competitiveness, pleasure seeking, and risk taking — and explains why people who experience flow regularly avoid these states, often without realizing it, when they want to enter flow.

Building a Skyscraper with Mind-Hooks

I write this chapter from Frankfurt am Main, Germany's financial heart, a city often nicknamed Mainhattan for its skyline of skyscrapers, stock exchange, and restless ambition. Like New York City in the U.S., Frankfurt am Main concentrates wealth, competition, pleasure, and risk into a small geographic space, while also offering deep reservoirs of art, culture, and meaning-making.

When I moved to Frankfurt for work, I was fascinated by the size and energy of the place. But cities like Frankfurt am Main and New York City magnify the very behaviors that quietly pull you away from flow: the urge to compete, the chase for quick pleasure, and the seduction of risk.

Here's a skyscraper analogy related to finding flow. Building a skyscraper requires a lot of hands:

>> The project owner has the vision and negotiates with sponsors, banks, architects, engineers, project managers.

>> After construction begins, contractors and subcontractors join in, coordinating laborers, foremen, superintendents, suppliers, and safety inspectors onsite.

During their work and daily life, these different professionals may fall into the trap of three behaviors or mindsets that prevent them from finding flow with their craft because of the effects that these behaviors have on the human brain and body:

>> **Competition:** They may get ahead of themselves, creating heightened stress hormones in their blood if they become competitive. Too many stress hormones prevent flow. (You can read more about the role of stress when you want to find flow later in this chapter and in Chapter 4 where I introduce our 'body orchestra'.)

>> **Pleasure:** They may become enthralled with the opportunities for quick pleasures that they can get in cities such as Frankfurt am Main and New York City. Unfortunately, those quick dopamine hits, one *unpredictable* splash after the other, although very absorbing, give your brain a very short attention span. Empty pleasure-chasing block flow.

>> **Risk:** They may begin to overestimate their abilities. In the pressure to move faster, higher, and more impressively, maybe they cut corners and ignore warning signs. The laborer may push safety limits while suspended high above the ground; the project owner might overleverage budgets or timelines in pursuit of scale or prestige. Risk-seeking, gambling and drama definitely break flow.

Any activity that you do that benefits from flow can be negatively affected by these mind-hooks. I'm not saying that you should never be competitive, constantly deny yourself pleasures, or stop the thrilling adventures that come from risk-taking. Your life has different domains, and competitiveness, pleasure hunting, and taking risks play important parts in some of those domains. However, if you want to experience flow, try to avoid these three mind-hooks when you do your flow activity.

Meeting Three Greek Gods of Mind-Hooking

In Chapter 5, I introduce three gods from ancient Greek mythology that personify the mind-hooks that prevent flow. They are:

>> **Nike, Goddess of victory:** She's all about competing and winning. The *victory paradox*, where you strive to be faster, better, and more. Your mind stays hooked on the final prize; you *want* it – you forget to stay in the now. If you take a look at the list of the 10 Flow Elements (Chapter 2), you'll see that Goddess Nike prevents you from tapping into most Flow Elements. For example, 2 and 3 (*have clear goals* within the current action – not the future – and *receive reliable feedback* about how the action is going – not just at the glorious end).

>> **Dionysius, God of pleasure:** He's all about wine, party, and pleasure hunting. His pleasure trap makes you chase the next quick hit. Little God Dionysius makes it difficult for you to focus on collecting the Flow Elements – for instance, Flow Element 5 – *intrinsic rewards*, as when you do the action for the joy of the action itself and not because of the reward that you get out of it.

>> **Tyche, Goddess of fortune:** Think gambling, risk-taking, drama, and sensation seeking. This slippery slope keeps you searching for ever greater heights of thrill. Goddess Tyche also prevents the Flow Elements to soothe your mind into the flow-zone – for instance, the drama she produces can make Flow Elements 9 and 10 that we saw in Chapter 2 completely elusive (*lose ruminative thought loops* and *worries*). Letting Goddess Tyche play our body orchestra is more likely to introduce more looping negative thoughts into our mind, than less – and that's bad for flow.

By naming these Gods of Mind-Hooking, you can recognize them as characters that have entered your thoughts as though they've entered a room. You can say, "Ah, Nike is here again to challenge me," or "Dionysius has come to distract me with his pleasure promises." Develop a voice in your head that analyzes your current behavior and pits it against your chances for finding flow *now*, considering the amount of Nike, Dionysius, and Tyche presently rushing through your brain and blood.

These three characters enter your body from the outside world through your behavior, which you can control (even if it sometimes feels like you can't).

Don't invite any of these three Gods into your brain and body while you do an activity that you want to find flow with because they cause you to lose several of the ten Flow Elements that you need to achieve flow (I talk about these Flow Elements in Chapter 2).

The human brain's passion for movement, pleasure, thrills, and drama can send your mind spinning into bad habits if you don't watch out.

Mind-Hook 1: Competing with Goddess Nike

You might recognize the name *Nike* as a shoe brand. But she's the ancient Greek Goddess of battle, competition, and victory. She rewards winners with her golden laurel wreath – which is also her symbol. Olympic athletes worship her. But when she shows up in your thoughts, your brain triggers the release of stress hormones, such as adrenaline and cortisol, into your bloodstream, priming your body for competition.

Many people grow up being told to outperform. For some, all of life is competition — even an amicable ball game on the back lawn with the neighbors can become a high-stakes fight. If you have Nike as your mindset, you steer your body orchestra (discussed in Chapter 4) into a "stress symphony" – as when your blood is rushing with adrenaline and other stress hormones, playing your heart into an accelerated drum roll.

But too much of that type of competitive absorption, too much focus on winning and these *extrinsic* rewards (which don't come from the joy of doing the action itself, but from some final external reward like winning, points or final achievement), can have a very negative effect on your health and attention in the long run — and it doesn't give you healthy flow because it interferes with the ten Flow Elements that I discuss in Chapter 2.

Disrupting flow and immunity with competitive stress

In 2014, Dr. Martha Newsom and her colleagues from Oxford University were at the FIFA football (soccer) world cup in Brazil collecting saliva samples from the Brazilian fans to see whether the stress symphony was at work in these spectators. Research shows that the stress hormone cortisol skyrockets in football players and other athletes, as well as in professional dancers and other artists during mayor competitions or when they're on stage. But this study wanted to see whether the fans also have stress hormones in their blood. The results showed that just *watching* their team loose made fans' stress levels skyrocket.

High stress hormone levels trigger the stress symphony playing inside you. When you're in the fight state, you're certainly absorbed. However, inside your body, a prolonged exposure to the stress-hormone cocktail prevents flow. For flow, you need Flow Element 1 (absorption), which gives you *sensory decoupling* (lessening the connection between inputs from your senses and your conscious mind; see Chapter 2). When in a state of stress, your senses are on high alert — basically the opposite of sensory decoupling.

The stress symphony injects a high level of arousal into the brain, which can distort your memory systems (discussed in Chapter 4). This mechanism doesn't discriminate between memories; whatever it activates carries the same negative feeling. It conjures up the most dreadful of thoughts, opening the gates for rumination and worry (so, making Flow Elements 9 and 10 impossible – *lose ruminative loops and worries*).

And it can also make you aggressive. Police statistics show that aggressiveness of football fans spikes after a heated match.

The insula (which I talk more about in Chapter 4) is a fascinating structure in your brain that, unlike muscles, you can't flex at will — even though it would be useful if you could. It plays a key role in your immune response. Simply put, exposing your senses to activities that activate the insula in the right way helps regulate immunity. Roughly speaking, your immune system has two modes: T1 and T2. By *regulate*, I mean the insula and other body systems help switch the immune system between these two states:

>> **T1 immune response:** The response when your mind and body are calm. You want T1 activated during flow — it sets your body to restoration and wellbeing, designed to keep you safe from viruses and other pathological agents.

>> **T2 immune response:** The response Nike activates during fight, competition, or other stresses. T2 protects the outer body (from threats such as wounds and the pathogens that might enter through those wounds) by activating a barrier function, just as it did when human ancestors fled sabretooth tigers hundreds of thousands of years ago. Examples of T2's action is quick blood coagulation when you scratch yourself or mucous that block your orifices like nose or ears to avoid penetration of pathogens.

REMEMBER

Your immune system always wants to keep you safe. It doesn't suddenly turn evil, or 'off'. But what you tell it through the behaviors that you carry out through your body (whether you choose these behaviors and situations, or if circumstances force them on you). (Part 4 talks about finding flow in not the most calming environments — for instance, when you're in the hospital: having a flow–habit can give you the ability to switch on the recovery state, even when you're in a stressful situation.)

WARNING

Your behavior activates T2 if you experience stress over long periods or if you're lonely for too long, which can cause you to develop skin problems or allergies. Loneliness can activate T2 perhaps because, evolutionarily speaking, isolation was dangerous. (See Chapter 6 for more on socialization and flow.)

Putting Nike on the bench

Of course, you can potentially find absorption by doing sports, working on the scaffolding of a high-rise building, or designing the architecture project of a skyscraper. But if you want healthy, invigorating flow, make sure to keep Nike in check. Nike can often provide Flow Element 1, complete absorption. However, you can't get the sensory decoupling (explained in Chapter 2) needed for Flow Element 1 when you have Nike leading the show. Instead, your senses are attuned to outside input, and you're hyper-aware of every step that you take and what happens around you — this alertness to the outside is key for competition.

Flow, on the other hand, makes you lose your sense of self; you become the movement (Flow Element 8, a fusion of your actions and awareness), and perhaps even have this strange feeling of being part of something bigger than yourself. But most importantly, you can't experience intrinsic reward (Flow Element 5) if you let your mind focus on winning. Nike is the personification of the final victory, the ultimate extrinsic reward.

TIP

If you can't remove the stressful or competitive elements from your work, find a hobby that lets you practice the Eight Guiding-Star behaviors of flow (outlined in Chapter 5) and reap the health and productivity benefits of flow there. Unsure which activity to choose? Flip to Part 3 for ideas or check Part 5 for some unusual suggestions. Dance and the arts can lead to flow especially well because you can enjoy them without needing to involve competition. Consider reading a book, visiting a museum, taking a dance class, or finally starting to take those piano lessons that you've always wanted. As long as you keep the Flow Element 7 in check (your skill and the challenge of the task should be in balance, so it shouldn't be too hard nor too easy). Even in a first ever dance class you can find flow if the level is matched to where you stand – at beginner's level.

REMEMBER

For flow, send Goddess Nike to the bench. Stay in the moment. Say bye to the wanting-stiving side of the wanting-liking principle. Invite the liking side (you can read about this principle in Chapter 4). Do the movement for the joy of doing that movement. In so doing, you are letting the *endocannabinoids* (neurotransmitters that are involved in giving your mind a feeling of flowy satisfaction) rain down in your brain, activating the continuous positive affect that will help you tap into the flow state.

Mind-Hook 2: Going for a Good Time with God Dionysius

Dionysius is the ancient Greek god of wine and grapes, fertility, and ecstasy. His symbol is a wine leaf. When you let him direct your body orchestra (which you can read about in Chapter 4), he sprinkles excitement transmitters everywhere and drives you to seek as much pleasure as you can possibly get. For him, it's all about the quick and easy delights.

He represents a mind-hook that prevents you from tapping into flow because all the quick hits of dopamine in your reward system teaches your brain to jump around like a confused rabbit. Good luck with finding Flow Elements such as absorption in that state. You simply can't hold your attention on the task for long enough to make the 10 Flow Elements happen in your brain.

Finding things deliciously addictive

In Chapter 4, you can read about two interrelated parts of the reward systems in the brain. One part is particularly *hedonistic* and very focused on maximizing pleasure *now* (we could call this part of the reward system "pleasure-driven"). The second part is *eudemonistic*, meaning that it tries maximize not just short-term pleasure, but also on maintaining a good life long-term (we could call this part of the reward system "meaning-driven"). To understand why the flood of dopamine that you get with quick-and-easy pleasures is bad for flow, consider the experiments that Professor Burrhus Frederic Skinner (1904–1990) conducted in the 1950s and '60s to examine how the environment affects behavior.

Rats and other mammals (including humans) have a hedonist portion of the brain, which controls the encoding of rewards as they relate to basic needs (such as food, water, sex, and shelter) that help with survival. This part of the brain is preoccupied with maximizing pleasure, no holds barred. This motivation can distract from flow. Professor Skinner wanted to study how rats reacted to promises of pleasure in the environment, and use that information to understand how behavior can be modified by changing pleasure promises in the environment. The 'experiment' involved many rats over the years and many many separate experiments. To give you an overview, let me focus on one experiment with one rat, the rat Barnaby (not his real name). This experiment involved three stages:

>> **A basic reward connection:** Skinner placed Barnaby the rat in a box that contained a lever connected to a food dispenser. Each time Barnaby pressed the lever, a food pellet appeared. Barnaby quickly learned the rule: Press the lever, get the reward. (This method of learning is called *positive reinforcement.*)

>> **Spacing out rewards:** After Barnaby knew the rule, Skinner changed the *contingency* (the consequence of Barnaby's behavior of pressing the lever) by programming the food dispenser so that Barnaby got a pellet only every third time he pressed the lever. Although Barnaby became frustrated, he still got the pellets in a regular pattern; so even though he got pellets less regularly, they still came predictably.

>> **Making rewards variable:** Finally, Skinner made this schedule completely variable — Barnaby still received a pellet 30 percent of the time (as in the previous condition), but now, at *random* intervals. Sometimes he got a pellet twice in a row, sometimes none after many lever presses. Barnaby began to press the lever over and over again. He wasn't pressing the lever constantly because he was hungry; he always had enough food and water. This intermittent positive reinforcement caused a very paradoxical effect in Barnaby's brain, making him addicted to the dopamine hit that he would get in his brain at a positive lever press.

The same processes occur in the human brain when you doom-scroll or gamble: When rewards arrive unpredictably, your brain gets hooked. The inability to predict when the reward will come makes the behavior almost irresistibly compelling.

In Chapter 4, I discuss how hyper-stimulating the hedonistic part of the reward system, simply put, gradually cuts off the neural communication with the eudemonistic (meaning-making) system. With Dionysius at the party, tolerance develops. What you used to find fun and exciting stops delivering pleasure. The mind narrows its focus to one thing only: the next opportunity for a hit, not for pleasure, but to avoid feeling discomfort. We develop a compulsion. Here, the reward ceases to feel good, you just need it to exist and you get edgy when you don't have it. These withdrawal symptoms are the tell-tell signs that you have gone beyond tolerance, and are on the way to a behavioral addiction.

Professor Skinner and many other scientists have questioned whether humans have a free will at all because they can be so easily looped into bad habits if they are presented with an environment that gives them inconsistent cues that promise pleasure.

Behaviors that chase pleasure can be as damaging to flow as junk food is to the body. You can see this dynamic clearly in the bright lights of the big cities like Frankfurt am Main and New York City: gambling, sex, sugar, and drugs available all over the place. Time and space dissolve, much like in flow. But with hedonistic pursuits, money, self-respect, and agency also dissolve. These environments hook the mind, and flow remains persistently out of reach.

Putting Dionysius on pause

You might worry that you can't identify when a behavior, person, event, or situation can be a Dionysian trap. For example, when you scroll through social media, you can't predict what you'll see next. A cute cat? A clever craft? An attractive person? The same unpredictability hooked Barnaby the rat in Skinner's experiment (discussed in the preceding section). It provides a variable reward pattern. And when you post on social media, it works the same way: You don't know who will reply to it, like it, or share it.

In Chapter 4, I discuss how cues from the outside world get into your brain through sensory receptors. During the brain's processing of these *cues* (inputs from your environment), it decides what value to assign a particular cue.

And your brain is susceptible to quick hits from cues that suggest pleasures — whether food, sex, or cute kittens — that act as potent *primary reinforcers* (input that your brain assigns an strong hedonic value to). Your brain assigns such cues to an immediate reward — which makes you seek those cues over and again.

Throughout evolution, these primary reinforcers helped humans survive. Evolution selected for brains that don't give up on plea-sure, especially when rewards are unpredictable. A variable reward schedule only strengthens the chase. But for most people in modern life, they face an abundance of these cues every day. Your brain was built to seek pleasure relentlessly, not to resist it.

REMEMBER

Personalized ads that appear in your social media suggest only what you like. They are designed to appeal to the hedonistic portion of your reward system, to create bad habits in your brain. The more you consume the products advertised, the more revenue the companies advertising them receive. The more you let bad habits form in your brain by compulsively using their apps, the richer they get.

You can silence Dionysius from time to time by actively seeking intrinsic motivation, Flow Element 5 (see Chapter 2 for talk about the Flow Elements), which has you seeking secondary (rather than primary) rewards. *Secondary rewards* are rewards that matter to you beyond a quick dopamine hit, that connect to your personal memories and systems in your brain that resonate with your sense of self. So these rewards delight both the hedo-nist and the eudemonist reward systems in your brain (which you can read about in the preceding section, "Finding things deliciously addictive"). Here are some small tricks that can help you focus on intrinsic rewards, instead of extrinsic ones:

- **» Avoiding targeted online ads:** Where you can, choose your online cookie settings so that you don't get personalized ads. Personalized ads overstimulate your hedonic hotspots. The sell is often that accepting personalized ads "gives you want you really want". Yet the truth is that this simply means that ads appeal to the hedonistic hotspots in your brain (making you "want" things badly), luring you into addictive behaviors with time and repetition.

- **» Adding steps to online orders:** Deactivate the auto-complete function for credit cards when you're shopping online. This gives the eudemonistic part of your reward system a few instants more to connect with the prefrontal cortex and your memory systems, to down-regulate the urge to hit the buy button.

- **» Putting social media on the back burner:** Place the icons of social media on secondary screens of your mobile phone so that you control the cues — you don't get prompted to open the app when you should really be doing something else. This is something that psychologists call 'environmental control' where you control which cues enter your senses. If you don't *see* the app, the chocolate, the new car — they are less likely to make you *want* them and hook your mind into chasing after the pleasure-promise.

- **» Keeping the unhealthy at bay:** Don't have sweets and fatty foods at home (you can more easily avoid the cues than resist them, especially if you already have a bad habit). The more you indulge in hedonic foods (something that neuroscientists call hyper-palatable foods because the special mix of ingredients makes them so irresistible that our brain can't but motivate us to eat more of it) — the more you have an unrestful mind.

- **» Ignoring TV ads:** Turn down the volume and look away when commercials start during the show that you're watching on TV. Again — simply control the environment. Don't let the cues enter your brain to begin with. If your ears don't *hear* the pleasure promise from the ad — your mind doesn't *want it* and it doesn't get hooked.

- **» Keeping track of your screen time:** Put a timer function on you TV, phone, and computer to monitor your screen time. Your brain is attached to your body and your body needs regular movement. Screens suck us in and make us forget our body. Getting back into the body makes you rediscover the joy of moving and removes some of the seductive allure of little God Dionysius (you can read more about the benefits of regular movement in Chapter 6).

REMEMBER

I'm not saying that you shouldn't, at times, succumb to Dionysius. Of course you should! He's a reliable companion to lift your mood instantaneously. Just be sure to keep an eye on his addictive side. I speak more about avoiding the Dionysian pleasure-junkiness in Chapter 10, where I discuss the flow pyramid — it works very much like a food pyramid; eat least from the top, most from the bottom. (Dionysius sits way up top in that flow pyramid.)

TIP

If anything or anyone (like, a potential love interest) behaves inconsistently or unpredictably — take a step back, disengage. If you notice *urges*, compulsions to seek or consume something, disengage. You can easily develop a bad habit with these urges, craving them more than they deserve. And they (or it) can hook your mind, leaving you no space to tap into flow.

Mind-Hook 3: Living on the Edge with Goddess Tyche

Tyche (pronounced *tie-kee*) — the ancient Greek goddess of chance, fate, and sometimes luck — is unpredictable, as likely to lash out as she is to bathe you in the golden glow of her wheel of fortune. She's the embodiment of your brain's love of novelty and sensation. Her symbol is the wheel of fortune.

In Chapter 3, I talk about how all people have different levels of need for sensation. Everyone's nervous systems simply differ in terms of how quickly they return to baseline after a thrill. Neuroscientists use an instrument called an *electroencephalogram* (EEG) to measure how slowly or quickly the electrical activity of a person's brain returns to normal humming after it receives a novel cue. Quickly adapting to new cues provides a person flexibility and openness to new experiences. This can make you resilient to deal with novel and challenging situations. However, this ability can also make a person more prone to seeking thrills, drama and novel sensations in life, especially if their life isn't so exciting to begin with.

For example, a doctor with a high sensation-seeker need may benefit from working in the emergency response team to get their sensation-seeker need quashed and feel balanced in other aspects of their life. While the same doctor in a routine-practice clinic would suffocate in boredom and be a liability to himself, his family and perhaps even his patients – because, according to his nervous systems' need for stimulation, he might be seeking thrills and excitement in all the wrong places.

Blocking flow with risk and thrill

Some people love to watch the goriest horror movies for the thrill that they get. Although most sensation seekers actually want the relieving feeling after a thrill, rather than the thrill itself.

They let Goddess Tyche hook into their curiosity and unleash floods of adrenaline while they throw themselves over the cliff, up the mountain, to the depths of the ocean, or wherever. And when it's all over, they relish the neurohormonal cocktail of *endogenous* (internally created) opioids and pain-killing substances that make muscles relax and reward them with an all-numbing feeling of relief.

REMEMBER

Like Nike (see the section "Mind-Hook 1: Competing with Goddess Nike," earlier in this chapter) and Dionysius (discussed in the section "Mind-Hook 2: Going for a Good Time with God Dionysus," in the preceding section), Tyche has a skillful hook on the mind, and when she stays at the controls too long, flow becomes elusive. Although Tyche may hook you firmly into one single activity and make you feel very absorbed, this feeling isn't flow, it's absorption that puts your body into a state that looks very much like a stress response (see Chapter 4).

Dr. Siri Leknes and her colleague Dr. Irene Tracey from Oxford University published a paper in 2008 that suggests that the systems that process pain and pleasure overlap in the brain. This may explain why people sometimes seek the stress or pain of a horror movie, the cold of Mount Everest, or the risks of diving with sharks. Of course, the brain processing is much more complicated than that. But humans may at times seek some (almost) painful thrills because they know what kind of juicy reward-kick they feel as a result.

But too much fascination with a thrill can interfere with free will. You may think that you have it all under control, but those low-level systems of pain and pleasure are governed by the hedonistic part of the reward system (which you can read about in the section "Finding things deliciously addictive," earlier in this chapter). After you form a bad habit, you have to really work to get control of it. Also, when you're in Tyche's grasp, your attention is entirely stuck on the outside world, so your mind can't decouple (a part of Flow Element 1, absorption) and find flow.

The data shows that sensation seekers have a higher risk for:

>> Physical injury

>> Financial ruin

>> Heartbreak

>> Drug addiction

>> Gambling addiction

When you take risks, you're also more likely to bond to the wrong people who might not be good for you in the long run, or the connection could bring your job in jeopardy if you start becoming unreliable for example.

In Chapter 6, I explain *arousal misattribution* — the phenomenon in which people perceive those around them as more attractive when they're in a stressful or dangerous situation. Escape rooms and similar high-arousal activities have Tyche written all over them. People may bond because of these events, but not always in ways that serve long-term wellbeing or healthy work environments.

Another Tyche-related risk is what clinical psychologists call *the risk of disclosure.* It's the risk you run if you disclose what's personal to strangers. You never know who has your best at heart. If you disclose your dreams, fears or even your wins, you risk humiliation, ridicule and social exclusion. Choose wisely who you disclose to. Trauma researchers like Professor Anke Ehlers from the University of Oxford caution strongly against public disclosure of trauma. Contrary to popular belief, evidence doesn't support the idea that sharing trauma publicly heals it; in fact, the risks include re-traumatization, ridicule, and shame. Hobby communities can be a source of flow — however, if you include personal disclosure in the mix of colors and fabrics, Tyche may come leaping at you from the paint cabinet.

As you can read about in Chapter 6, when I discuss Guiding-Star flow behavior 2, social connection, you must share vulnerability carefully. Share with the wrong person, and you can get hurt. That uncertainty is part of Tyche's appeal, but also her danger. She's a true mind-hook and flow will remain persistently elusive if you're enthralled in her spinning wheel of fortune and dismay.

REMEMBER

When you're in danger, your brain can't do sensory decoupling, which is necessary for Flow Element 1, absorption. Your senses stay alert, scanning for threat. Flow requires the opposite: the ability to turn inward and let the intuitive mind take over. It also requires rumination and worries to subside (Flow Elements 9 and 10) — which is impossible with Tyche around. Rather, she stirs up the pot to the point of boiling over!

Resisting Tyche to find flow

In German, Tyche has found her way into the common language. *Tückisch* means nasty, malicious or treacherous if it's a person, or slippery, foggy or unclear if refers to a road. So, watch out — is the road ahead of you *Tyche-ish*? Are you gambling with your livelihood, your family's livelihood? Your health? Are you risking it all for what you think is love? If the road is Tyche-ish, it is not the road to healthy flow.

Don't reveal that you're seeking flow, unless you already have that habit firmly anchored in your brain and feel secure about it. The comments and opinions of others, often spurred by envy and jealousy, can fragment your attention and deflate your aims – and your flow along them. Jealous, petty minds, more often than not, try to tear down your dreams. For instance, they might say that your achievements aren't special or that they certainly wouldn't sacrifice their time on something like that. Or they may use the standard attack on flow states: "I don't have the luxury to take time out of my day to just let my mind go idle; some of us need to work." For a flow-filled, meaningful life, you must make your flow practice your safe place, the corner into which you curl up and submerge yourself, to be authentically you, without any risks. Risk-taking is for other parts of your life – and there, they are a good thing.

The human brain is so susceptible to thrills because Tyche made our ancestors explore and able to deal with some level of uncertainty. In a dangerous prehistoric world, Tyche rewarded those who explored.

Tyche's hold on the human brain (that sweat spot of overlap between pleasure and pain) essentially drives human innovation and progress — personal, economic, social, and scientific. Without it, no one would have built cities, bridges over cliffs, tunnels into mountains, railways, or anything else. Risk-taking made Homo sapiens thrive.

But even though risks can arise naturally, when people start to seek them deliberately, the risk becomes the end in itself. Tyche tempts us with novelty, adventure, and stimulation in abundance. The same drive that propelled our species can now lead to overstimulation, restlessness, and a mind too unsettled to enter flow.

By all means, satiate your thirst for thrills — whether through movies and arts, skydiving, or some other way (just be sensible). However, make sure to have a separate, unrelated flow practice in your life, away from the thrills.

Cultivating Flow Through Your Muse

The modern world offers plenty of opportunities for the three mind-hooks discussed in the section "Meeting Three Greek Gods of Mind-Hooking," earlier in this chapter, to hijack your attention. You need to steer clear of the gods of mind-hooking if you want to obtain flow.

People who tap into flow regularly create meaning-making activities in their life, which very often are the same activities that give them flow. Those activities counteract the pull of the extrinsic rewards of the mind-hooks. They connect with the eudemonic part of the reward system, looping in the personal memories, and the sense of self. This means that these activities provide you with personal relevance and the all-important *intrinsic* motivation (Flow Element 5) — along with all the other Flow Elements (see Chapter 2).

In addition to their gods, ancient Greek mythology included nine muses who inspired thinkers and artists, and encouraged flow. The ancient Greeks believed that the muses draw your attention away from the everyday, letting your mind meander creatively, allowing you to find new ways of seeing things; these muses were the origin of the English word *muse* (meaning to ponder deeply). From a neuroscientific perspective, when a person muses, we can say new, perhaps surprising neural connections form inside their brain.

In many big cities, the arts and wealth go together. Perhaps because the Arts offer a refuge from the constant pleasure "junkiness" of modern cities like Frankfurt am Main or New York. Even in the European Central Bank—the maximum expression of wealth and extrinsic rewards—we can connect with over 500 works of contemporary art. Drawings, paintings, sculptures, photographs, and installations by artists like Nevin Aladağ, Ólafur Eliasson, and Giuseppe Penone provide opportunities to pause, reflect, and experience aesthetic emotions (explore these special emotions that open our mind to new experiences and thoughts, in Chapter 8).

Pick a sculpture and notice what memories or associations arise when you look at it. You can tap into flow by observing how a sculpture moves you, not in finding a particular interpretation of it. Try this in any gallery or museum, letting your mind make new connections. Muse!

Chapter **10**

Stringing It All Together: Owning Your Flow

Humans all have an *Achilles heel* (a phrase that comes from Greek mythology, where a hero was invincible except for one heel) that prevents them from feeling flow — the brain's tendency to get firmly gripped by cues that trigger flow-stalling behaviors. You need to set the right *intentions* (Guiding Star of Flow 8, explained in detail in Chapter 8) for your flow practice.

To set these intentions, you don't need drama and big speeches; you just need to set boundaries and curate a pathway to flow for your mind. In Bonus Chapter 1, found at `www.dummies.com/go/flowfd`, you can read about cues in your head, your surroundings and your family/friendship groups that may help you tap into flow — or not. Be a sniffer dog in the service of your flow and identify good and bad cues for *your* flow.

Construct a protective palace for your flow practice, including boundaries for cues that set your mind spinning, and a *flow-altar* that presents pleasant, flow-triggering cues to your mind so that you can find flow.

In this chapter, we look at how you can create a flow altar with your flow practice. I also introduce the Phoenix Cycle, a tool to maintain skill-challenge balance (Flow Element 7; see Chapter 2 for all ten Flow Elements) and keep flow alive.

Creating Flow Cues: An Altar for Flow

To help change the cues in your mind, deliberately introduce new cues that you find engaging, interesting, and associated with activities that bring you into flow. Over time, these cues can become part of habit loops that reliably support focused, rewarding action.

Fundamentally, you want to design your environment so that it contains cues that repeatedly prompt the actions and complex behaviors that will bring you toward flow. When you consistently pair specific sights, sounds, smells, textures or other sensory cues (remember that we have eight senses — see Chapter 4 for how to appeal to all of them with your flow-altar) with a flow-bringing activity, your brain makes the association. Eventually, the cue alone can prepare your mind and body for flow. (I talk more about this kind of association in your brain in Chapter 7.)

Designing a space for flow

Choose or create a space that you can consistently associate with your flow practice. Make this space feel safe, calm, and supportive of focus. You don't need to find a large or special place (you may just turn in a specific direction, or away from something), but it does need to be stable enough for your brain to recognize it as the place where this activity happens. You can add cues to that space like a focus point (a stone, plant, color, etc.), add sounds that you only listen to when you seek flow, etc.

Pay attention to how different environments affect you. Some spaces support concentration and ease; others trigger vigilance or distraction. If a space makes you feel exposed, rushed, or unsettled, it works against flow. If you don't yet have an ideal space, you can gradually shape one by adjusting lighting, layout, sound, and objects so that it feels more aligned with the activity that you want to practice.

Your flow-"altar" can be something as simple as carrying a knitting pouch in your bag (create it so you love how it looks, feels and sounds!) which you then pull up when you want a flow-break. You turn toward the white wall with no distractions and you submerge yourself into the textures, colors and repetitive movements you're your hoop-loop-stitch.

While you return to the same space and repeat the same actions there, your brain begins to anticipate the activity. Over time, simply entering the space (or pulling up that needle pouch) can bring you closer to flow.

Acknowledge the space as part of your practice. The more consistently you pair it with a specific activity, the more strongly it cues flow when you enter it.

Start simple. A flow trigger should be a basic, easily repeatable cue that helps you begin the activity. For example: a specific notebook, a particular chair, a familiar scent, or a consistent piece of background sound. You don't want to create stimulation, but to reduce friction and signal readiness.

Designing your flow space with intention

When a cue becomes part of a habit loop, your brain responds automatically. Habit loops are explained in Chapter 7, but you can also check the section "Identifying Your Habitual Cues" in online Chapter 1. The moment your senses register the cue, it activates stored associations in memory and prepares the corresponding action. If the action leads to satisfaction, engagement, or relief, the loop strengthens. For example: A specific object can cue you to start your creative work, which gives you a sense of satisfaction or absorption. Over time, seeing the object alone can prime your brain for the activity.

Through these associations, environments can quietly shape behavior. By designing your surroundings with intention, you allow your brain to more easily do what you want it to do.

Setting cues in interest-driven learning

Flow practices work best when personal *interest* drives you to do them (see Chapter 2 for Flow Element 5 "Intrinsic Reward," as when the activity itself matters to you), rather than external pressure like exams or extrinsic rewards like "winning." When you focus on cues that draw you into the activity itself (absorption, Flow Element 1 — see Chapter 2) and allow the activity to provide feedback while you go (Flow Element 3), you shift learning and practice away from performance or outcome fixation and toward curiosity, engagement, and enjoyment.

You're likely already setting up your environment in small ways that make it a positive place for you: choosing clothes you like, arranging your workspace, decorating your home. Make some of these cues specific to your flow practice so that they reliably trigger the actions that you want to repeat.

Check out the section "Identifying Flow Triggers" in Chapter 2 for inspiration from pre-historic humans' flow-practices.

Think of this process as becoming attentive to how your brain learns. Notice which cues support focus and which disrupt it (we practiced this in the preceding sections when you wrote down your habitual distracting cues). And place helpful cues in plain sight. Remove or reduce those that pull you away. Over time, these small adjustments add up to a space, and a habit structure, that supports flow.

Focusing on Engagement, Not Completion: The Phoenix Cycle

To build a skill that can become a flow practice, you must refuse the idea of being done. Flow depends on continued engagement, not completion. For this reason, the Phoenix Cycle is a useful model: it has no endpoint and always gives you a place to re-enter the practice. The Phoenix Cycle is called like this because it follows the life cycle of the mythological creature by the same name which transitions through 3 stages constantly — it starts as a newly-hatched ugly chick, transitions to adolescent bird and then becomes a glorious, golden beauty, only to light up in fire and fall to ashes. Of the ashes, the ugly chick re-hatches and the process starts anew. Be like that in your practice. Simply never stop re-hatching. And make *that* fun. See Figure 10-1 for an illustration of this process.

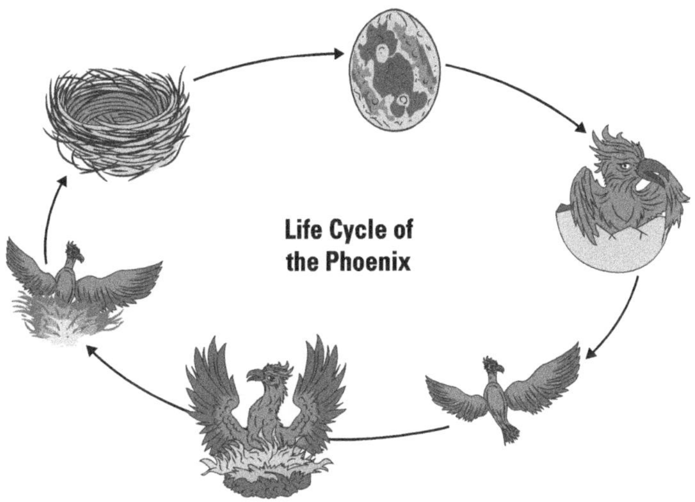

FIGURE 10-1: the Phoenix Cycle of learning a new skill.

John Vinycomb/Wikimedia Commons/Public domain

For flow, the Phoenix Cycle describes how you can learn and relearn skills in a way that keeps your brain engaged, always taking it to the next level. Each new skill within your practice is another Phoenix Cycle. It supports the skill–challenge balance that makes flow possible (Flow Element 7 — the activity never becomes too boring nor too hard). This also prevents stagnation or avoidance. (You can read about all ten Flow Elements in Chapter 2.)

Following the Phoenix Cycle

The Phoenix Cycle learning model involves these elements:

>> **Copying:** Every skill starts with copying. Painters copy others' paintings to practice, musicians copy phrases, dancers copy movements, writers copy structures or sentences. This copying doesn't imply a lack of creativity; the brain uses it to build the basic neural habit loops required for a skill. With time and repetition, the copying helps the skill transition from effortful explicit memory systems into implicit systems.

>> **Practice and refinement:** You repeat the basics, adjust details, and gradually increase complexity. This phase strengthens habit loops and builds fluency. Many experienced practitioners deliberately return to simple exercises at the start of each session to warm up the brain and body. The English painter William Turner is known to have returned to the 1st year live drawing classes at the Royal Academy in London, every morning, to tune his skill.

>> **Expression:** As you build your skill, you start being able to use the activity for expression (Guiding Star of Flow 5 — see Chapter 7). Variation, interpretation, and originality emerge. Expression feels rewarding because it expands your repeated practice and it is a channel for ruminative thoughts to be "expressed" into the activity you're doing, to get it "off your chest." Flow often appears most reliably in this phase, when challenge and skill are well matched.

>> **Slowing down:** Eventually, the practice reaches a point where progress slows or interest drops. This element doesn't represent failure; it just gives you a signal to restart the cycle — with another aspect of the skill; another dance move, a new musical piece, another technique, etc. Simplify again, copy again, and rebuild from the basics. The cycle continues.

Supporting flow with the Phoenix Cycle

Flow requires continuous adjustment between skill and challenge. The Phoenix Cycle keeps that balance moving. By returning to basics when you start to feel overwhelmed, you avoid overload. By expanding when ready, you avoid boredom. The cycle also removes pressure to reach a final outcome, which reduces performance anxiety and supports intrinsic motivation (Flow Element 5). Simply keep the cycle moving. Practice your skill at times and act as a beginner at others. You need to fill both roles throughout the cycle. Always, and on repeat. Flow doesn't come from mastery alone, but from staying engaged in the process.

For your flow practice, you need to:

>> Accept that you must return to beginner phases.

>> Use repetition to stabilize habit loops.

>> Let expression emerge naturally from practice.

>> Avoid the idea of a final goal or finished state.

3
Integrating Flow into Daily Life

Apply flow principles to everyday activities such as learning, cooking, and working.

Lean into what you're already doing for more flow

See how different domains — from sports to writing to science — can become flow-rich.

Follow real-life examples that show how people build flow into their routines.

Start small, stay present, and develop sustainable flow habits.

Chapter **11**

Reaching Flow While Learning a New Language

E ven if you're not interested in learning a new language, please don't skip over this chapter. You can think of learning any new skill or subject like learning a language. It requires learning a new vocabulary (movements of the mouth or other parts of the body), a set of rules (technique), a way of thinking (new meanings): You learn new words that you then string together into sentences, you get familiar with the grammar rules and sentence structure — and, little by little, you build a more sophisticated vocabulary while you go. At some point, you start to really express yourself and understand complex meanings in this new language, perhaps even enjoying literature and poetry in that language.

In this chapter, you can get guidance on how to find flow while learning a language. And I point out how you can use the same principles to learn any skill.

For language learning, the *For Dummies* series offers books that can help you learn many languages in fun and accessible ways. Check them out!

Getting to Flow with a New Language

Like with any skill that you want to learn, you can most successfully master a language if you practice it in a way that you find fun. With time and repetition, the new skill passes from explicit, effortful memory systems to implicit memory systems (which I talk about in Chapter 7), meaning that, little by little, your new skill becomes automatic and you start to expand your fluency, having more natural conversations without having to plan every sentence that you want to say in the new language.

During this process, you run the risk of getting ahead of yourself, comparing yourself to others (extrinsic motivation, which definitely doesn't help flow — see Chapter 2 for more about the role of intrinsic motivation in flow). You can also end up chasing quick gratifications — like when you know a list of words by heart (so that triumph causes a rush of dopamine in your brain) — but can't use them in context in a sentence, so you haven't really developed your language skill that much. Also, you may come across mind-hooks that can distract you from flow (see the section "Dodging Language-Learning Mind-Hooks," later in this chapter).

But you can use the eight Guiding Stars of Flow (introduced in Chapter 5), behaviors that can help guide you to flow, while you learn a new language. (The section "Following the Guiding Stars of Flow in Language Learning," later in this chapter, points out the role of these "star" behaviors.) And you can use the *Phoenix Cycle*, where you learn and relearn skills in an endless loop, to help boost your learning process. (Chapter 10 goes into detail about the Phoenix Cycle.)

Being Authentically You in a New Language

To find flow, you need something that you like submerging yourself into. To appreciate a good book, you need to understand the language it's written in. This need applies to all activities — such as learning how to read music or follow a recipe. So the metaphor of language learning is really useful to understand the process that you want to go through to find flow with any activity.

Expressing yourself is one of the *Guiding Stars of Flow* — those behaviors that can help you achieve flow — which I discuss in Chapter 5. (Expression is Guiding Star of Flow 5.) Activities that give you flow do so because they link very deeply to who you are — into your authentic self (see more about the science of authenticity in Chapter 7). They really appeal to something inside you, however small — a love for systems, a love for specific smells, movements, textures. This special *you*-element allows you to express yourself within that activity — whether in the way that you arrange the landscape on your model train tracks, the columns in your spreadsheet, the dance movements you do, or the colors of the fabrics that you sew. Expressing yourself with your flow activity stokes your intrinsic motivation (Flow Element 5) — one of the ten Flow Elements discussed in Chapter 2 — and makes the activity deeply rewarding for your brain.

Humans have a tremendous need to express themselves, and research suggests that self-expression can improve physical and mental health. Expression can help you release negative feelings and share positive ones. Think back to the last time you said something or "got something off your chest" that made you feel so good, whether it was airing a grievance or sharing an insight. People can express themselves in a number of ways:

>> Verbal language

>> Writing

>> Movement (such as dance and sports)

>> Other creative movements (such as crafts, coding, and arts)

Neuroscientific studies show that the neural pathway that controls part of your vocal apparatus, the *larynx*, which enables humans to speak, also controls arm movements (including gestures). (I go into more detail on this connection in Chapter 7.) For your brain, similar neural pathways regulate both body language and spoken language. For flow, use your body-language in ways that you love.

Dodging Language-Learning Mind-Hooks

Whenever you're brand-new to something, you can feel helpless, like learning the new skill is a lost cause.

In today's highly interconnected societies, where people often migrate to other countries or have to communicate with people whose native language isn't the same as their own, you may find yourself surrounded by a completely new language landscape and have to learn a language particularly fast or particularly well.

Whether you're cast into a new language landscape by an exchange program, through migration, or by falling in love with someone whose primary language is different than yours, avoid the three Gods of Mind-Hooking (which you can read more about in Chapter 9).

In Greek Antiquity, three Gods personify exactly what to avoid when you want to find flow with any activity. Goddess Nike of victory stands for a competitive mindset. God Dionysius of celebration and wine lures you to chase empty pleasures, while Goddess Tyche of Fortune is the drama queen. Her risky allure is all-absorbing, but also a true flow blocker. You may be successful by letting these three gods guide you in other parts of your life, but these three behaviors, personified by the gods, break your flow, guaranteed. Regardless of the way that you approach your language learning, they can lurk around the corner. In the following sections, I offer some methods to avoid them.

Avoiding Mind-Hook 1: Learning without competition

To learn a language, you do need to memorize lists of words in that language and their translations in your own (see Chapter 5 for more on the Guiding Star of Flow 4, technique practice). However, you can't speak that language (or master any other skill) by rote memorization. Some schooling systems rely heavily on students learning lists of words by heart, making vocab tests part of the school curriculum; and many children receive top grades in these exercises but can't really use the language because they can't speak any full sentences or have a conversation.

Perfectionism concerns may kick in while you try to actually use the language, so you lose your motivation because you essentially inhibit yourself. Inside your head, you may feel like a superstar — but when you open your mouth, you sound like a beginner.

Don't get ahead of yourself — the mind-hook of competition (personified by the Greek goddess Nike of Victory) may tempt you to strive for winning and perfection, which leaves you discouraged by every mistake.

As soon as you let competition, comparison, and judgment into your mind space, your body releases adrenaline and other stress hormones. When you're in a stressed state, you can't use several of the Flow Elements (discussed in Chapter 2), including absorption and intrinsic rewards.

Avoiding Mind-Hook 2: Aiming for meaning, not gadgets

You lose your language-learning flow if you buy many books and gadgets, never using any of them in depth. All you need is one book, a notebook, and a pen. Buying too many tools to support learning gives you a pleasurable dopamine release in your brain the moment you make the purchase because it makes you feel like you're working toward your goal. But this external pleasure bringer actually demotivates you when it comes to doing the hard work of achieving real skill learning. (I equate this mind-hook with the God Dionysius, who represents quick, easy pleasures and indulgences.) You get a brief high from carrying the goodies home or downloading the new app, but then the heavy realization strikes: You're still nowhere near learning the language. And you feel depleted because after spending all that money, you face a stark dissonance between what you thought you had and what you really have.

Instead, research thoroughly what book or app can help you learn the language. Some books rely heavily on grammar language — so to use that kind of book, you need familiarity with grammar terms, such as verb tenses, prepositions, clauses, and so on. If you don't feel comfortable with that approach, find a book designed for people who want to learn a language without having to know the ins and outs of grammar terminology.

THE GOOD AND BAD OF LANGUAGE-LEARNING APPS

Language-learning apps such as Duolingo have the potential to either limit your chances of success through mind-hooking or help you reach flow by sparking the Guiding Stars of Flow (discussed in the section "Following the Guiding Stars of Flow in Language Learning," in this chapter). You can use them to consolidate word retention and establish some sentence-structure know-how, but they also feed you unpredictable dopamine hits through the shiny awards and cha-chings that you receive after every completed lesson. They are unpredictable because you never know whether your responses were right or wrong before you hit the button. As explained in detail in Chapter 9, this unpredictability hooks your mind — it's little God Dionysius promising that *maaaybe* you'll get a great, exuberant reward.

In Chapter 9, I discuss the risk of falling into addictive behaviors with anything that provides a reward that can become an aim in itself — to get the highest score on the test, to collect the shiny app prizes on the screen — instead of focusing on learning the language. You get hooked on the rewards, not on the language.

Here's the right mindset for language learning:

>> Set your intention to learn the language (or other skill), but not to be able to do it perfectly. Perfection takes a very long time to reach, and you need to have fun even before that glorious day in the distant future. So focus on the process, not the final outcome nor on external prizes. Focus on building mastery, not on reaching perfection. Stay within the doing.

>> Approach learning without letting the opinions or abilities of others pressure you. Keep your language learning for yourself — the eyes of others who know you may not be helpful. And don't chase their admiration or approval — it may never come.

>> Take action regularly that builds your knowledge (Guiding Star of Flow 4, technique practice), but don't make the goal too big. Break it down so that you can enjoy the process, piece by piece. Aim for learning a word, a sentence, a rule, an expression — don't aim for giving a Nobel prize speech in that language.

>> Learning this language provides you with a new way to see the world; it changes you. Other people's language levels or their appreciation about your skill have nothing to do with it. This is about *you*.

REMEMBER

Avoiding Mind-Hook 3: Shielding your vulnerability from unnecessary risk

Taking risks isn't inherently bad. Humans have the ability to strive and make wonderful things happen because they dare taking risks. And in learning a language, you do have to take the risk of failure — can you really succeed in understanding this new way of communicating? But you must stay aware of the effect the stress related to this risk-taking (the third mind-hook, personified by the goddess Tyche) can have on your physical body and your ability to find flow.

When learning a language, you run the *risk of disclosure* (the potential negative reactions and effects of sharing information about yourself), which I talk about in Chapter 9, if you share that you're learning a language with other people who might negatively judge you. Your risk-taking can hook your mind on the worry that you face ridicule and that you're not good enough.

You may feel this less-than self-judgment if you're the biggest beginner in the room: Say that your partner is a native speaker and you're new to the language. You may feel like you're too far behind them in that language to have meaningful conversation, and they may get impatient with your incomplete understanding. You face the same risks if you're the slowest in your jogging group or can't quite finish that knitting project at the speed that your friends can.

To avoid letting the mind-hook of risk-taking ruin your language-learning flow, know that:

>> You'll have days of failing and of wanting to abandon it all because you're frustrated. Remember back to the playful days of your childhood and youth. Failing was just part of the learning process — you didn't stop trying to learn to walk because you fell over from time to time. This just motivated you to try even harder. Shift your focus a little: You didn't practice walking *to* walk but to do other things for which you needed walking (get to the corner where the fun toys were, for example). Now you're learning a language, not to speak, but to communicate or to understand something. Perhaps shift a little in the type of materials that you use for studying. If the materials you're using to learn a language discuss quantum mechanics but you really love flowers (or vice versa), consider finding language learning materials that use vocabulary that you're intrinsically interested in, *flowers* or quantum mechanics.

Make this your motto: Keep calm and play more.

>> People will judge you — you can't avoid that. Be prepared so that your self-esteem doesn't take a hit. Develop an "I don't care what you think" attitude toward people who are arrogant and rude about your language learning. And don't disclose that you're learning a language in situations that might invite criticism and judgment.

>> Choose wisely whom you disclose to — make sure that they realize your effort and give you positive and supportive feedback.

When you have a lot of pressure to learn a new language, Tyche will be your constant companion. You *will* feel fear, judgment, risk, and pressure. Make peace with her, acknowledge her. But don't let her make your vulnerability a block against finding flow.

Following the Guiding Stars of Flow in Language Learning

While you venture into a new language world, you need to maintain an open mind about what you'll find there, and you need to avoid trying to apply the parameters of your native language world to that new world. Stepping into a language-learning process requires that you understand that you'll change — which happens when you learn anything new.

I see this process of learning a language a bit like traveling in space — thrilling and somewhat painful. You start out completely lost, without any real understanding, and you see the world as you know it from a distance. But new connections form in your brain. If you follow the eight Guiding Stars of Flow (outlined in Chapter 5), they can help you navigate your language-learning trip.

Guiding Star of Flow 1: Moving for language skill development

Movement is Guiding Star of Flow 1. In Chapter 6, I explain why movement and exercise are so important for our brain and for learning any skill, also for language learning. So get moving while you learn your new language. Perhaps reserve 30 minutes a day where you walk while rehearsing your language skill. You can practice counting — each step a number. Or narrate your walk in your new language, what you see and what you feel.

Conjugate verbs to a beat (if the language you're learning has clear conjugations), such as the rhythm of your walk. You can carry a small booklet that has all the verb forms so that you can check them in case you run blank or question yourself.

Because you're seeking flow with a mostly sedentary activity (which language learning is, at its base), find ways to fire up the neural pathways of the movement systems of your brain — it fires up the rest of your brain and helps you make connections (which you can read more about in Chapter 6).

Guiding Star of Flow 2: Learning a language with social contact

You can naturally make language learning quite social, and social interaction is Guiding Star of Flow 2. You need other people around so that you can hone your language skill. Humans are born with the predisposition to learn a language, but depending on what language landscape you grow up in, you use your capacity for imitation to assimilate the words and the sentence structures of that language. As an adult learner, you use the others around you who already speak the language as models, and you imitate them. You just need to be careful that you don't allow the mind-hook of risk-taking to interfere with finding your language-learning flow (which I talk about in the section "Avoiding Mind-Hook 3: Shielding your vulnerability from unnecessary risk," earlier in this chapter).

REMEMBER

You need to set the right settings in your mind to avoid ruminations and worries (Flow Elements 9 and 10, which you can read about in Chapter 2) so that you can focus your attention on language learning. Social contact helps reduce a whole range of stress messenger substances in your body, so you can more easily avoid these negative thought patterns. For language learning, social contact therefore serves a double function — you can use it to get the settings right in your brain for flow and practice the imitative process that you need to learn a language.

Guiding Star of Flow 3: Creating a language-learning routine

A language-learning routine can bear fruit — and routine is the Guiding Star of Flow 3. By following a routine, you connect neurons related to that activity.

With any skill that you set out to learn, you start by copying. With time and repetition, this skill passes from explicit, effortful memory systems to implicit memory systems — meaning that, little by little, a new skill becomes automatic and you start to expand your fluency. You can have more natural conversations, without having to plan every sentence that you want to say. At some point, you start to genuinely express yourself in that new language.

Create your language routines around pleasant activities so that your mind finds it easy to stick with it. Perhaps you read some German texts in the early mornings and practice your comprehension while you have your coffee before work — ten minutes can be plenty to allow your neurons to get excited and connected. Or maybe you set up an afternoon walk routine where you identify things that you pass in Japanese. When you build a routine for flow, pay special attention to having the right cues around so that, with time and repetition, the cues help usher your mind along the pathway to flow. I explain this process in detail in Chapter 7.

TECHNICAL STUFF

ADJUSTING TO A NEW LANGUAGE'S STRUCTURE

With language learning, you start by copying words, sentences, and texts. You copy, copy, copy. Like a parrot. Vocalize, write. Copy the sentences you've written over and again, listen to a native vocalize them. Vocalize words and sentences yourself. Use a podcast, try to talk to a vendor. Your brain starts detecting beginnings and endings of words, generating little habit loops for all words, then for sentences, in a process called *categorical perception*. All languages have specific patterns in their sentences:

- Some languages have the structure Subject–Verb–Object (SVO), such as English: I (S) have (V) a book (O).

- Other languages use Subject-Object-Verb (SOV) structures, including Turkish.

(continued)

(continued)

- In some languages (for example, Spanish), you often omit a word for the subject completely because the verb form relates who you're talking about. **She** has a cat (in English), but *tiene un gato* (in Spanish: "Has a cat").

Another aspect of grammar that varies between languages is the use of articles:

- Some languages (such as English) have articles — the word *the* in the sentence *He loves the book.*

- Other languages don't use articles at all (like Turkish).

- Then some languages have different articles, depending on the object — for instance, in Spanish, a masculine noun (*libro,* meaning *book*) uses a masculine article (*un*), but a feminine noun (*mesa,* meaning *table*) uses a feminine article (*una*). Both *un* and *una* translate as *a.*

While you repeat these patterns in your language-learning routine, you start expanding your neurons' ability to detect these regularities and categories. Slowly, random gibberish starts sounding a little less so.

Guiding Star of Flow 4: Upping your language skills with technique practice

Some people are more flow-prone than others (see Chapter 3), and perhaps some people have an advantage when it comes to learning a language (they may have grown up bilingual or have already learned other languages). But setting the right habits in the brain beats all previous talent for something (as discussed in Chapter 6). Arguably, to reach real excellence in something, you do need both some talent (or genetic predisposition) and drive to form the right habits.

So, the technique practice (Guiding Star of Flow 4) that you set up when you start learning a language matters. People who already speak more than one language have an advantage because they have practice in how to learn a language. Languages don't just magically appear in their brains: They do put in the hours of study time. But they know how to approach the process of learning a language. They know of the frustrations and what can give them joy. They know what it means to learn different verbal tenses of a new language — speaking in the present tense, or in past tense about yesterday, or about tomorrow's future.

You can follow a Phoenix Cycle (see Chapter 10) with your language-technique learning, developing skills in an endless loop. Start by learning verbs in present tense (words that mean *I do, I have, I speak*), repeating them so they stick in your memory. Then, expand the number of verbs that you learn. Start using those verbs in sentences, expressing yourself when you use them in simple conversations or simple dialogues.

Then, go back to the beginning — learn to use the same verbs in past tense (*I did, I had, I spoke*). You expand your ability to express — for example, you can tell your friend what you did yesterday.

You come back to the fragile beginner stage again, this time learning the future tense (*I will do, I will have, I will speak*). You again expand with new verbs and express — perhaps planning the party you'll have tomorrow.

You can repeat this cycle, over and again, for all the different aspects of the new language that you need to learn. Learn how to learn a language, and then apply that to each cycle you take.

Keep the skills-challenge balance (Flow Element 7, discussed in Chapter 2) while you learn your language. For flow, the activity you do can't be too hard, nor too easy. Depending on your native language, you may find different languages more or less difficult to learn. A native English speaker tends to find Korean or Chinese the most difficult to learn because of how very different those languages are from English, and they find German or Dutch the easiest to learn because they belong to a language family similar to English. Factor in the difficulty of the language that you're trying to learn when you plan your copy-expand-express cycle because if the task is too difficult, flow remains elusive.

LANGUAGE MOVEMENT

In Chapter 6, I explain that the brain perceives everything as movement. Learning a language involves learning new movements: mainly movements of your vocal system — led by a physical structure called the *larynx*, a cartilaginous construction in your throat that helps you breathe, swallow, and produce sounds by interacting with the vocal cords. You need to learn new muscle modulations for your vocal cords, and your brain needs to learn to sequence the sounds it hears into words. Learning a language is a process of habit formation. It takes time. Be patient. And if you accompany the concepts that you're learning with some sort of physical movement — such as mimicking running when you use the word that means *to run* — you help your brain form the right links.

Guiding Star of Flow 5: Expressing yourself in the new language

Expression is an obvious aspect of language learning, and a very important one. Expression (Guiding Star of Flow 5, introduced in Chapter 7) can help prevent ruminative loops and worries. But expression can also help strengthen the right habit loops in your brain (stoking Flow Element 8, reducing the gap between action and perception) and make the activity intrinsically rewarding (Flow Element 5) so that it matters to you. (Chapter 2 discusses all ten Flow Elements.)

You can express yourself in the language that you want to learn through the arts that use that language:

>> Choose a song that you love that has lyrics in that language.

>> Watch a soap opera in that language that has subtitles in your native language.

>> Read an easy-reader book in that language (some publishers offer the classics of a language in an easy-reader format).

>> Read books that you already know translated into the new language (if you already know what happens, and what objects are used, you don't need to use the dictionary so often, which helps you with reading flow in the new language).

Of course, you can't understand all of the meaning of what you're experiencing yet. So, you express yourself through the choices that you make and the preferences that you have, which makes the activity that you're involved in matter to you. Choose something in the language that you want to learn because you like listening to or reading it — that way, you get both a feeling of pleasure and of meaning.

REMEMBER

Language learning through music, movies, or books that appeal to you stokes your intrinsic motivation (Flow Element 5) and helps your brain learn words in context and not coldly in lists of words that you memorize by rote. You do sometimes have to do this list learning. But if you can spice it up with some stories, songs, and soaps, you can have greater success at finding flow while learning the language.

Watching a movie

Watch a movie that has dialogue in the new language, with sub-titles in your own language. While you enjoy the movie, your brain is learning to detect the edges of the words in the new language. Slowly, these neural connections can help you in other contexts. Because you find watching a movie or a soap opera that you actually like more rewarding than, say, reading a dry story about a dog in your language-learning book, your brain retains this type of information more effectively. Your brain attaches meaning to these words in a more personally relevant way, linking it to other experiences already stored in your memory systems, than if you learned them in the context of reading a boring book.

Writing down the lyrics of a song

You may find this process tedious, but try it with a song that you really love and want to understand. Listen, stop, write down what you understand. Then start again: Listen, stop, and write down what you understand. Resist the temptation to check what the actual lyrics are online until you're done. Then compare. Try to understand every word.

Because the song has a personal significance for you, your brain can more easily stay focused (Flow Element 1, absorption) and remember the words that you hear. And you may tap into flow because this activity stokes your intrinsic motivation (Flow Element 5) and reduces the perception-action gaps (Flow Element 8). The human brain reacts with an urge to groove along when it hears rhythm and when you try to sing along to lyrics.

Learning languages from books that you love

You can find easy-reader versions of novels in most languages in bookstores and online. While you read a story that fascinates or captivates you, your mind becomes intrinsically engaged.

You can also choose a book that you know well — say that you love J.R.R. Tolkien's *The Hobbit* — and then read it in the target language. You already know the book so well that you don't need to check a dictionary constantly for what the words mean; you already know what the author conveys in your language, so you can use that knowledge to help translate the text. This leaves your mind free to flow a little, within the story that you love so much — and all the while, your brain gets familiar with sentence structure, verb tenses, new words, and so on.

Conversations

Of course, after you have a better understanding of this new language, you can have long, flow-filled conversations with people in that language, where you can express your thoughts and opinions. You can start with the patient shop keeper in the corner shop and speak about the weather, or ask your cab driver about their favorite song or foods, and so on.

Guiding Star of Flow 6: Using your imagination in language learning

You definitely need your imagination (Guiding Star of Flow 6) to learn a new language. Imagery is a complex mechanism of your brain, in which it basically draws on large-scale connections between distant brain regions via the *associative cortex* (the surface of your brain — the wrinkled bit you see in pictures). These connections help you imagine flying cars — and concepts as they relate to different sounds in a new language.

Chapter 7 talks about how different people have different levels of imagery vividness. Even if you have a somewhat low level of imagery vividness, you can use external prompts to stoke your imagination while you learn your language. And finding that level of imagery that works for you can help you tap into flow.

You need to practice conversation while you learn a language, ask questions and reply to questions. To practice having a conversation, you need to role-play a situation many times. Adult language learners don't get the same experience as a child learning a language, who can get things wrong repeatedly without negative consequence. In the wider world, adult language-learners don't find such situations as often as they need them. So, you must create them.

You need to have interesting made-up situations so that you can keep your mind focused and absorbed (which can help you reach flow). Come up with scenarios that you find interesting, such as planning a party or asking for directions to the cinema in your city (use a real map and a real landmark that matters to you), and convey your intention in that scenario by using your new language. You can practice these conversations alone (imagining the responses you get), or you can practice with a partner who either knows or also wants to learn the language.

Guiding Star of Flow 7: Finding aesthetic emotions with language learning

The Guiding Star of Flow 7, aesthetic emotions (such as awe) increase arousal, which helps oxygenate the brain (giving it the fuel it needs to work). Also, you tend to better remember something if you feel slightly aroused when you perceive it. Experiencing aesthetic emotions also makes you more receptive to self-transformation, including learning a new language.

REMEMBER

While you learn a new language, plan to invite some aesthetic emotions into the process. Flip back to Chapter 8 for a list of emotions to aim for. Consider researching a culture associated with the language that you're currently learning. Enjoy this process of discovery and finding new ways of seeing the world. You may feel curious, fascinated, and perhaps even moved. Stoke your intrinsic motivation (Flow Element 5) with these aesthetic emotions.

Your mind must *like* the moment and your *doing* within it, in order to achieve flow. You can invite some aesthetic emotions into your language-learning practice to achieve this.

Perhaps choose colored sheets of paper or notebooks that have images on them that you like. Read literature and movies that interest you in that language. And, if you're in a country where that language is spoken, visit its museums and galleries, theaters and cinemas, bookshops and art shops.

Guiding Star of Flow 8: Setting a language-learning intention

As a rule of thumb, and for any skill that you're learning, set very short-term intentions (Guiding Star of Flow 8, discussed in Chapter 8), a maximum of ten minutes away, that you can achieve and that don't invite the three Gods of Mind-Hooking (discussed in the section "Dodging Language-Learning Mind-Hooks," earlier in this chapter). For flow with language learning, don't set your mind to compete with anyone, seek risk or sensation that could poke your heart the wrong way, nor chase after language certificates by learning lists of words by heart without context. These aims don't provide valid flow-induction goals, nor intentions.

Flow Element 2 (discussed in Chapter 2) involves having clear goals about what you're trying to achieve. In addition, to fulfill Flow Element 3, the activity itself has to give you reliable feedback about how it's going; so you can't set an intention about anything grand. You can't get direct feedback while practicing a language about how you're progressing in relation to passing your final exam. Your brain goes into a wanting state where you strive, which means you're unlikely to find flow.

Some people naturally don't get ahead of themselves — perhaps that's what makes them *flow-prone* (meaning that they can find flow particularly easily). (See Chapter 3 for discussion of flow-proneness.) They enjoy the moment and their activity in it; and if they don't, they find a way to create enjoyment.

Connecting Emotionally to Your Language Flow

Learning a new language takes sweat and tears. You're in a process of metamorphosis. The schemas that you know don't necessarily apply to the language that you want to learn. Everything about this new language seems entirely random at first because the regularities that your brain knows don't work. But your brain has a regularity detection mechanism — it loves to look for patterns. When it finds them, it relaxes — and you get to experience Flow Element 10 within your language practice (you lose the sense of unpredictability and feel in control). So don't get ahead of yourself. Give your brain time (and repetition) to detect the regularities that exist in any language and that reveal themselves while you go. That's when the door to flow opens up.

Chapter **12**

Finding Flow with Athletic Movement

The human brain likes to categorize and sort by features — cats versus dogs, ambulance sounds versus music. That instinct to box things helps people make sense of the world, but it also leads to some problems — especially when you try to define subtle differences in things that are quite similar. You might approach them in the wrong way. Sports, dance, and yoga are examples of activities that you may try to classify as different. But for your brain, they aren't. They are all *athletic movement* — with varying degree of exertion and different movements perhaps, but athletic movement nonetheless. This allows us to look at them together.

In this chapter, I look at sports, dance, and yoga as flow activities and how the eight Guiding Stars of Flow (which you can read about in Chapter 5) can apply to these physical pursuits. Find out how to follow these stars through your physical activity, whether it's a sport, dance, or yoga. This chapter also offers suggestions about how to stay clear of the mind-hooks that you can find within your exercise regimes (flip to Chapter 9 for discussion of mind-hooks) so that you can let your mind achieve flow.

Finding the Similarities in Sports, Dance, and Yoga

How you categorize the physical activity that you enjoy can depend on many factors. Perhaps you think that dancing includes more of an aesthetic element and rules about the proper poses and movements, while sports focus on the outcomes, not how you look doing it. In yoga, you focus on how poses and movements feel, not how they look, and you don't have any tangible outcomes, such as goals or points.

However, for developing your pathway to flow, rather than thinking of what differentiates them, think about what makes them similar. For flow, sports, dance, and yoga have a lot in common, actually. For instance, they all involve *aerobic exercise,* when you bring the heartrate up over a certain number of beats per minute (BPM).

According to The American Heart Association, the threshold for a type of exercise being aerobic depends on your age. If you're around 20 years of age, aerobic exercise is between 100 and 170 BPM, while for a 70-year-old it would range between 75 and 128 BPM.

If you talk to any football player, yoga practitioner, or dancer, they also agree on another thing: Practitioners recognize their activity as beautiful and that it also gives them other *aesthetic emotions* (which we will see in the section "Guiding Star of Flow 7: Aesthetic emotions," later this chapter).

These activities also share that you can practice them competitively — or not. It is important to remember that competitiveness creates a focus that prevents you from finding real, healthy flow (I call competitiveness a "mind-hook" and describe this in the section "Mind-hook 1, Nike: Comparison and competition," later in this chapter). Focusing on extrinsic rewards such as winning, prizes, and admiration may well absorb your attention — and that can be healthy and important for some aspects of your life. Yet, it's not a mindset that can help you find healthy flow.

You can see a small difference between sports, dance, and yoga in the ease with which you can practice them non-competitively. You can definitely practice dance and yoga non-competitively. With sports, that's harder — they're often competitive by design (you collect points or goals, aim to be faster or lighter, and so on).

Letting the Stars Guide You in Your Exercise Practice

A section about stars may at first seem counterproductive in discussion of flow because of the mainstream use of *stars* to refer to competitive rewards or achievements. However, you're not trying to *reach* the Guiding Stars of Flow. You use them to set direction, like navigating on a boat over stormy seas, using the stars as a navigation aid.

The purpose of the eight Guiding Stars of Flow is simply to orient your thinking (to guide you) so that you can invite the ten Flow Elements into your practice (see Chapter 2) and find healthy flow. The following sections examine how you can incorporate some (or all!) of these Guiding Stars into your physical endeavor to help you achieve flow.

Guiding Star of Flow 1: Movement

Because the human brain expects you to move regularly, if you don't, it tells you about it. Your body will be sending signals of danger to your brain before you know of it. It arrives there as arousal that may confuse you, make you restless. Regular movement therefore appeases ruminative thoughts (Flow Element 9), and helps you feel in control (at least some of the time; Flow Element 10). I give more details about how body and brain are intertwined and why movement is so important for flow in Chapter 6.

Perhaps you have another activity like crochet or drawing as your flow activity, but you struggle to find flow sometimes? Your brain may be missing Guiding Star of Flow 1 (movement). Crochet and drawing don't involve much physical movement, so to set the settings for flow in your brain, perhaps consider adding a small exercise regime to your day. A 30-minute walk in the evening can do wonders to still your mind and set the settings for flow for next time you sit down for the next loop stitch.

An exercise regime contains movement by definition — but for flow, don't push your body too hard (the negatives of which I talk about in the section "Mind-hook 1, Nike: Comparison and competition," later in this chapter).

Guiding Star of Flow 2: Social contact

To set the right settings in your brain and body for flow, you need to have healthy social contact. In Chapter 6, I discuss the special magic that happens when people smile at you, make friendly eye contact, or move with you in unison, or when you solve a problem together. These social nuggets for your brain appease it and help set the settings for flow.

If you practice your exercise activity solo, such as running alone in a forest or dancing at home by yourself, just make sure that you have positive social contact somewhere else in your life.

In any subcommunity, including sports, dance, and yoga communities, you can find people who have similar interests and personalities to your own. It can provide a nice alternative, perhaps, to your normal everyday crowd, a place where you can be more yourself with a specific social focus.

But watch out for unhealthy community interactions (discussed in the section "Mind-hook 3, Tyche: Drama and risk," later in this chapter).

Many times, positive in-person social contact can be difficult to obtain. During the COVID-19 pandemic (2020–2023), most people had to practice sports, yoga, and dance alone. But people got inventive, by doing remote Zoom dance or yoga classes or *co-running* (running sort of together via an app). Find ways to connect with people who practice what you practice, whether online or in local clubs and classes.

Guiding Star of Flow 3: Routines and rituals

To escape the unpredictability of life (Flow Element 10, feeling in control), you need to build routines or rituals, such as a brisk walk every early evening or a dance class every Wednesday. The more kinetic and multisensory your routine, the more it can guide you toward flow.

Go through what you've done in the past few weeks. What physical activities do you do recurrently? Maybe you

>> Walk the dog in the park every morning.

>> Do yoga every Tuesday, dance class every Wednesday, and walk with your mom for 30 minutes every evening.

>> Play a rec league softball game followed by a drink with your teammates on Friday evenings.

After you identify some physical routines or rituals that you perhaps already have in your life, try to analyze the cues and movements or actions that go with them. For example, for your ritual of entering the gym:

>> **Cue(s) that start off the ritual:** You see the clock strike a specific time (a visual cue). Or you feel a specific way in your body ("I feel edgy"), a cue that comes to you via your *interoception*, the sense of your body from within.

>> **Action that follows:** Begin stretching.

>> **What you feel as a result:** Your body releases tension, which acts as a reward.

If you flip back to Chapter 7, you can read more about how your brain creates habits through the cue-action-reward loop. The reward you feel encourages your mind to perform the action again the next time it perceives the cue (because it got a reward last time it did it). And routines and rituals are the result of many habit loops. The elements of the preceding list outline the three elements of a habit loop. You string together your rituals and routines from these kinds of habit loops, and you can create new ones for your flow practice. Refer back to Chapter 4 to identify which senses can most effectively create your habit loops. The more senses you involve in your rituals and routines, making them *multisensory* experiences, the stronger the loop can become.

Write the elements of your routine or ritual down to get a good picture of how they work together (see Table 12-1 for an example of how to categorize these elements).

TABLE 12-1 **Cues, Actions, and Rewards of Routines and Rituals**

Routine/ Ritual	Cues	Movements	Rewards	Senses Involved
Enter yoga studio	The time of day, the yoga mat, the lighting, the items that you encounter only here, the smell of incense, the music or chanting, the tea or mint-water they serve you, the sensation of the yoga mat on your feet and hands.	Stretching, the movements of your yoga practice (the sun salutation, warrior pose, and so on).	Your body releases tension. You feel joy because the movements feel right *while* you do them. You enjoy the smell of the incense *while* you inhale.	All of them! (Sight, smell, hearing, proprioception, exteroception, interoception, taste, and touch.)

The more senses that you can involve (and pay attention to), the better. If you associate the cues from your sports venue, dance studio, or yoga room with the movements that you do there, you can potentially create a special link between the cue and the action. With the time and repetition, the cues become *flow triggers* — you start feeling an urge to do the moves when you perceive the cues.

For example, for people who do yoga regularly, as soon as they see the mat and perhaps smell the incense (so common in yoga studios), their minds already get ready for flow. Similarly, when soccer players see a soccer ball, they enter a state where only they and the ball exist. For ballet dancers, it's perhaps the sight of the ballet barre and the sound of piano music that brings them immediately to the doorstep of the flow state (and ready to do barre training).

Use cues that you genuinely enjoy. For your brain to want to return to a moment, it must like being there *while* you're at it (check out the Liking-Wanting principle, which I cover in Chapter 4). Think in terms of aesthetic emotions (more on these in the section "Guiding Star of Flow 7: Aesthetic emotions," later in this chapter). Which cues evoke beauty, joy, energy, fascination, surprise, or a sense of wonder for you?

REMEMBER

If you find the word *routine* too rigid and off-putting, remember this isn't a dogma. You want to provide circumstances that train your brain to tap into flow, so tailor them to your brain's need and offer it a *ritual* instead. (For flow, use what terms and phrases work for *your* mind.)

Table 12-2 shows an example of how a dancer, Anna, uses cues strategically in a daily Argentine tango exercise ritual. You don't need to dance Argentine tango to find this table useful; I offer general tips for each sense. And you can find a worksheet in the online Cheat Sheet for this book (just go to www.dummies.com and search for "Flow For Dummies" to find it). On that worksheet, fill in the spaces with your own exercise regime, following the Argentine tango example.

Whatever cues you use, tailor them to your likes. Be weird. Make it unique and memorable to your brain. Of course, don't make it too complicated — you want a *simple* trigger for flow without too much effort.

Combine this routine from time to time with specific technique practice sessions (see the following section). You can even make your technique practice your routine or ritual: Two stars for the price of one!

Sense	Cues Anna Uses	Tips for You
Touch	Loose skirt of Lycra; warm, tight-fitting top	Do something to your hair that's different from how you usually have it (change the feeling).
Sight	Black clothes, golden shoes	If possible, arrange something golden (if you like gold — or another special color for you, if you prefer) as a focus point during the exercise ritual.
Hearing	Argentine tango music from the 1920s to 1950s	Perhaps craft a playlist of songs that you love and can use to practice.
Taste	Flavored lip gloss	Have a specific food item or drink (for example, a coffee) before you start.
Proprioception	Tango heels, changing the center of gravity feeling in Anna's body from how it usually feels	Wear a particular pair of shoes that make your limbs feel a little different in terms of balance and center of gravity.
Interoception	The body's morning-feeling for Anna's 8 a.m. dance class	Look for the inner nudge within your body that reminds you that it's time.
Exteroception	The wooden floor of the dance studio	Go to a different place altogether or create an altar for your tango ritual in a familiar space. (I speak about how to create altars for flow in Chapter 9.)
Smell	A specific perfume	Light a scented candle where you practice.

Guiding Star of Flow 4: Technique practice

Technique practice helps you build skill, creating habit loops (discussed in Chapter 7) that make this skill second nature. You fuse action and awareness (Flow Element 8), reducing the perception-action gap; you become the movement.

Here's the difference between the Guiding Stars of Flow for routines and rituals (see the preceding section) and for technique practice:

REMEMBER

However, you don't have to link your routine or ritual to your exercise regime and flow practice. The routine or ritual can be anything, from very simple to very complex movements — you focus on the cues and the regularities, giving your brain a sense of control (Flow Element 10) because the surroundings and what you do inside them are familiar and predictable.

When you go to your sports, dance, or yoga practice, you practice different elements of that activity, including specific technique practice. Perhaps you work on perfecting specific movements, positions, transitions between movements — racket grip, passing the ball, shooting a goal, and so on. Every practice has a specific set of elements that constitute its technique repertoire. And practicing its technique builds mastery, which you need for tapping into flow. You might find flow the first time you take a dance class — and then you go back and can't seem to find it. That's beginner's luck. When you do something that you happen to love for the first time, you may feel like you *are* the movement in a strange, absorbed way. To recreate this moment again and again, on demand, you need to build mastery.

Technique practice also fuels your Flow Element 7, the skills-challenge balance. Continuously increase your skill. Even the grand masters and geniuses keep practicing their technique every day. World-famous golf player Tiger Woods put it very simply: "No matter how good you get, you can always get better." Think of ways to keep up the challenge in your technique practice without overwhelming yourself. Hovering in that sweet spot is flow-triggering.

Technique practice doesn't involve you spending hours mind-numbingly repeating movements. Athletes are very clear about this. NBA basketball player Kobe Bryant famously said, "It's not about the number of hours you practice, it's about the number of hours your mind is present during the practice."

No matter your flow activity, you always need to make small adjustments to correct your technique and take the movement to the next level. Get creative with how you can incorporate the search for these adjustments in your technique practice. And, as

I explain in Chapter 7, ritualistic technique practice, such as when you practice your tennis forehand return over and over by using a ball machine, or do your ballet technique barre every morning, and so on — all of these familiar movements on repeat act as washing machines for the mind. They help you trigger Flow Element 9 (lose ruminative thought loops) and Flow Element 10 (feel in control), setting the settings for flow in your brain.

Guiding Star of Flow 5: Expression

With Guiding Star of Flow 5, expression, I don't want to pull you away from technique practice (which I talk about in the preceding section). But technique practice on its own (such as when you obsess only about the correct or beautiful move, and you do only that move with your practice) can never lead to a flow practice. World-famous contemporary dancer and choreographer Martha Graham once said, "Great dancers are not great because of their technique; they are great because of their passion." Technique makes you do the movements correctly — and that's important. You need mastery for a reliable pathway to flow. But to build a reliable flow practice, you must figure out how to be authentically yourself when you practice, expressing yourself and perhaps your needs, feelings, thoughts, or dreams with your activity.

When you start to incorporate the technique of your sport, dance, or yoga practice in your implicit memory systems, you can start expressing within the language of that practice. However, it's never too early to express. You don't have to first learn *all* the technique before you can express. In fact, some teaching models in dance emphasize that you start from expression, like a child that learns to speak and just babbles as best it can, and little by little starts learning the rules. The processes of technique practice and expression can totally go in parallel.

To get a feel for expression, practice your sport, dance, or yoga somewhere that you don't usually practice it. If you're a ballet dancer, go to the club and move however the music inspires you. For yoga, perhaps practice your usual studio sequence at home.

Without anyone watching, you likely own the movements in a different way because you don't have the thought of another's gaze in the back of your mind. (Don't put a mirror in front of you. Instead, tune into your *interoception*, the sense of your body from within, and appreciate what it feels to be you now.)

WARNING

Being expressive in a sports activity can get difficult. The objective of any sport is to compete, either with yourself or with others. You use emotions in an instrumental way, as tools to trick opponents or to communicate with teammates, again with the object of winning; and you mostly aim to suppress or otherwise manage your own emotions. However, you do express yourself through the clothes and shoes that you wear and the hairstyle that you adopt. You can use this form of expression in sport as a starting point. With time and repetition, your personal expression may come in how you do the moves of the craft in difficult situations.

Look for a balance between technique practice and expression — and perhaps take a look at Chapter 7, where I explain why expression through the body is like a language too — a body language.

TAILORING EXPRESSION TO WHO YOU ARE

Chapter 3 discusses that you need to tailor your flow practice to who you are. For example, if you're alexithymic (you have difficulty identifying and labeling feelings in yourself and others), the idea or expressing emotions can sound incredibly odd. Perhaps think of this expressivity as being very *you*, as a space where you can really be yourself. You do the poses and movements in ways that make you feel good. That's expression, too. And you may look for feelings such as being relieved or satisfied during that activity, like a cleaning of the soul.

Guiding Star of Flow 6: Imagination

Lionel Messi, an Argentine professional soccer player regarded by many as one of the best of all time, said, "I like to imagine things. Like the opposing defenders and what might happen. And obviously in your imagination it always turns out for the best." This quote explains wonderfully how previous imagery of a situation can prepare the neural pathways of the actions that he later needs so that he has a fraction of a second's advantage in the game. In Chapter 8, I explain the science of how your body aligns along mental imagery.

Imagining can help you align your physical body for specific activities in a sport, dance, or yoga practice. For example, imagine someone pulls you carefully upward by the hair at the back of your head. While imagining this adjustment, you probably breathe in and relax your facial muscles a little and your shoulders, and activate your diaphragm.

Dancer Wellness, a book by Donna H. Krasnow and M. Virginia Wilmerding (Human Kinetics), contains a chapter that explains the neuroscience about how to apply different types of imagery to your dance practice (which you can also use for any sports and yoga practice), including simple exercises to try.

People who experience flow regularly usually have a very clear motivation to use their imagination like a tool on their pathway to mastery. But they don't often realize that this very action makes them more likely to tap into flow. The imagination is always very *multisensory* (meaning it involves many senses).

For example, professional golfer Jack Nicklaus once said, "Before every shot, I go to the movies inside my head. Here is what I see: First, I see the ball where I want it to finish. Then, I see the ball going there, its path and trajectory. The next scene shows me making the kind of swing that will turn the previous image into reality. These home movies are a key to my concentration and to my positive approach to every shot."

Guiding Star of Flow 7: Aesthetic emotions

When you achieve flow, you sort of lose yourself and feel part of something bigger than yourself. You can't consciously aim for that state on purpose, of course. But you can aim for things that give you *aesthetic emotions* — when you feel emotions and sensations such as wonder, awe, being moved, curiosity, challenge, or interest. Checking whether you feel aesthetic emotions also helps you evaluate the flow possibilities for a practice. In Chapter 8, you can find a test to determine how different aesthetic emotions rate with regards to your sport, dance, or yoga practice.

Importantly, for the exercise in Chapter 8, don't focus on what you feel when you see someone else playing the sport, dancing, or performing a yoga routine perfectly on stage or TV. These emotions can help you identify what might work as your practice. But if you start rating these emotions in terms of dreaming of that wonderful moment when you'll be as good as them, you point yourself away from flow and toward the mind-hook of competitiveness (see the section "Mind-hook 1, Nike: Comparison and competition," later in this chapter).

Aesthetic emotions open you up, making you ready to invite new sensations and feelings into your practice and opening your mind for flow. They focus your mind into a meditative state, and off you go, *flow*.

Guiding Star of Flow 8: Setting an intention

When you tap into flow, the activity you're doing gives you reliable feedback about how it's going (Flow Element 3). To get this type of feedback, you must set your intention in the right way. Never get ahead of yourself. For Flow Element 3 to happen, you must be entirely *with* the activity. For Flow Element 2, you need a very clear goal with the activity you're currently doing so that your mind stays put and doesn't fly ahead to the glorious end pose or the praise.

Ask yourself, what's the exact next step, move, position? And how can you inhabit it fully, with your full attention tuned to this intention? Staying so focused on the movement can also help you achieve Flow Element 1 (absorption).

The biggest challenge with intention setting is finding an intention that's interesting enough for your mind to stay tuned to it, not dreaming ahead or imagining other glorious moments. Choose an activity that you really love (Chapter 8 offers ways to get to know yourself and your mind's likings a little more).

You can also help your mind love the intentions that you set by making the activity intrinsically rewarding to you (Flow Element 5). Perhaps you can create the practice in ways that your mind loves (for instance, by using beloved cues and altars — see Chapter 10 for how to create a flow altar).

One way to create intrinsic motivation, helping your mind stay put on an intention (because your mind just loves to stay there), involves triggering the meaning-making systems in your brain (read more about these in Chapters 4 and 9) with your activity. Separate from your actual practice of the activity, consider searching for information about your sports, yoga, or dance practice. You can set your intention to:

>> Understand a mechanism in a specific kind of tennis serve.

>> Know the history behind the ballet move *pas de chat*.

>> Research the conceptual background of your yoga poses.

Next time you arrive at your exercise practice, your memory systems are powered with this knowledge, connecting deeply with your meaning-making systems, as well as triggering rewarding feelings through the exercise. These connections help with keeping your intention on the very movement that you're doing, step by step.

Use the Phoenix Cycle (discussed in Chapter 10) to expand your flow practice by increasing your knowledge of that practice. You make the practice yours because you create those connections through elements that matter to you.

Moving Away from the Three Gods of Mind-Hooking

Can a person practice sports, dance, or yoga without feeling competitive, being surrounded by drama, and chasing external rewards? Yes and no. As I discuss in Chapter 9, it largely depends on what you want to achieve with the activity. Many ways of practicing these physical activities are competitive, or you need to set your intention to external rewards. For achieving flow, however, you need to approach the practice a little differently.

Sports players, yogis, and dancers who experience flow regularly make sure to stay clear of three mind-hooking behaviors when they want to tap into flow. To help you remember what these are, I give you a character from Greek Antiquity that personifies that behavior. The three mind-hooks are:

>> **Competition:** Personified by the Greek goddess of victory and competition, Nike

>> **Chasing quick pleasures:** Personified by the god of celebration and pleasure, Dionysius

>> **Seeking empty thrills and drama:** Personified by the goddess of fortune, Tyche

Know where these mind-hooks may be lurking so that you can avoid them on your flow path within your sport, dance, or yoga practice.

Mind-hook 1, Nike: Comparison and competition

Don't compare yourself to others in whatever physical practice you do. Comparison and competition create a mind-hook that can prevent flow. Of course, the whole point of sports for some people is the competition. And that's fine. But with that mind-set, you probably can't find flow while participating in that sport.

With sports, you face the most difficulty in remaining free of the mind-hook of competition. But it's not impossible: You just need to love the moves you do for the act of doing them (the serve, the *pas-de-chat*, the warrior pose), not for an ultimate goal (such as winning, points, goals). Check out the section "Guiding Star of Flow 8: Setting an intention," earlier in this chapter, for how to set a flow-inviting intention.

For flow, do what you do for *intrinsic rewards* (Flow Element 5; stuff that connects you with your sense of self), not for extrinsic rewards (winning, points, or goals). The competitive mindset brings you absorption but not flow because of the mix of chemicals that striving, wanting, and comparing sets loose in your bloodstream. While your mind is trying to disengage so that it can float effortlessly (Flow Element 6), competitive goddess Nike hooks you firmly in the present.

Dance because you love dancing, run because you love the feeling of running, do yoga because you really connect with yourself when you do it. This approach stokes the liking aspects of the Liking-Wanting principle (which I talk about in Chapter 4) and sets the stage for flow.

Mind-hook 2, Dionysius: Empty pleasure seeking

You can easily fall into the trap of getting stuff for your physical exercise practice that you don't actually need because of the burst of pleasure you get from acquiring it (a mind-hook). Yoga studios often sell things that they promise can help you get better at yoga — I promise, they won't. Also, expensive dance gear or sports equipment doesn't come with the skill and talent; you still have to work for those. By all means, purchase some gadgets to create cues for your routine or ritual (see the section "Guiding Star of Flow 3: Routines and rituals," earlier in this chapter). Just don't make those acquisitions your goal.

The pleasure-seeking mind-hook can also appear at the gym. Regular trips to the gym can help you boost your physical practice for sports, yoga, or dance. For instance, you may have to build strength in your arms and legs to improve your pitch. Perhaps your dance teacher recommends that you build strength in your upper body to help you perform dance lifts. But if you go to the gym regularly, don't make the number of crunches you do or the size of the weights you lift the objective. Little god Dionysius is tempting you away from the flow path when you start striving for the post-able selfie of you striking a pose, sharing the distances you run, seeking admiration and likes, doing it for the money, and so on. This striving can deflate your flow balloon in no time. Do karate because you actually enjoy the feeling of the moves, not for the cool pictures that you can post afterwards.

TIP

Create your practice so that you keep going, even on days where things seem hard. Here's an inspiration for when you lose motivation, from golf legend Tiger Woods: "Days when you just don't have it, you don't pack it in, you give it everything you've got."

Create your physical practice so that you keep going, even on days where things seem hard. Keep your motivation by creating a practice that you simply love doing for the sake of it, not because Dionysius blindly stimulates your pleasure systems after a cheap win.

Mind-hook 3, Tyche: Drama and risk

The mind-hook of risk-taking and drama (personified by the goddess Tyche) can negatively impact your quest to find flow with a physical activity in a number of ways:

>> **Risk of injury:** In sports, dance, and yoga, you must challenge yourself, sure. But if you constantly risk injuring yourself, the risk-taking goddess Tyche hooks your mind in the present and prevents it from finding flow.

>> **Fear of failure:** This mind-hook can also appear in relation to a fear of failure. In sports, dance, or yoga, you can't totally manage the *risk of disclosure* (showing your vulnerable self through what you do) because your body discloses with every movement. But you can potentially practice the sport, dance, or yoga alone, where no one can judge you. Create that judgment-free bubble wherever you

practice so that you feel like you're all alone and it doesn't matter whether you fail.

Failure gives you an opportunity to learn, nothing more — but also nothing less. To get better, you must, at times, fail. That's when your brain realizes that you must change something. Your brain forms new connections while you try a different approach, and you begin to build mastery.

>> **Unsafe social contact:** Although you need healthy social contact to find flow (see the section "Guiding Star of Flow 2: Social contact," earlier in this chapter), you may find yourself in social settings that you join for your sport, dance, or yoga practice that block your access to flow:

- *Recognizing mismatched connections:* While you sweat together, whether in sport, dance, or yoga practice, scientific measurements show that bodies exchange much biochemical information, which your conscious mind can interpret as finding a soulmate. However, science also shows that only time can tell whether this person is really friend or foe. Take care of yourself and make sure you have that coffee (or many coffees) together to really get to know each other.

- *Keeping it professional:* People who own these businesses probably treat you, the paying customer, well. But this friendly behavior can potentially create emotional dependencies. Trainers, masters, and teachers often come physically very close to you during practices, you move in synchrony with them, you focus on the same things — so very likely, your brain waves and other physical rhythms synchronize, leading to feeling emotional connection. Don't let your mind focus on that feeling of connection, otherwise it stays hooked on the moves of the teacher more than on your practice. Remember why you're at their business: to learn your practice, nothing more.

- *Staying focused on your practice:* Some trainers, masters, teachers, or other personnel around sport, dance, or yoga businesses sometimes cross a line because of the hierarchical asymmetry of that relationship. They can hook people to their business if they flirt with their clients and make those clients feel special. This type of connection makes your practice very conditional on that person, which makes flow remain elusive because you're constantly hooked on anything to do with that authority figure. Remind yourself that your brain reacts naturally to authority, and then focus back to your practice.

To steer clear of Tyche's mind-hook in your practice, remember the strong social binding effects that happen in a community because of synchronous movements and attending to similar things (see also Chapters 6 and 9) — don't mistake them for real connection.

TIP

Each community has a set of rules, both spoken and unspoken. When you're new to a group, try to figure them out. You can do an Internet search for those community rules, ask other more experienced practitioners, or simply take your time, observing the community, asking questions, and seeing how people react and interact with each other.

BUILDING AWARENESS

If you're in a leadership role, keep in mind the risks for people's flow and the reputation of your business posed by unsafe social contacts (which I talk about in the section "Mind-hook 3, Tyche: Drama and risk," in this chapter). Develop a framework within which you can have a conversation about this tendency to form unhealthy social contacts with your employees. Such initiatives exist already. For example, the president of the German Association of Dance School Companies (*Wirtschaftsverband Deutscher Tanzschulunternehmen*), Christoph Möller, and his team have devised a certificate for dance school personnel after they go through an awareness-building work-shop. The certificate is a physical copy that managers can hang on the walls in the dance school as a constant awareness builder. Look out for such awareness campaigns in your sports, dance, or yoga studio; ask teachers, other practitioners and perhaps friends who might know about this issue, and help to create awareness.

If your physical activity community doesn't provide you with a safe haven, make sure to seek another social community where you can feel safe. You need social contact (discussed in the section "Guiding Star of Flow 2: Social contact," earlier in this chapter), otherwise this absence chips away at your self-worth and flow will never come. You can also help yourself stay clear of Goddess Tyche by engaging in a little self-reflection to determine what you can do to fit in better within the social community of a physical practice space — which can help you contribute to creating that social community that you want to join:

>> **Find your fit.** How's your technique? There's nothing wrong with being a beginner. Nothing at all. But choose your group so that it matches your level.

>> **Put in the effort.** Are you practicing enough to improve your moves? If you're not, those people who do practice probably find you a little tedious, hanging behind, stepping on their feet, bumping into them, and so on. A sports, yoga, or dance community doesn't owe you unconditional love. Everyone needs to work on their technique so that you can all enjoy the moments together.

REMEMBER

If you never learned any dance style before, you likely learn somewhat slower than people who took ballet classes as kids or learned martial arts when they were young. It's totally fine and normal. Craft a good technique practice ritual for yourself for outside the regular classes or practices. (Flip back to the section "Guiding Star of Flow 4: Technique practice," earlier in this chapter, for the importance of technique practice.)

>> **Be friendly.** Most people don't take arrogance well. And most also don't enjoy people-pleasing. Aggressive outbursts are frowned upon in most communities. Effectively interacting with any group of people requires a difficult balance, but you can find many etiquette books or etiquette influencers that can help you figure out how to show your best within different types of communities, be they an Argentine tango community or a football association. Some communities actually have their own etiquette guide if you ask for it.

>> **Keep yourself clean.** In places where you practice closely together with others, you have to be mindful of your body. Sweating is totally okay — it happens when you exercise. (Some would say it's the prize for hard work!) But if you didn't shower for a day or so before starting your activity, you may not smell the best — and people probably won't want to get close to you, so you feel excluded for a reason that you could so easily change. You might not care about your own smell, but other people do — and bad odors can pull a person out of flow immediately.

FLOW AS A PIECE OF SOAP IN THE SHOWER

I love this quote by the American psychologist George Mumford: "You can't enter into flow by wanting to get in flow." Say that you're a hobby practitioner of a sports, yoga, or dance style. If you try to aim for flow, you invite all the Gods of Mind-Hooking (see the section "Moving Away from the Three Gods of Mind-Hooking," in this chapter) and flow remains elusive. It's like squeezing a piece of soap between your hands in the shower. It persistently jumps out of your grip. And the more you try, the soapier and slipperier it gets. Follow the eight Guiding Stars of Flow instead (which you can read about in the section "Letting the Stars Guide You in Your Exercise Practice," in this chapter). On the other hand, professional yoga, sports, or dance coaches often say that their once-beloved practice that always gave them flow no longer does. The extrinsic rewards have taken over (God Dionysius), and the risks (Goddess Tyche) overwhelm the joy — not to mention the competitiveness element (Goddess Nike). In that case, see whether another practice could become your flow practice. If you're a professional dance teacher, for example, you may already have a lot of movement in your practice daily (Guiding Star of Flow 1). It can become too much movement (Goddess Tyche), and flow will remain elusive. So then, perhaps take a look at Chapter 13, which talks about finding a flow practice in arts and crafts.

Chapter **13**

Finding Flow with Arts and Crafts

Arts and crafts offer a particularly fertile ground for flow, whether you act as a creator yourself or as someone who just enjoys the arts and crafts of others. Both creating and admiring arts and crafts naturally invites many of the ten Flow Elements (discussed in Chapter 2), like sustained attention (Flow Element 1, absorption), sensory engagement (Flow Element 8, the perception–action link), and a balance between effort and enjoyment (Flow Element 7, the skill–challenge balance). They give the brain something concrete to work with (Flow Elements 2, 3, and 10; clear goals, reliable feedback, and feeling in control), while also allowing space for curiosity, experimentation, and immersion (Flow Element 5, intrinsic motivation).

In this chapter, you can see how best to develop a flow practice by using arts and crafts, following the eight Guiding Stars of Flow (which you can read about in Chapter 5). I look at practical ways to structure your involvement in arts and crafts so that flow becomes more accessible, repeatable, and sustainable over time. If you want some inspiration for what arts and crafts activity can work for you, check out Part 5, where I discuss some options.

Dive into arts and crafts — don't overthink or aim for perfection. Just start, whether by copying a favorite image or experimenting with materials.

Setting Your Mind to a Cycle, Not a Goal

When you pick up those paper-clipping scissors, that pencil, or a paintbrush, set this intention in your mind about what you're about to do: Think cyclical, rather than linear. Although you do want to produce something beautiful at the end, of course, you also want to simply focus on that process of creating. A mindset that can help you with this is that you simply refuse to be done, instead cycling back to the beginning of your creative process, over and over again. (This describes the Phoenix Cycle, which I detail in Chapter 10.) This intention basically helps you not to get ahead of yourself. It is about *process* over *progress*.

STRIVING TO BE A CHRISTMAS TREE

A short Christmas fable by Hans Christian Andersen, "The Fir Tree," offers a quiet warning about what happens when you fix your attention on a final goal, like recognition or a prize, rather than the act of becoming. In this story, an impatient little fir tree wanted to grow up. Year after year, it sees larger trees cut down and taken away for use as Christmas trees, where they were decorated with candles and beautifully crafted ornaments. They became the center of everyone's attention.

The families surrounded these trees, faces joyful and awash with the beautiful golden glow of the candles. The people forgot their worries and quarrels that day, and those Christmas trees were at the center of all this happiness. The little fir tree saw these Christmas trees receive so much respect and reverence, and it couldn't think of anything else than becoming a Christmas tree.

When the day came, the fir tree it didn't much like the painful cut of its trunk and separation from its roots. Then the glory of being a Christmas tree came — and passed. When the little tree was lying broken and drying with all the other wood to be burned, it thought back about the choices it made.

Goals and recognition can motivate you, but in any activity, they pull you out of flow when they become the point of the work (focusing on extrinsic rewards). Flow lives in staying rooted in the making itself, not in rushing toward the moment of display. Don't aim for glory and praise for what you do in your arts and crafts if you want your brain to tap into flow. Don't be the Christmas tree.

At the point in his career where the English romantic painter William Turner created very high quality works of art, every morning, he still took the 11 o'clock live drawing class at the Royal Academy with the first-year students, copying from a model. He was okay with starting over every day anew and with never being done learning and repeating the actions of his craft. Important artists such as Da Vinci, Michelangelo, Picasso, Van Gogh, and Matisse copied from other's work first so that they could learn and master their art — and then to expand and innovate their own work and, finally, to express. This pure enjoyment of the simple act of *doing* (copying, tinkering, expanding, etc.) is golden for flow. And if you manage to do this, you're in good company!

Do an online search for "The Good Samaritan by Eugène Delacroix," and then search for Vincent van Gogh's painting named "The Good Samaritan (after Delacroix)." Compare the two. Delacroix painted his version (from 1849) in the style of a Renaissance painting — the dark red colors, the greens and browns, all the black. When you look at Van Gogh's version (from 1890), he created a mirror image of Delacroix's piece, but expressed his own style with his signature bright colors with blues, yellows, whites, and light reds. If drawing is your thing, get your favorite drawing out and try to copy it. That's the best start.

Acknowledge that you copy from others' work; otherwise, you're appropriating that work without proper due to the original artist. The name of Van Gogh's painting included "after Delacroix" for just that reason.

Crafting Your Way to the Guiding Stars of Flow

When I introduce the concept of the Guiding Stars of Flow in Chapter 5, I compare them to the actual stars that sailors have always relied on for navigation to give themselves a sense of direction. You can use the behaviors that make up the Guiding Stars of Flow to reach your destination too — flow. The following sections outline how you can find these Guiding Stars of Flow while participating in an art or craft.

In Chapter 4, I introduce what I call the Liking-Wanting principle. The liking part of that principle, simply put, is enjoying the present moment, giving you a pleasant feeling of satisfaction and well-being. Wanting something involves a striving feeling, an urge, perhaps even a state of craving. To reach flow, you need to like what you do, making the present moment matter to you.

Of course, you can find much well-meaning advice out there that tells you to focus on the present moment. If the present moment wasn't so boring, you'd probably be there more — right? The key is to develop an arts and crafts practice that makes the present moment interesting enough that you want to stay in it, which helps you tap into flow. Set your mind to meaning-making. Artists, art critics, and art historians can sometimes help you open secret doors to the meaning hidden in shapes, textures, and colors of an artwork.

The art historian Dr. Beate Kemfert is the director of the modern art museum Arts and Culture Foundation *Opelvillen Rüsselsheim* in Germany, close to Frankfurt am Main. When she describes an artwork, her words can both educate and trigger a firework of aesthetic emotions in the spectators (see more about aesthetic emotions in the section "Guiding Star of Flow 7: Aesthetic emotions," later in this chapter). People on her museum tours have described her talks like being introduced to a living being, an organism that has a past; a present, including motivations and feelings; and perhaps a future within their own life.

She generally starts by introducing the title of the visual artwork and the name of its artist. But then she focuses on textures and colors, reliefs and their meaning. Dr. Kemfert's words make the organism in front of viewers come to life, seeming to breathe and wink at them. The spectator may even picture themselves inside it. When you want to view arts and crafts to find flow, don't worry about being a beginner and not knowing anything at all. Find what appeals to you, and take it from there.

REMEMBER

In arts and crafts, materials — such as paper, canvas, wool, and paints — are more than objects, they're portals to meaning. While you engage with them — as a spectator or creator — your brain links the activity to your body and sense of self, activating multiple systems that make the process matter to you. This association primes your brain for flow. Being present in this way taps into liking — while reducing the distracting urges of wanting.

You can't control the neurochemicals involved in liking and wanting directly, but you can choose behaviors, such as a mindful art practice, that reliably encourage them. Eight behaviors which I call the eight Guiding Stars of Flow guide you on this path.

Guiding Star of Flow 1: Movement

Most people do arts and crafts while sitting down or otherwise being in resting positions. So unlike dancing as a flow activity (which I talk about in Chapter 12), to make arts and crafts practices flowable, you likely need to put your attention first to collecting Guiding Star of Flow 1, movement, through a different activity — perhaps a run, walk, or other aerobic exercise.

Your brain needs 150 to 180 minutes of aerobic exercise per week to remain healthy (more on that requirement in Chapter 6). As soon as you compromise on these numbers, you increase your risk for all kinds of physical and mental health ailments. When it comes to flow, lack of movement triggers arousal in your brain that can take the form of ruminative thought loops and worries, both of which make flow impossible. (In Chapter 2, I introduce the ten Flow Elements, two of which describe ridding yourself of precisely these types of looping thoughts: ruminations about the past and worries about the future. Regular movement helps you let go of these thoughts.)

Whether you combine your time doing your arts and crafts practice with an obligatory walk in the evening, or whether you go for a run, dancing, or a swim, (the type of aerobic activity doesn't matter), having a regular movement practice in your life will be a game changer for your ability to tap into flow. You'll see that after a few weeks of those regular 30-minute evening walks, it will become easier for you to focus on the present moment while crafting, guiding you toward flow.

Guiding Star of Flow 2: Social contact

The human brain has wonderful systems that log social information, such as smiles, gestures, others' tone of voice, and other social cues. These systems also allow you to learn from, cooperate with, and respond to others by integrating the social information that you perceive with your senses, with your emotions, and actions. Because these neural systems that encode the social information also regulate our health and well-being, social contact supports both survival and meaningful interaction. This is why social contact is Guiding Star of Flow 2 (you can read more about how social contact plays an important part in finding flow in Chapter 6).

Often, art brings people together, it connects them. You may experience a shared aesthetic emotion in a gallery, sense the people involved in the creation of a work, or discover stories behind a piece of art that resonate with your own life. Whether through the artist, their influences, or those we enjoy the artwork with, appreciating arts and crafts can link you to others in multiple ways.

Enjoying others' art, as much as crafting and art-making yourself, can provide social interaction. As a crafter, you can join a club or group that meets regularly to practice your craft. Connect online to a crowd that cares for the same practice that you do. If you want to connect to the art of other people, perhaps go to an exhibition in your town.

An art museum curator may invite spectators to meet the artists whose work hangs in the museum, either directly or indirectly. For example, art historian Dr. Kemfert (introduced in the section "Crafting Your Way to the Guiding Stars of Flow," earlier in this chapter), in working to set up the exhibition *See with Different Eyes* at the *Opelvillen Rüsselsheim*, connected with art historians, art experts, museum curators, family members and heirs of the artist. They all shared a common interest — the subject of the proposed exhibition, French painter Hélène de Beauvoir (1910–2001), the less-well-known sister of the famous feminist and author Simone de Beauvoir.

Every single person had something new to tell her, to show her, or to recommend to her for further study. Dr. Kemfert put it all together — the paintings, as well as the stories behind the making of the paintings — so that she could share all of that later, with the museum visitors.

No real boundary exists between arts and crafts for your brain. An exhibition may contain an oil painting that also has bits of fabric or woolen threads. Art or craft? It doesn't matter, as long as it appeals to you. Whether you create artworks yourself or enjoy the creations of others, mix and match what helps your mind tap into flow without worrying about labels.

Your crafts community, knitting group, museum club, or other friends you meet for practice provide soothing agents in the service of your flow. If you prefer to practice your skill alone, that's fine, too. Like with Guiding Star of Flow 1, movement (see the preceding section), if you don't get your positive social contact through your arts and crafts hobby, just make sure that you follow this Guiding Star in a different part of your life. And of course, you can still reach out to other people to talk about your projects or share your work.

Because of the bonding effects that happen when you engage in arts and culture, they often help you identify your community. Some crafts and arts are most familiar in a particular cultural group. If you want to find a new flow hobby, perhaps look to another cultural group — their practices can open up a whole new social community for you.

Guiding Star of Flow 3: Routines and rituals

The brain loves predictability. When you worry, feel uncertain about a choice, or simply can't make sense of what's happening, your brain comes unhinged. Routines and rituals can give your brain back control, and an arts or crafts practice can give you a stellar pursuit to provide your brain with delicious immediate experiences of control and predictability (Flow Elements 2 and 3). At the same time, these multifaceted practices help you avoid the risk of going stale and dying of boredom.

If you don't already practice an art or craft, consider taking one up to give your brain calming experiences of predictability. Per-haps you have a very stressful life and crave something that can calm your nervous system instantly when you need it. All arts and crafts contain important cues that you can use for a daily routine or ritual to put your brain at ease. (Chapters 16 and 17 also discuss developing a flow practice if your life is stressful or has you on edge.)

To set up a routine or ritual for your flow practice (which I talk about in detail in Chapter 7), give your senses something daily (perhaps several times a day) that your brain knows and loves. (Flip back to Chapter 4 for discussion of your eight senses.) Here are some ideas for cues related to your favorite arts-and-crafts activity (and *For Dummies* books that can help you try these activities out):

>> **Needle arts:** Knitting, crochet, sewing, and embroidery. Always carry a needle pouch. Have the colors, textures, needles, and patterns ready for you when you want to craft. When your mind unhinges, make the moves of the craft to calm yourself. The sound of the thread and needle can provide a clicking beat that signals familiarity

immediately. Former American First Lady Michelle Obama writes in her memoir *Becoming* (Crown) how "these clicking needles on repeat" soothe her mind and give her calm when she knits. Consider *Knitting For Dummies,* 3rd Edition, by Pam Allen, Shannon Okey, Tracy L. Barr, and Marly Bird (Wiley), or *Embroidery For Dummies,* by Amanda Fox (Wiley).

>> **Visual arts:** Drawing, painting. Choose utensils and materials that you enjoy — the smell of charcoal, the texture of paper, the sound of pencils rattling in their case. Even simple items, such as a familiar notebook or a plastic pencil box, can create a small sensory cocoon around you. *Drawing For Dummies,* by Brenda Hoddinott, Jamie Combs, and Jamie Platt (Wiley) might give you some inspiration.

>> **Three-dimensional arts:** Woodworking, whittling, sculpture. Crafters all over the world use a multitude of fabrics, textures, and materials for arts and crafts practices. Explore these options with the objective in mind to find something that you love doing, something that delights your senses and that you're naturally drawn to. Perhaps check out *Woodworking For Dummies,* by Jeff Strong (Wiley).

>> **Paper crafts:** Origami, scrapbooking, paper engineering. You can easily carry these crafts with you at all times. Perhaps get a lovely little pair of scissors that you use only during the flow routine or ritual and that easily fold into your handbag or backpack, always reachable when your mind unhinges. *Origami Kit For Dummies,* by Nick Robinson (Wiley), or *Scrapbooking For Dummies,* by Jeanne Wines-Reed and Joan Wines (Wiley) can offer a guide.

>> **Museums, galleries, and other exhibits:** Build a routine around the museum down the street from your home, the gallery that you pass on the way to work, or just some statue (or other landmark or natural sight) that appeals to you. You just need a flow routine that gives your mind a break from the unknown; you aren't looking to become the next big art critic.

Guiding Star of Flow 4: Technique practice

Routines (Guiding Star of Flow 3, discussed in the preceding section) can help you develop Guiding Star of Flow 4 — technique practice. No matter what Instagram videos want you to believe, you need to practice the technique of any skill. No one wakes up one morning and just can do amazing drawing, knitting, quilting, or other arts and crafts. And the technique practice can actually give you the routine itself — so you get two for one! Bargain. I explain this Guiding Star in detail in Chapter 7.

Flow very much involves letting go and letting the craft take over. However, you need experience through technique practice to really be able to let go while you perform those actions.

Your brain learns movement sequences (such as the movements involved in folding an origami rose or drawing a hand). When you repeat an action — say, quilting something — your brain at first spends a lot of energy to remember each movement; perhaps you have to check from a model that you're copying or read up on proper methods. But if you repeat these actions, your brain recognizes the repetition and starts to pass this movement sequence from effortful explicit memory systems into implicit, more automatic (and procedural) memory systems.

All the movement sequences that you know well and that you pay little attention to during your day (such as walking, driving a car, or riding a bike) passed through this first effortful conscious execution into the implicit memory systems because you repeated them over and over again. This transition to implicit memory systems freed up mental space so that you could do other things at the same time (walk and talk, drive and sing, and so on). Conscious repetition makes your brain want to free up mental space to do other things, which can help you take your practice to the next level.

Mindless repetition of a movement (such as when you watch TV while rehearsing the line with charcoal) can't create mastery in your brain. For Flow Element 2, you need clear goals while you act, and the act that you're doing must give you immediate feedback about how the action is going (Flow Element 3). You have to put your mind to it — otherwise, inattentive technique practice can't help you find flow.

In December 2025, a review titled "Recent discoveries on the acquisition of the highest levels of human performance," carried out by Arne Güllich and colleagues, appeared in the scientific journal *Science*. This review looked at the life stories of about

34,000 adult star performers in different areas of expertise (the most renowned classical music composers, Nobel laureates, Olympic champions, the best chess players, and so on). The data showed that early talent was rarely a predictor of later excellence. Those young talents got selected into prestigious expert schools and reached a peak quickly in one domain. However, those people who qualify as *exceptional adults* (meaning that they excel throughout their life time — those Nobel laureates and Olympic champions) had a multidisciplinary background and practiced more than one skill repeatedly (unlike those students at prestigious expert schools). So don't cry about lack of talent: Instead, do as those exceptional adults did, practicing the technique of different skills that you love — and with this practice, little by little, get better.

Guiding Star of Flow 5: Expression

Guiding Star of Flow 5 (see Chapter 7) is all about expressivity. Think of expression in terms of your native language. You don't think about the act of writing or speaking anymore while you write or speak. You write or say what you want to say. This *expression* is possible because the skill you need to communicate in that language is logged into your automatic implicit memory systems thanks to the technique practice (discussed in the preceding section) that you did when you were a child. You want to achieve exactly that effortless expression with the arts and crafts skill of your choice.

Think back to how much repetition you had to do to automate skills such as writing or speaking. How often did you draw the letters of the alphabet before you felt comfortable? And today, you string it all together into sentences that express how you feel and who you love. You need a lot of repetition to automate a skill — and then, at some point, you pass over that invisible line and start expressing. Movement stops being movement — instead, you feel like you *are* the movement (that's Flow Element 8, the fusion of the perception-action gap, explained in Chapter 2).

With arts and crafts, you can express yourself by:

>> Your actions on the paper, canvas, wood, and so on

>> How you respond to art around you

» Feeling connected to an artist when their work reveals something about them

» Choosing subtle variations in how you create, what colors or materials you use, and many other actions that you do

» Doing what you like to do — you're expressing a preference

» Examining the constraints of technique and craft, and then breaking them in new ways to free yourself from the accepted bounds of your art or craft

REMEMBER

By choosing the activity that you do, and the moves that you get comfortable with through your routine and technique practice (see the two preceding sections), you have at your disposal a space where you can be totally yourself, free from the bounds of convention and social rules and norms; what existentialists may call being authentically you.

WARNING

One important thing when it comes to art as a flow activity, particularly as pertains to expression: Never fake your response. Be truthful about your reaction to art. Don't pretend that you see anything in it if you don't. Out of politeness or pressure from perceived authorities on the subject, you might feel like you have to pretend to like something. Perhaps flip back to Chapter 8 to read more about the science of authenticity.

To develop a pathway to flow, you need to provide honest, genuine expression of your preferences, dreams, and thoughts. This authenticity brings you back to yourself. Therefore, for flow, please don't worry about fulfilling social conventions.

Guiding Star of Flow 6: The imagination

People who experience flow regularly make sure to use the imagination as a tool. Even people whose imagery is quite opaque find ways to use the mind's eye to their advantage. Of course, you can't just decide to be imaginative. As you can read in Chapter 8, to effectively use your imagination, you must identify which of your eight senses can give you the most imagery or find models that you can copy from.

Perhaps your *interoception* (that's your awareness of the body from within) can feed your imagination. Sensations from inside the body — heart rate, arousal, warmth, chill, butterflies, and so on — can act as triggers for your imagination, which you can then express through your art. And if your mind feels blank, don't worry: You can always use external imagery, sounds, or textures as inspiration. The imagination is a tool, and like any tool, you can train it to support your flow practice.

Many artists have expressed how important the imagination is to their practice and how they use it on purpose. Michelangelo (the famous sculptor and painter from the Renaissance) said that painters don't paint with their hands, but with their brain. Leonardo da Vinci (the Renaissance polymath) described the imagination as "the rudder and the bridle of the senses." And Edvard Munch (a renowned painter from the turn of the 20th century) said, "Nature is not only what is visible to the eye, it also includes the inner pictures of the soul."

Play (and cultivating a playful mind) is a big part of flow. The good news is, you can easily play when it comes to arts and crafts — whether you play with mud, clay, paint, paper, or something else entirely — let your imagination guide you (refer back to Chapter 8 for inspiration).

Guiding Star of Flow 7: Aesthetic emotions

Aesthetic emotions, such as awe, feeling moved, surprise, curiosity, wonder, and so on, usually bubble up when you do, see, or otherwise perceive with one of your eight senses something that you *like*. With an art or craft, the texture of a knitted sweater may surprise you or the colors of a painting make the shapes look to you like real water, frozen on canvas.

Flip back to Chapter 8 and examine and rate aesthetic emotions that you feel with particular crafts or arts activities. See where you have the highest scores of the emotions that you need most at present. Tailor your flow activity to your needs.

Say you're browsing a thoughtfully curated exhibition of a previously overlooked artist (for example, the exhibition about

Hélène de Beauvoir that you can read about in the section "Guiding Star of Flow 2: Social contact," earlier in this chapter). You can experience all kinds of aesthetic emotions as a result of visiting such an exhibit. Maybe you feel a sense of wonder and surprise because of the scale and skill of the work. While you engage with the artworks, you may also experience *pleasedness* — finding some pieces beautiful, funny, or intellectually satisfying. You might also feel transformative captivation — curiosity, interest, and intellectual challenge — while the works pull you fully into the experience.

Venture out into the arts or crafts practice that you want to develop into your flow practice. Pay attention to the aesthetic emotions that the activity itself, the community around it, the usual place of practice, the utensils, the colors, the textures — everything about it — evoke in you. What fascinates, enchants, and sparks your interest? Do you feel a mental challenge to stretch beyond yourself?

Make sure that your nervous system relaxes around the activity. If it stimulates you in good ways, but also perhaps makes you fearful or sad, you may find this activity an interesting pursuit, but it can't help you find flow. Read more about this fine balance in the section "Protecting Your Craft Flow by Avoiding These Three Behaviors," later this chapter.

Guiding Star of Flow 8: Setting an intention

For flow, you need to set your intention on the next task at hand; don't get ahead of yourself. (Setting an immediate intention is Guiding Star of Flow 8, which I explain in detail in Chapter 8.) For example, if you want to learn a new origami pattern, copy from a specific model of origami. Focus, not on the finished product, but on each fold. Did you do Fold 1 correctly? Yes. Fold 2? Yes. Fold 3? And so on.

People who experience flow easily set their intention on the very next task at hand; they don't get ahead of themselves (Flow Element 2, keeping clear goals). This focus helps them collect Flow Element 3 (getting reliable feedback on whether they're doing it right through learning signals rewarding their brain).

Process over progress is a mantra that can help you here. In the section "Setting Your Mind to a Cycle, Not a Goal," earlier this chapter, I look at how important it is that you chose a flow activity that *really* appeals to you so that your mind *likes* to stay put for fold 1, fold 2 and fold 3 of your origami, for example. If you're not enjoying the action itself, perhaps try out a different art or craft that does make your mind stay put — delighted, curious, interested — *as you do it.*

To expand your skill, and to keep your intention where it belongs — in the *now* — focus on copying a more complicated model, over and over again. After you have the skill logged safely in your implicit memory systems, your hands will suddenly try new ways to fold, to snap the edges, and so on. Suddenly — a completely new shape emerges.

Protecting Your Craft Flow by Avoiding These Three Behaviors

When you engage with arts and crafts solely for the sake of doing, your brain, senses, and body focus fully in the present, building skill, identity, and aesthetic pleasure — independent of competition, immediate reward, or sensation-seeking. Repetition, ritual, and attention to your materials help your brain enter flow while reinforcing intrinsic satisfaction (Flow Element 5 — see Chapter 2).

But three behaviors can disrupt flow, which I call *mind-hooks*. I characterize these mind-hooks as ancient Greek gods (discussed in Chapter 9):

>> **Goddess Nike:** Competition

>> **God Dionysius:** Pleasure

>> **Goddess Tyche:** Sensation-seeking

It comes naturally to some people to avoid these three mind-hooks. Others are hopelessly driven by competition, desire for immediate pleasures, and sensational drama. Of course, the behaviors symbolized by these three gods play an incredibly important part in life and business — and our ancestors survived *because* they competed, sought reward, and were attuned to social upheaval. So, these behaviors aren't inherently bad. But for flow, you need to steer clear of them. Inside your blood and brain, they make the stress symphony ring out (which I talk about in Chapter 4).

Keeping Goddess Nike's crafting competition at bay

Avoid competition in your flow activity: It belongs elsewhere. Even a visual artist who's competitive professionally, when they actually create their art, sets the intention for the next step only. Focus on the stroke, fold, stitch, or trace in front of you. Bills, gallery attention, or comparing yourself to others creates feelings of stress and drains your capacity for flow. The artist Jochen Maiwald, in Santanyí, Spain, personifies how to stay clear of the competition mind-hook. He paints with all his attention on the next fleck of gold, or the next fish in his motif: no competition, no thought of the bills, no comparing to others. He trains his attention to last, using beloved cues and feeling a need to express.

TIP

Only the present intention matters with flow. Striving for outcome triggers adrenaline and sets you on edge. Rituals, cues, and repetition help the brain stay present and flowy. (See the section "Crafting Your Way to the Guiding Stars of Flow," earlier in this chapter, for how to follow these Guiding Stars.)

Steering clear of God Dionysius' much-loved but unnecessary extras

Don't become a pleasure junkie, falling prey to Dionysius's mind-hook. The painter Jochen Maiwald (discussed in the preceding section) makes a point to avoid the urge to amass pencils, paper, or paints unnecessarily. This unnecessary acquiring doesn't bring flow — rather, it likely deflates your motivation.

Start with very few things, just the basics. Carry a small pouch with essentials for your art or craft. Browse, dream, imagine, but delay acquiring extras. Mr. Maiwald travels with a small pouch of crayons and a notebook of paper — just enough for him to practice and work when inspiration strikes. Succumbing to the pleasure hunting mind-hook deflates flow faster than you can imagine.

Keeping your crafting free of drama queen Goddess Tyche

Flow requires letting go. Your nervous system must feel safe for skills to move from effortful, explicit memory to implicit, automatic use. (I talk about the science of creating implicit memory for a skill in Chapter 7.) Risk, uncertainty and sensation-seeking (the mind-hooks of the drama-queen goddess Tyche) — treacherous tools, toxic paints, or dramatic social exposure — can over-arouse the nervous system. Keeping your senses on high alert prevents sensory decoupling, which you need for Flow Element 1 (absorption).

Structure your arts and crafts practice to feel safe. Follow mindful, repetitive techniques. Pay attention to your *interoception* — the sense of your body from within — to detect early distraction or overstimulation. Even if your final outcome is uncertain or imperfect, the process itself produces flow.

Deciding on Your Art or Craft

If you love the idea of arts and crafts as a flow activity, but you don't know which type of art or craft can work for you, take time to explore. Here are some ways to get started:

>> Do an online search for options (felting, quilting, drawing, and so on) and see on what pages you stay longest and where you feel aesthetic emotions such as interest and curiosity.

>> Go to shops that have the elements of each hobby and see where you stay longest. Browse the shelves, ask shop attendants for ideas — and see where you get aesthetic emotions.

>> Check on social media for groups and channels dedicated to the different options — for example, someone doing pottery by using a potter's wheel.

>> Browse (online or in an arts shop) through different painting and artwork styles; see which one appeals to you. Then check museums and galleries for exhibitions, read up on the backstory, and perhaps book a guided tour.

>> Listen to your interoception and your memories. Is there an arts or crafts item that keeps popping up in your mind, even hours after leaving a shop or homepage where you learnt about it? What item is it? Your mind may be telling you — this is your art!

REMEMBER

You want to find what appeals to your authentic self. You may feel very tempted to immediately buy a lot of kit. Don't. Start with just the most basic utensils if you're a beginner and acquire more only when you have a need.

If you're already experienced in your practice, perhaps you can go deeper in expressing yourself through it (see the section "Guiding Star of Flow 5: Expression," earlier in this chapter). If the expression doesn't come naturally (which often happens), ask around — a teacher, a community, or experts in shops and galleries. (Perhaps you need a little more of Guiding Star of Flow 4, technique practice?) Focus back on yourself, what you feel and prefer. Perhaps you have a message to yourself that you can transform into colors or textures. You can invent metaphors for thoughts. You can color-code your feelings, give them shapes and textures. Or you can choose an arts exhibition that appeals to your state of mind or emotional turmoil in this moment in time. And remember: *process over progress*. What you *like* doing for the sake of *doing* it, will generate flow.

Chapter **14**

Flowing on the Page

Humans are storytellers and have always been. Archaeological evidence suggests that humans have told stories in words and pictures — and later in writing — ever since the dawn of civilization. Something about a well-spun narration catches your mind like no other thing in this world — whether you're the consumer or creator of such stories. You can get several elements of the flow experience by producing or consuming stories and narrations.

In this chapter, you can browse the different types of story-flow and see the important elements of story immersion that act as flow triggers. To increase your chances of finding flow with your story activity, eight behaviors, which I call the Guiding Stars of Flow (see Chapter 5), can help make your brain more likely to tap into flow.

However, stories of all sorts, whether you're writing, reading, or seeing them, can also trigger behaviors that I call *mind-hooks* because they pull at your attention and prevent you from finding flow (you can read more about these behaviors in Chapter 9). You have to navigate the seas of information around you carefully.

Flowing through a Story

Think about the last time you sat with a good book and felt completely immersed. Did this experience become flow? Here are some ways that you may experience the Flow Elements (described in Chapter 2) while reading a book:

>> **Flow Element 1:** You effortlessly get absorbed in the activity. You don't see, hear, or feel anything else; it's just you and the story.

>> **Flow Element 2:** You have a clear goal. You know what you're trying to achieve — reading the next word on the page.

>> **Flow Element 3:** You receive very reliable feedback. You understand each word, and your brain rewards you with little dopamine showers.

>> **Flow Element 4:** You feel time and space disappearing around you. You don't realize two hours have passed until you look up from the page.

>> **Flow Element 5:** You feel very connected to the activity and find it meaningful. You feel intrinsically rewarded, emotionally engaged, and expanded by the story; you love it.

>> **Flow Element 6:** It all feels effortless. You don't have to consciously remember the meaning of the words; reading just happens.

>> **Flow Element 7:** You have a perfect balance between your skill and the challenge. Your reading skill matches the difficulty level of the book.

>> **Flow Element 8:** You feel so engaged that the boundary between perception and action blurs. You feel part of the story or otherwise fully connected.

>> **Flow Element 9:** Your worries and unpredictability vanish. You feel in control of your reading, even if everything else around you is a mess.

>> **Flow Element 10:** Ruminative thought loops disentangle themselves. Intrusive or repetitive thoughts don't bother you anymore while you read.

Everyone loves a good story, whether a historical account, a romance, or a drama. Greek mythology, for example, personified abstract ideas as characters: gods, muses, and other figures. These characters kept the Greeks' minds engaged while helping them understand phenomena such as weather (Zeus), inspiration (the Muses), or memory (Mnemosyne). (The section "Mindsets That Block Flow," later in this chapter, makes use of some ancient Greek gods to personify behaviors to avoid if you want to find flow.)

Today, stories come in many forms — books, comics, podcasts, TV shows, movies, plays, and social media. I group all these forms of storytelling together because they all involve a listener or reader experiencing narration of events — and someone telling or writing the tales.

Telling Tales with the Eight Guiding Stars of Flow

Say that you want to reach flow through reading or writing stories, but sometimes it works and sometimes it doesn't. You can follow the eight Guiding Stars of Flow to increase your likelihood of experiencing flow.

These are Guiding Stars only. Don't use them as a dogma. See what works for you after you identify them and how they relate to finding flow. You need to tailor a flow activity to who you are.

Guiding Star of Flow 1: Movement

So many people forget about the brain-body connection. As I explain in detail in Chapter 6, your brain gets incredibly restless when you don't move enough; it interprets inactivity as a warning sign. As a consequence, your body goes on high alert, so you can't get absorbed into a task, and ruminative loops spin on repeat inside your head.

Some people have flow activities such as dancing — so they get the necessary aerobic exercise within that flow practice. However, for bookworms and writers who sit for hours on end, hidden within a book or a story, you can't use that activity to follow your movement Guiding Star.

Consider a 30-minute walk each evening and some stretching during the day to prevent orthopedic strain from all the sitting. And you can actually work on your story flow while you work out — audiobooks provide perfect companions for some solitary sports activities. Or perhaps you'd enjoy a daily treadmill routine. Set it at an incline while reading an engrossing magazine (Smithsonian or BBC History?) while you sweat. Or you could check out Bonus Chapter 4 (www.dummies.com/go/flowfd) for inspiration about how to find flow with different forms of exercise like yoga, dance or sports.

Guiding Star of Flow 2: Social contact

The human brain has special systems that regulate the immune system and other neurohormonal processes in a person's body; the same systems process social information such as smiles, gentle touch, and reassuring social gestures. Therefore, in order to stay healthy and be able to tap into flow, you need healthy social interaction.

You can read more about the science of our social brain and flow in Chapter 6, but briefly, it is important to set your mind to actively seeking positive social interactions in relation to your story-flow activity. Although reading a book or writing a story is very solitary, you can find social interaction through story-related activities. For social contact through reading flow, for example:

>> **Join a book club.** Online or in person. Bond with the group members by reading and discussing books together.

>> **Join a cinema club.** Many cities offer these sorts of groups, usually structured in a way that you chat about the movies after you watch them. You might prepare for the movie by reading up on the plot and the background story; maybe even discuss it beforehand with the people in the club.

>> **Read together.** Meet with a friend for coffee and reading. A regular café routine, where you just sit together and read, can provide you the social connection you need. Your senses detect when you have a non-threatening human next to you. Some therapists call this *body-doubling,* and it refers to actively seeking to calm your nervous system by having a friend nearby.

>> **Game nights at your local pub.** You can find wonderful, complex board games that include loads of storytelling, where you enact or otherwise play entire stories.

>> **Join a poem recital community.** Love poetry? See whether you can find a club for poem lovers close by. Go see what they're up to and whether you feel you fit in.

WARNING

Reading social media can't give you the social connection that you need for flow. I talk about the negatives of social media in Chapter 9.

Guiding Star of Flow 3: Routines and rituals

You can easily access the third Guiding Star of Flow, routines and rituals, when you practice story-based activities such as reading and writing. As I explain in detail in Chapter 7, your brain links cues to actions (such as an alarm clock waking you or hunger leading to a snack). These cue–action patterns create a stable mental environment, letting your mind flow naturally.

When life is unpredictable, your attention stays on the outside, scanning for potential problems, which makes finding flow difficult. Predictable cues let your senses decouple from distractions (Flow Element 1) and allow you to fully merge action and awareness (Flow Element 8).

My advice to establish routines comes with an important caveat: Some people actually have too much routine and ritual in their life. Their mind may operate robotically, repeating all the well-known cues (the alarm clock buzzing) and actions (get up, go to work). So aiming for Guiding Flow Star 3 can also involve breaking some routines, if your life has too much repetition. You can decide to have an impromptu reading session of a book that you've always wanted to read (intrinsic motivation — Flow Element 5) or attend a creative writing course where you learn the craft of writing from a completely new angle (skill-challenge balance — Flow Element 7).

Create an altar that functions as a flow trigger, especially if life includes a lot of uncertainty (see Chapter 4 for more on setting up a flow altar). Use cues and actions that you already do habitually, and create a small, reliable space in your life — a physical space or simply a mindset that you can get into wherever you are — where you experience the same cues and take the same actions. Consider making this altar a spot in your room or house, where you go to read, giving your brain a respite for flow. Research links regular reading routines with better focus, better problem solving, improved sleep, and even a lower risk of dementia in the long run.

Research shows that to most effectively get the cognitive effects from reading and writing, do both activities on paper — in the real world, with your hands, in an embodied way (because of the important brain-body connection that I talk about in Chapter 4).

Reading

The repetitive movements of your eyes over the page while you read can act as a washing machine for your mind. Because the actual mechanism of reading (your eyes traveling over letters and words) is very predictable, you can guarantee Flow Element 10 (feeling in control when everything else feels uncertain). You can also place some specific reading cues for your senses (see Chapter 4 for ideas of how to appeal to all eight senses) so that you can use these cues like a portal back to the calm serenity of your reading nook.

Writing

Flow Element 9 involves ruminative thought loops disappearing when you're in flow. However, the more uncertainty you have in your life, the more likely you are to ruminate. Expressive writing can help. Research led by Professor James Pennebaker from the University of Texas in Austin has shown exciting results from expressive writing practices (see the sidebar "Trying an expressive writing ritual," in this chapter).

Expressive writing is a simple practice where you write freely about your thoughts and emotions around stressful or uncertain experiences, without worrying about grammar or style. Studies show that when people do this for some weeks, their immune markers improve, they have a better wound healing, they need fewer doctor's visits — and they have better sleep, concentration, and general well-being. Having an expressive writing ritual in your life can help you manage the things that overwhelm you and glue your attention to the outside world.

Help your mind let go by having a regular expressive writing routine or ritual in your life. Curate it so that you love it — use a specific pen (chose a beloved color and texture that appeals to eye and hand), perhaps put on a specific sound scape (music, chanting, white noise, and so on), use a specific notebook that you love. Assemble cues for your expressive writing altar so that your mind associates these cues with the action of writing and the rewarding feeling of getting it off your chest. By establishing these cues, you can later use them to find your way back to flow.

TRYING AN EXPRESSIVE WRITING RITUAL

You have your own story to tell. Combat the things that haunt you, weigh on your shoulders, spin on repeat in your mind, scare you, infuriate you, numb you, or otherwise emotionally drain you. Download these thoughts onto a page, through the repetitive writing-motion of your hands.

(continued)

(continued)

The original experimental set up in the 1980s by Professor Pennebaker and his team at the University of Texas in Austin was simple. And you can use that simple template today. Don't overcomplicate things:

- Write two to three times per week. Hand write, with a pen and paper, not a keyboard.

- Write for 20 minutes straight without lifting the pen from the paper, only to move from word to word. (Never mind grammar and correct punctuation — no one is going to see this.)

- Write what you feel, no complicated descriptions of plot and scene.

- You want to download what's bugging you, so focus on how the situation makes you *feel*. Perhaps start the session by writing, "It makes me feel . . ." And then continue the sentence. You don't even need to specify what *it* is. You can do that later, or not at all.

- After your 20 minutes of writing, throw away what you wrote. An expressive writing practice is for you only.

I talk more about this kind of practice in Chapter 7.

Guiding Star of Flow 4: Technique practice

You can probably already write and read (if not, check out the sidebar "Learning to read and enjoy reading," in this chapter). Reading and writing are the main technique practice that you need for story flow. I explain more about the science of technique practice in Chapter 7.

But perhaps you want to take your story-related flow activity to the next level, which makes Guiding Star of Flow 4, technique practice, important to consider. Here are some examples:

>> **Improve your typing skill:** Handwrite your thoughts when you want to really connect with yourself, then copy that handwritten content to the computer as typing technique practice.

LEARNING TO READ AND ENJOY READING

For the National Year of Reading in the United Kingdom (U.K.) in 2026, the Government's Department for Education (DfE) in collaboration with the National Literacy Trust focuses not only on all the people who already read and write avidly, or otherwise enjoy story activities. They also acknowledge the many people who can't read and write, or who learned these skills later in life. I heard a woman speaking on BBC Radio 4 about what a revelation it was for her to learn to read and write in her 50s. Now a grandma, she derives the greatest pleasure from reading fairy tales to her grandchildren.

So perhaps you're listening to this book as audio because you can't read. Then technique practice (Guiding Star of Flow 4) can help you develop your writing and reading skill! Find a teacher, a book, or a course and get started. If you want to learn to read, check out Chapter 7 for more information about technique practice.

>> **Read a novel in not your native language:** Do some grammar and syntax training (technique practice!) of that language so that you can limit the distraction of stumbling over words, diving deep into the meaning of the novel, collecting Flow Element 5 (intrinsic rewards).

>> **Write a screenplay:** You might need to join a creative writing course to learn the craft aspects of writing a screen play (how to create conflict, believable dialogue, and so on).

>> **Watch old English plays by Shakespeare and others:** Before going to the theater, learn a bit about old English, about the geopolitics at the time, the type of society, and so on, to really grasp what's happening on stage.

Guiding Star of Flow 5: Expression

Humans have a natural drive to express their preferences and express themselves. Both the poem-writing author who pours their disagreement about the politics of their country into rhythmic lines and the reader who identifies with and understands this poetry are expressing themselves.

You can express yourself though what you write, but you can also express yourself through the choices that you make in reading material and stories. Engagement with stories, regardless of genre and medium, is a meaning-making exercise, if you make sure that it appeals to you deeply.

Perhaps the activity with which you want to find flow doesn't involve story engagement. But if your activity (say, soccer) doesn't give you many opportunities to express yourself genuinely, perhaps you can collect your "Guiding Star of Flow 5: Expression," via the books that you read, theater that you choose to attend, or expressive writing practice that you do. You want to follow each Guiding Star in your life, but that doesn't mean that you need to collect them all within one activity.

Guiding Star of Flow 6: The imagination

The imagination is a tool that you can use to increase your chances of tapping into flow. When you imagine, you use a mechanism in your brain that co-activates several systems at the same time — those of perceptions, memories, and sense of self. I explain more about the science of the imagination in Chapter 8.

Story activities can act as wonderful triggers of the imagination, especially those that leave the world-creation to our brain, such as books, spoken stories, and poems. Theatrical plays can also leave a lot to your imagination while you watch an actor bring a whole world to life on an empty stage. So the story arts do a good job of taking care of Guiding Star of Flow 6, imagination.

Imagination can help you with Flow Element 5 (intrinsic motivation) and Flow Element 1 (absorption) because the imagination is so multisensory; and it also gives your brain a way to feel in control of what happens next (Flow Element 10). You can read more about how imagination feeds into these Flow Elements in Chapters 15 and 16, which talk about how flow can help you spin a cocoon of bliss around yourself against hardship, and how you can use stories and the imagination as tools to confront stress.

TIP

Do you have children or know children you want to arm with the wonderful shield of the imagination? The book *Rosie's Superpower: The Power of Imagination,* by Rosie Phillips Davis (self-published) will show them the way into the phantasmatic happy worlds of the imagination.

You can use your imagination, as inspired by reading, watching a movie, and other story-based arts, both as simply a tool to tap into flow, but also as a wonderful way to insert new cues that can act as a boundary to negative aspects of your life.

Guiding Star of Flow 7: Aesthetic emotions

Do you remember the last time you felt awe, were moved to tears, or got the chills when reading or hearing a story? Perhaps you experienced these *aesthetic emotions* (Guiding Star of Flow 7) because of something that you really loved — or something that you found really horrible.

These feelings while you experience a story (whether you read or write it, watch or listen to it) cracks open the sticky coating that assembles around your mind during your everyday life, and these cracks make you more receptive for flow. They open up your mind, allowing for playfulness and being authentically you.

Aesthetic emotions — such as surprise at a plot twist, curiosity about a phantasmatic device found in a fantasy world, or wonder at the description of a dramatic situation in a tragedy — tell you that you're on the right path to find flow. In Chapter 8, you can find out more about the science of aesthetic emotions and you can fill in a grid of aesthetic emotions that can help you identify which activities may give you more aesthetic emotions.

Guiding Star of Flow 8: Setting an intention

Set your intention (Guiding Star of Flow 8) when it comes to story arts to the next possible action that's part of the activity. With a book or a poem, your intention should hover at the next word, the next sentence — don't let your mind run ahead to finishing the chapter or the book.

With the story arts, you can pretty easily set an intention conducive to flow, which helps with your brain's need to feel in control from time to time in your life (Flow Element 10). Your brain already has reading habits in place, so you have a perfectly balanced skills-challenge principle (Flow Element 7).

Your mind naturally flows along a good story if you set the right intentions — understand the next sentence, plot twist, scene, and so on. To read about why the right intention setting is so important to finding flow — and why getting ahead of yourself blocks your flow — flip back to Chapter 8.

Mindsets That Block Flow

The human brain's creativity has helped humans find shelter, food, and security for millennia. These survival systems sit very deep inside the brain and are extremely absorbing. They catapult you into a state of high alert, pump the body with stress hormones, and narrow your attention to what feels most urgent: useful in situations of real danger, but exhausting for the brain and problematic for flow.

In Chapter 9, I personify these behaviors — what I call *mind-hooks* — as ancient Greeks gods: Goddess Nike (competition), god Dionysius (pleasure), and goddess Tyche (risk and drama). In relation to story arts, it is like with all other flow activities — you want to navigate around them. If you let them poke at your mind, they will hook you firmly in the present and flow will remain elusive.

You can experience fun and thrills by indulging the three Gods of Mind-Hooking within the story arts. And I by no means suggest that you shouldn't watch horror movies or read lightweight romance novels. But for healthy flow, make sure to have some movies, stories, and other narratives in your life that follow the eight Guiding Stars of Flow (discussed in the section "Telling Tales with the Eight Guiding Stars of Flow," earlier in this chapter) so that, in the long run, you can benefit from the health and well-being that flow can provide to your brain and body.

Mind-Hook 1: Keeping competition out of your story time

Success is never guaranteed. If you have a creative writing practice for flow, that's great. However, don't get ahead of yourself. If you start to write while imagining yourself holding the final manuscript in your hands, or already receiving awards for your book, you'll find flow elusive. You have to actually enjoy the process of writing in order to achieve flow while doing it.

If you let goddess Nike poke your mind with thoughts about winning the Pulitzer Prize or social media feeds about writers who supposedly wrote a whole book in six weeks, you lose your peace of mind and your flow.

You can find similar competition risks for your flow in the other story arts. Perhaps you read a book because others say it's wonderful and you want to compete with them when the topic of conversation touches the book. Moments in your life lend themselves to competition, but others definitely don't. For flow, choose books, movies, plays, and so on, that you love; never mind what others think about them.

Mind-Hook 2: Avoiding insubstantial story pleasure

Some stories let you collect only the cherry on the cake: A rapid succession of images, with no deeper content, stokes your attention and curiosity, providing a dopamine reward in your brain at every turn. The cliff-hanger endings make you succumb to the Netflix effect, where you keep watching the next episode, and then the next episode — although you have other things to do or need sleep.

These empty rewards keep you hooked, but they can't help you reach healthy flow. The story arts have potential for meaningful rewards, but like any activity, Dionysian versions out there offer no depth, just addiction.

Mind-Hook 3: Closing off risk and drama for story flow

Involving risk taking and drama in your story arts can prevent you from achieving flow for a number of reasons:

WARNING

>> **Risk of disclosure:** Say you tap into flow while writing in a café. But when you start writing, people might look at you, wondering what you're doing. Friends may ask what you're writing and whether they can read it. Goddess Tyche offers you the tempting risk to expose your vulnerable self to social scrutiny. Whom you disclose to by showing what you love doing, can judge you. Choose well. Your flow activity should, first and foremost, be yours.

Don't sit to read or write somewhere you fear judgment; don't share what movies or plays you enjoy if you fear ridicule or drama.

>> **Risk of bad writing:** Each time that you pick up a text to read, you face a risk to your ability to tap into flow based on how the text is written. The author might use words that unsettle you or content that sets off ruminative loops in your mind or triggers a flashback to a traumatic experience. Or perhaps, it's just not very well written. Poor writing can hook your mind because it's not organized logically and doesn't have the right rhythm.

TIP

For flow, make sure that you read books that have well-crafted sentences. If you keep stumbling over sentences while you read, this book can't help you find flow, regardless of who recommended it. Similarly, if you go to a Shakespearean play without knowledge of old English, you likely can't experience flow because you don't have a good skill-challenge balance (Flow Element 7).

For flow, you want to get absorbed (Flow Element 1); however, if a story puts you entirely on edge and triggers survival mechanisms, you can't experience flowy, healthy absorption.

4

Adapting Flow to Real Lives and Challenges

Use flow to navigate unfamiliar, stressful, or constrained environments.

Tailor flow practices to different life roles, health conditions, and responsibilities.

Adapt flow strategies for neurodiversity and mental health challenges.

Figure out how to make flow work for you — even when life is complicated.

Chapter **15**

Creating Flow in Times of Extreme Change

People's nervous systems differ in terms of how easily their senses adapt to change. Some people move town and country without the slightest concern; for others, a move triggers a near mental breakdown. So, the first step is perhaps to accept that not everyone adapts at the same pace. Don't compare yourself to others who may be more used to changes or are born with a nervous system that adapts to novelty easily — or have developed specific strategies to soften the sharpness of their uncertainty. According to decades of scientific research into flow, being able to *let go of ruminative thoughts and worries*, and *feeling in control*, are important elements of flow (you can read more about all ten Elements of Flow in Chapter 2). But, of course, that's really hard to achieve when life is currently happening "on the edge." You can't just decide to feel flow: You need to set the settings for flow in your brain and body so that you invite flow to your mind.

In this chapter, I talk about how to develop strategies to deal with the great unknown through a flow activity and to allow the ten Elements of Flow to take hold. Whether it is an improvised ballet barre exercise between boxes in your new apartment, your hands in the familiar soil of your garden, or a yoga session within the unknown of a prison — I offer advice about how to include what I call the eight Guiding Stars of Flow into your life, no matter what. (The eight Guiding Stars of Flow are eight *behaviors* that can help you find flow; see Chapter 5.)

Ancient survival systems take over in times of stress and change, creating a stress response that works against flow (see more about the workings of this response in your body that impacts your mind's ability to find flow in Chapter 4). This chapter is also about three behaviors that you better avoid in uncertain times, if you want to find peace of mind and flow. You can read more about them in Chapter 9.

Finding Flow in Your Changing World

What happens in your brain when everything around you is unfamiliar, new, unexpected? When you choose extreme change or novelty — visiting a far-away country, for example — you may feel out of your comfort zone, but you likely love it. You feel awe, wonder, curiosity, surprise at every step — and your mind flows. You chose the change and anticipated it.

But, what if you didn't? It's different when you're thrust into the unfamiliar, such as when you have to go to hospital, to immigrate, or are imprisoned. Just finding yourself in a new town after a move for work can absolutely kill your flow.

REMEMBER

You can find it harder to feel in flow in some circumstances than in others. Chapter 2 talks about the ten Flow Elements and the science behind them. One of these, Flow Element 10, involves feeling in control and escaping unpredictability. You may struggle to find this Flow Element in a brand-new, unexpected circumstance.

To let go and allow the mind to flow, you must give yourself a feeling of control. But how do you do that when everything around you and inside you feels chaotic? Unusual situations fixate your attention on external cues, making absorption (Flow Element 1) difficult. Stress hormones narrow your focus further, pulling you away from what you find intrinsically meaningful (Flow Element 5) and from developing the skill-challenge balance that supports flow (Flow Element 7). The following section discusses using the Guiding Stars of Flow to keep yourself pointed in the direction of flow.

Staying on Course with the Eight Guiding Stars of Flow

The eight Guiding Stars of Flow can help you find a flow state in uncertain and perhaps daunting times, such as when you or a loved one is:

>> In the hospital or undergoing life-changing medical interventions

>> Caught in an immigration or asylum process

>> Imprisoned or accused

>> Required to travel a lot for work

>> Recently moved to a new city or country

REMEMBER

Think of the Guiding Stars as navigation aids, not destinations that you must reach. Like sailors used star patterns to cross stormy seas in the Middle Ages, these flow behaviors can help you orient yourself in uncertain conditions. Don't look at the Guiding Stars as a dogma or a set of rules. Playfulness matters — especially when everything around you feels strict and daunting.

Guiding Star of Flow 1: Movement

The first Guiding Star behavior is movement. To clear your head-space for flow to take hold of your mind, you have to get rid of anxious, worrisome, and ruminative thoughts. Of course, you can find this removal difficult to achieve normally. In more traumatic times, you may find it almost impossible. You likely have terrible thoughts circling on repeat in your mind.

Because of how your brain and body are looped together, you can have some say in what's going on within your skull by choosing wisely what you do with your body. Literally. Movement can trigger the most wonderful restorative processes in brain and body (read more about this special movement–based brain–body connection in Chapter 6). No matter your circumstance, find a way *to move*. Consider these options:

- **In hospital:** Listen to music that you love through your headphones or ear pods and move along to the beat; you can do everything from a 30-minute walk through the corridors (or outside the hospital), doing movements with your arms, to a finger ballet with your loved one while you lie in bed. Just move. 80-year-old Konrad from Germany who has cancer goes for daily walks — in his ear pods: the rhythmic drumrolls of the songs of his youth — the Scorpions, the Beatles, Cat Stevens . . . and sometimes, it's audiobooks. While his body moves, his mind eases away into the stories of Johann Wolfgang von Goethe or Frank Schätzing, depending on his mood.

- **In an immigration/asylum process:** Walking, sports, gym, yoga, dancing, running, swimming — these activities are absolutely key to your mental (and physical) health — and they set the settings for flow, too. Political prisoners Salvador from Peru and Dame Dibaba from Ethiopia both took up running to combat the depressive and anxious feelings that come with being caught in the bureaucratic limbo.

- **Imprisoned:** If not provided by the authorities, make sure to have some daily exercise routine in your cell to keep yourself going, walking, doing. British national Linsay Foreman currently (2026) unjustly imprisoned in Iran, shared on a BBC Radio 4 phone-interview from Evin Prison that she does yoga sessions in her cell every day.

- **Traveling a lot for work:** Bring your yoga mat, your dance shoes, or your sneakers — regardless of where you are, you can move, either in your hotel room, in the hotel gym or pool, or out on the streets. Demand that your employer provide you with a pass for local fitness venues. Doing familiar exercises in unfamiliar places also helps to take the edge off the unknown. This is the trick: Do things you always do, also when away. Perhaps your thing is hot yoga? There are communities that do exactly the same 26 postures at 39°C for 90 minutes in almost any major city. You dance Argentine tango? Google "tango milonga + [name of the city you're in]" and you'll get your daily fix of familiar cues. Bring the few little items that identify this flow activity for you in your suitcase (the yoga towel, the tango shoes, etc.).

>> **New in town:** Immediately seek a place where you can practice the sport, yoga, dance, or other movement activity that you usually do. If you don't have any regular physical activities, start one. A 30-minute walk through the new streets can help you domesticate those looping thoughts, plus you can slowly familiarize yourself with that new place that you now call home.

In Chapter 6, you can find an overview of how many minutes per day your body and brain need to move to set the settings for flow in your mind. In Chapter 12, I discuss building a flow practice by using a sports, yoga, or dance activity.

Guiding Star of Flow 2: Social contact

The human brain has areas responsible for detecting positive facial expressions, smiles, soft-spoken voices, and a pat on the shoulder. And if you have a lack of these social cues, alarm bells go off and send hoards of negative thoughts into your mind. Those same systems also regulate your heartrate, immune system, and other aspects of your body functions. So, said very simply, a balanced social life — including enough hugs, smiles, and encouraging words — results in a balanced and healthy body and mind. And, it sets the setting for flow in your brain.

Being ill, alone, new, or otherwise separated from your social group can put your brain and body into a state of emergency. So, focus on the second Guiding Star of Flow, social contact, to collect enough social contact to set the settings for flow in your brain:

>> **In the hospital:** Consider joining group therapy sessions with other people who are in a similar situation as yourself. Alternatively, many hospitals have crafts, arts, creative writing courses, and other social activities on the schedule every day. Ask about them. And even if you don't want to talk to anyone, just being in the company of others can soothe your nervous system — something that psychologists call body doubling.

>> **Working through an immigration/asylum system:** When you feel that you don't have control over what happens to you, the fight-or-flight response in your brain may make you stay immobile for a long time or withdraw from people, or you may experience defensive outbursts of aggressive words without really understanding why. The reason for this behavior that may feel like "it's not you," is due to the three "degrees" of the fight and flight system: 1) *fight* (aggression), and if fighting it is not possible, 2) *flight* (withdrawal) is the next level. When flight is not possible, you will 3) *freeze* (stay immobile). Recognize the urge to isolate yourself, and fight against it. Read more about this response in Chapter 4. Safe social contact as in a hobby community can help you counteract this response of your brain.

Take advantage of opportunities in your new home country: language courses (see Chapter 11), or volunteer work. These activities can provide vital social input for your brain. Besides, they support integration (and immigration or asylum processes often recognize these activities favorably). While you engage in these positive social interactions, your brain frees up capacity — and your conditions for flow improve.

>> **Imprisoned:** Being imprisoned is a situation in which you experience an absolute loss of control over what happens to you. And some life situations can feel similar to an actual imprisonment — such as what most of the world felt during the COVID-19 pandemic from 2020 to 2023.

Inviting regular flow experiences to your mind can help with making space for thinking and planning, and just help you deal with the uncertainty. You need positive social contact to calm your nervous system. Join crafts, arts, or study groups within the prison, official or unofficial.

» **Traveling a lot for work or new in town:** You may not know anyone for much of your day. If you flick to the Chapters of Part 3 as well as Bonus Chapters 3, 4, and 5 (`www.dummies.com/go/flowfd`) and identify a flow practice that you also practice at home or before your travels, this practice can travel with you wherever you go. Prior to your trip, you can find out whether your new locale has a practice space for this hobby so that, when you arrive, you have a potential social community waiting for you.

Chapter 6 explains this Guiding Start of Flow, "Social contact" in detail and Part 3 of this book includes a variety of hobbies that can help you achieve flow; check them out to see whether one might work well in your new location.

Guiding Star of Flow 3: Routines and rituals

When everything around you is unknown and unfamiliar, your brain craves predictability. Many of the flow practices that I explain in Part 3 include predictable routines and suggestions for rituals that help your mind find this predictability. Repetitive movements, such as when you knit, write, read, dance, or otherwise swing your body regularly (as in golf, tennis, and so on), can help repair the mental damage done by uncertainty.

In Chapter 7, I speak in detail about how you can build an altar for flow that includes familiar cues that you always experience when you practice your flow activity (for instance, when you knit, you use a particular type of wool, your special needles, the familiar movements, and your chosen colors).

Check out the British charity Fine Cell Work (`https://finecellwork.co.uk`) to find out more about a wonderful initiative for prisoners to take back control over the uncertainty triggered by prison life.

To find flow, you sometimes need to extract yourself from the madness around you. In fact, you can stay within the madness physically, while you spin a pretty durable boundary around your mind by submerging it into the repetitive movements of a creative activity's routines.

Guiding Star of Flow 4: Technique practice

Flow Element 7, an appropriate skills-challenge balance, represents the wonderful feeling when you're completely focused on an activity that's neither too difficult nor too hard. The sense of achievement that comes from mastery boosts self-esteem, health, and well-being in many ways.

How can you find flow while learning something new, or work on a skill that you're already developing, regardless of your current situation? First, don't drain yourself with practicing something that you don't love or that you practice to fulfil the expectations of someone else. To achieve flow, you need Flow Element 5, the personal meaningfulness of the activity (intrinsic motivation).

TECHNICAL STUFF

You can read more about the neuroscience of technique practice in Chapter 7, including why habit beats talent and why this repetitive technique practice can make the skill pass into implicit memory systems in your brain. "Implicit" means that you don't have to put so much mental effort into what you're doing anymore, and you've freed up space in your mind to focus on other things within your practice. For example, on *expression* (see the next section), or on the imagination (see "Guiding Flow Star 6," later this chapter).

Guiding Star of Flow 5: Expression

If you feel like you don't have control because of the situation or circumstance that you find yourself in, find ways to express that hardship to get it out of your system. Ruminative thoughts and worries chip away at your self-esteem and prevent your mind from tapping into flow. (Read more about the power of expression and how to do it in Chapter 7.) When you're in unfamiliar situations, you no longer have the habitual cues that initiate your habitual movements (which I talk about in Chapter 7 too). You may feel a little like you're losing yourself.

This is all very daunting for your brain, trying to find flow when you seem to have forgotten who you are. So, you need to get back to yourself. Here are some ideas for how to do just that:

>> **Seek habitual cues.** Try doing habitual movements, listening to habitual sounds, and seeing habitual visual cues. You can't always access these cues, of course, but consider what defined you in the past, what movements you used to do, and what you used to smell, taste, and see.

   Chapter 4 discusses all eight senses; and Chapter 10 explains how to craft an altar that incorporates your cues as a means of expression. Try to bring familiar and loved cues with you in the great unknown.

>> **Engage in expressive practices.** Engage in activities that you can use to express yourself. In the Chapters of Part 3 and in Bonus Chapters 3, 4, and 5 (www.dummies.com/go/flowfd), I explain the science of how expression with different activities can help your mind get rid of ruminative thoughts (Flow Element 9) and worries (Flow Element 10). Whether you "dance it out" like Dr. Cristina Yang (played by Sandra Oh) in *Grey's Anatomy* to cope with high-pressure situations (see Chapter 12), or purr your sadness into the strings of your instrument (see Bonus Chapter 5 at www.dummies.com/go/flowfd). *Expression* releases arousal and tension and sets the settings to flow in your brain.

   In Chapter 14, I introduce the "Expressive Writing" regime, developed by Professor James Pennebaker. His scientific work in the 1980s was inspired by his own experiences of stress and his mother's hypochondria. His research shows how "bottling up" emotions can lead to ill-health, and how, on the other hand, downloading them onto the page, improves mental and physical health. It also makes your mind flowier.

Guiding Star of Flow 6: The imagination

When in a situation that involves hardship or pain, you may find that questions about purpose and meaning fade a little into the distance. Your mind gets so busy with worrying about the future (the opposite of Flow Element 10) or ruminating about the past (the opposite of Flow Element 9).

Scientific studies show that people in hardship situations who insist on maintaining a practice that returns feelings of meaningfulness and self-relevance fare better in the long run.

You can use your imagination and spin your mind around a different image than your current reality. Reading, listening to an audio-book, watching a movie, and other story-based arts can provide a wonderful way to use the imagination to insert new cues that can act as a boundary to your stressful situation. (I talk about using stories for flow in Chapters 14 and Bonus Chapter 5, which you'll find at `www.dummies.com/go/flowfd`.)

You can use your imagination to tap into flow because it is so multisensory (which helps with absorption — Flow Element 1). Besides, imagining is a delightful way for your brain to feel in control of what happens (Flow Element 10), as well as to escape hardship and create meaning in your brain (Flow Element 5 — intrinsic motivation):

>> **Reading fiction:** Books can take you to an entirely different world in your imagination (such as *Lord of the Rings,* by J.R.R. Tolkien [William Morrow], *Harry Potter,* by J.K. Rowling [Scholastic Press]), others may give you a sense of revindication for things that are happening to you (including perhaps *Brave New World*, by Aldous Huxley [Chatto & Windus], or *1984* or *Animal Farm*, both by George Orwell [Secker & Warburg], and some books may resonate with your current situation (such as *Americanah,* by Chimamanda Ngozi Adichie [Random House]).

   British national, Nazanin Zaghari-Radcliffe was unjustly imprisoned in Iran for 6 years. After her release, at a 2023-Booker prize ceremony, she spoke glowingly about the book *The Handmaiden's Tale*, Margret Atwood's dystopian novel about the oppression of women by an authoritarian government. The book was smuggled into Evin Prison. When freed, she left it there in the "Secret Library," for prisoners that would come after her, because books "could transform my life and take me to another world." See Chapter 14 for more about stories as paths to flow and away from a current tough situation.

>> **A movement practice:** Your imagination can serve you deep states of absorption (Flow Element 1) in many ways.

In Chapter 12, I explain the science of how you can optimize movements through your imagination. Sports people and dancers call this "mental training," as when you rehearse movements in your mind before doing them, or imagine physical sensations like "walking in honey" (heavy and difficult moves), as opposed to "walking as if you're inhaling a beautiful perfume" (light and easy moves).

The reason why this works for absorption is because the imagination can be very multisensory (involve many senses, see Chapter 4). Besides, you can combine your Guiding Star of Flow 3 and 4 ("Routines and rituals" and "Technique practice") with this Guiding Star of Flow 6, "The imagination" — which in turn will help you with stoking Flow Element 7 (the skills-challenge balance). Now, as you keep expanding your skill, your practice will never be too easy nor too difficult. This allows you to enjoy *the movement* just for the joy of the movement itself (Flow Element 5: Intrinsic motivation), not for what you will perhaps get out of it at the end (like a prize, money, points or praise).

>> **History, foods, crafts, music and arts:** Experiment with combining creative pursuits that can stoke your imagination – getting your Flow Element 1 (absorption) in place. If you listen to your favorite song as you chop the salad, the cucumber can briefly be the microphone for *You're simply the best* by Tina Turner (1889), and the tomatoes can give a brief sprout of maracas to *Raspberry Beret* by Prince (1985). Combing arts and crafts that you personally truly enjoy, also help you with stoking intrinsic motivation (Flow Element 5), and can help you find Flow Element 4, where you feel so absorbed that time and space seem to disappear around you.

Susana Bravo is a professional filmmaker from the Island of Mallorca in Spain. To practice history which she is *not interested* in, but believes is important to understand current world-political events like wars and imprisonments, she combines it with something she is *very interested* in: art. For every historical event, she searches for an artwork that was painted around this time, or for another important art-historical event. For example:

War of the Spanish Succession (1700–1714): In 1700, *The Entrance to the Grand Canal, Venice* was painted by Canaletto (this work highlights the rise of the Venetian school). The year the war ended, **1714,** Claude-Joseph Vernet was born (an important French painter).

Second World War (1939–1945): In **1939**, Pablo Picasso painted *Night Fishing at Antibes* (this work is said to capture the tense atmosphere in Europe just at the outbreak of war. In **1945**, Edmund Kesting painted *Rubble at the Church of Our Lady in Dresden* (which represented of the horrendous destruction of war in Germany).

Spanish transition to Democracy (1975–1982): In **1975**, the Catalan painter Joan Miró created the artwork *Per Alberti, per la Spagna* in Rome (for Alberti, for Spain) as a symbol of anti-fascist resistance. In 1982, Pablo Picasso's work *Guernika* (an artwork that symbolized a protest against the brutal bombing of the town of Guernica by Fascist Italian and Nazi German forces during the Spanish Civil War, that he had painted in 1937) was finally exhibited in the Prado Museum in Madrid, marking the end of dictatorship and start of peace.

TIP

Combining different strands of practices that combine your senses and stoke your imagination — like crafts, history, arts and more — you can easily tap into flow, despite of what currently surrounds you. Read more about the neuroscience of the imagination and why it is so useful for tapping into flow, in Chapter 8.

THE IMAGINATION IN UNIMAGINABLE CIRCUMSTANCE

In the 1997 Academy Award-winning movie *La Vita è Bella* (Life Is Beautiful), a Jewish-Italian father, Guido, uses his imagination to spin a protective cocoon around his son Giosuè within a Nazi concentration camp, pretending that the horrors of the camp are, in fact, an elaborate game.

The imagination as a true shield for mental and physical survival also appears in Stephen King's book *The Girl Who Loved Tom Gordon* (Scribner), which follows a 9-year-old girl who gets lost in the

Canadian wilderness. She keeps her will to live while she fights fear, hunger, the cold, and even bears by using her imagination alone.

Writing the *Prison Notebooks* (Columbia University Press) allowed the political theorist Antonio Gramsci to maintain his sanity in one of Benito Mussolini's fascist prisons, where he was placed in 1926. As mentioned in the section "Guiding Flow Star 6: The imagination," this chapter, the British-Iranian dual national Nazanin Zaghari-Radcliffe, who was unjustly incarcerated in Iran from 2016 to 2022, said the fictional dystopian world of the book *The Handmaid's Tale,* by Margaret Atwood (Vintage), helped her maintain hers while imprisoned by a real authoritarian state that oppresses women.

Guiding Star of Flow 7: Aesthetic emotions

Awe, wonder, and interest fall into a special set of feelings — called *aesthetic emotions* — that give you incredibly magnificent experiences, stoke your motivation, and improve your mood. Especially if you're battling with many negative emotions because of your situation, seeking these aesthetic emotions can inject some optimism into your brain. This optimism helps you set your mental sails for flow.

If you flick back to Chapter 8 where the science of aesthetic emotions is explained in detail, you will find a test that will help you identify the aesthetic emotions that you most respond to, along with the activities that can give you those emotions.

TIP

You can use the three examples explained in the previous section about "Guiding Star of Flow 6: The imagination." Try them out and fill in the aesthetic emotions grid which you can find online (www.dummies.com/go/flowfd):

>> **Reading fiction.** Select from these three options (or, try out all three of them, one by one):

   1. *a book that takes you to a completely different world (perhaps a fantasy book)*

   2. *a book that has a topic that makes you feel revendicated (for example, a dystopian novel)*

3. *a book that resonates with your current experience (a memoir, or a novel by a survivor)*

What emotions do you feel for each of them? Use the emotion grid.

>> **A movement practice.** Select a physical exercise.

Practice mental training with your chosen activity, as explained in Chapter 8.

What emotions do you feel for each of them? Use the emotion grid.

>> **History, foods, crafts, music and arts.** Select more than one and work on combining them.

Practice the history example. Pick a historical period and start googling artwork examples for the years you're interested in. For example, perhaps you're interested in American history, but can't seem to remember the dates? Go on an expedition to link artwork from American art-history to these events. The moon landing was 1969. If you now google "Which important American artwork was finished in 1969?" One of the artworks you'll find is a light statue called Monument for V. Tatlin *by Dan Flavin. Google it and find out what intention the artist had when producing it, write down the "story behind" in a notebook, perhaps. Google the same as above and add "What was the artistic context at the time?" and you will be surprised what it will tell you about the social fabric of America of that time.*

What emotions do you feel as you do this exercise? Use the emotion grid.

Now that you have a list of activities. Check which of them gave you most and the strongest aesthetic emotions that *you* enjoyed (remember how important it is for flow that you feel intrinsically motivated, Flow Element 4). And did you feel transformation of time (Flow Element 4) for any of them? When time and space disappear around us, it's usually a good sign that the activity can be a good flow practice for us.

Some people enjoy to be made curious and surprised. Others prefer to be awed and made to feel moved and wonder. In Chapter 3 you can learn more about these differences between people and why different levels of uncertainty and stimulation may lead to flow in different people.

Guiding Star of Flow 8: Setting an intention

For flow, you need to focus on what's doable, given your current circumstances. You very likely have your mind galloping ahead to the hoped-for good outcome and happy resolution of your current situation (if you're in the hospital for an extended time or alone in a new country, for example).

To be blunt: This is the wrong approach for flow. While your mind focuses on an ideal future that may never come, you let your life slip through your fingers. Train your mind to focus on short-term goals that are doable and a maximum of ten minutes away so that you can invite Flow Element 2 (having clear goals) and Flow Element 3 (receiving clear feedback about how it's going).

One way to train your mind to stay in the now is by engaging in a hobby that naturally incorporates this short-term intention-building. Literally all of the activities that I propose in Part 3 offer you this opportunity.

You simply need to fill the waiting time with meaningful activities, and the final goal recedes into the shadows and lets you *live* now. In Chapters 4 and Bonus Chapter 2 (`www.dummies.com/go/flowfd`), I explain the Liking-Wanting principle and how focusing on *Liking* what we're doing *in the present* is much more conducive to healthy flow than insisting on *Wanting* something at the end of the process.

In six months, when you look back on the past six months — What would you like to look back on? Six months of worries, living in the worm-holes of social media, or having learned a new language, perhaps gained a language certificate and inscribed yourself into the course or university studies you always wanted to do while you were still back home?

REMEMBER

The process of achieving these two objectives (learning a language and starting to study), involves you taking many many small steps along the way, some detours, and some steps backwards. This means, you'll have the opportunity to set many small intentions in your day.

Challenges will be part of this process of becoming. But see these more like important data that you need to collect for your objective, rather than as something off-putting. After all, you're getting wiser about the overall roadmap with each dead-end street that you discover.

You can follow these steps, if you want to:

Learn a language:

1. Identify the language you want to learn

2. Seek information about how to learn this language where you are (online, in person, alone or in a group, Is there funding for it that you can apply for?)

3. Check out Chapter 11 for flow with Language Learning

Enrol at a course or university to start to study:

1. Identify the course you want to do.

2. Check the requisites.

3. Find out all the paperwork you need for this. If you're an asylum seeker, or waiting in an immigration process, some courses are available to you, but not all. In prison, it will be similar.

4. Follow the lead of the authorities here for what documentation you need.

5. Check out Bonus Chapter 4 (www.dummies.com/go/flowfd) for how to even find flow with this bureaucratic step-by-step, and then, with your studies.

Google "Can I study [name of course you want to do] in [name of closest largest city where you are or can get to] and what are the pre-requisites to enrol?" Likely this will take you to academies or university sites. Check which ones are private and which ones are public. Likely, the public ones are cheaper or for free, but you can also add to the above search terms something like "are there bursaries or scholarships?". Alternatively google "what types of courses are available for free for people who [insert your predicament, like "are in prison", "are asylum seekers", etc.]. You can do this!

And in six months, time will have flown, and you'll have six months of flow-filled activity to look back on — if you manage to set your intention to the little steps on your way. (And perhaps you'll even be holding a certificate of a language or some other skill in your hands, that will open doors in your new life!) See more details about the neuroscience of intention setting in Chapter 8. Keep your mind busy with something meaningful, while the mills of bureaucracy work their way instead of grinding your mind to flour. Grab some flour yourself and bake it how you want it. A flower doesn't bloom earlier because you keep running back to it to check. *Let it be* sang The Beatles. Our brain needs meaning-making activities to stay sane. Read more about this need of our brain in Chapters 4 and 9.

Avoiding Mind-Hooks If You Want Flow in Uncertain Times

Being on edge because of a life situation means that your brain is in survival mode. Scientific data shows that people who live within such uncertain bubbles have a higher risk to suffer from several mental and physical ailments. And healthy flow remains persistently elusive if you don't actively seek to guide your mind (which I discuss in the section "Staying on Course with the Eight Guiding Stars of Flow," earlier in this chapter).

Your brain is particularly receptive to unhealthy types of absorption because your senses attend to the slightest cues when on high alert as is typical in this survival mode.

With this enhanced radar inside your brain, you can very quickly burn out and suffer from overwhelm. This is the very reason why flow remains elusive, but at the same time, it is also why it is so important that you actively seek activities that can give you flow, despite the situation you're in.

Especially, when in this state of high alert, you are particularly vulnerable to cues that can set off very energy-consuming processes with regards to three behaviors that I call *mind-hooks* (which make letting your mind go into flow difficult, if not impossible). Greek mythology includes gods who personify these behaviors:

>> **Goddess Nike:** Competition

>> **God Dionysius:** Empty pleasures

>> **Goddess Tyche:** Risk and drama

Especially if you're in an emotionally draining situation already, you must navigate around these types of behaviors, especially if you want to use your flow practice. I explain these three Gods of Mind-Hooking in detail in Chapter 9, and also at the end of each chapter in Part 3 of this book where I present different flow activities. It is important to learn to spot these Gods of Mind-Hooking within our practice to create a healthy flow habit.

Combatting Goddess Nike to keep your focus on yourself

For your flow, it doesn't matter whether others get their discharge from hospital or their residence permits before you, are allowed to travel less for work than you, or can stay where they are instead of having to move to a new town. It's very difficult not to compare yourself to others. But to give your nervous system some peace, simply seek social contacts during the course of your day who don't face the same situation that you do.

Combatting God Dionysius to pleasures that are healthy for you

Perhaps you find few rewards and validation in your life at the moment, and maybe your situation seems to deprive you of the joys of life. Your mind feels stale and marred with negativity. To keep your spirits up, you may need to invite the Greek god Dionysius into your life with some pleasure-seeking.

But keep this pleasure hunter on a short leash. A certain group of pleasurable behaviors (which you can read more about in Chapter 9) are very addictive. And if you're not careful, especially in your vulnerable state of mind, you can get hooked.

In times of change, your brain is primed to create new habits — which includes creating bad habits, such as drug addiction, alcoholism, and gambling.

If you need sweeteners of your life, consider music, dance, singing, crafts, or art. (Part 3 talks about many options for flow activities that can give you a mental boost.)

Check out where you can see a stand-up comedian live or find them online. Comedy is born out of hardship. You can find comedians who experienced situations similar to yours — the same health issues, going through an asylum process, moving repeatedly, and so on. You can connect with their jokes and feel part of a community, all the while taking advantage of the laughter effect — a boost to mood and health alike. As you throw your head back in laughter, your worries suddenly recede into the shadows. And before you know of it, you flow.

Combatting Goddess Tyche to reduce risk and drama in your life as much as you can

You already have enough drama in your life that your brain stays glued to and ruminates about. That's an unhealthy state of absorption (see Bonus Chapter 2 at `www.dummies.com/go/flowfd`). Your mind is particularly open to absorb even more drama, which makes boundary setting particularly important.

If you seek drama and sensation, you are opening the gates of your vulnerable mind to arbitrary cues that you cannot control. Goddess Tyche is unpredictable. She may reward you or punish you.

Sometimes you can best avoid risk and drama by just literally staying away. Don't read news about the topics that trigger you; don't follow fellow patients, applicants, or colleagues on social media who are going through something similar to your experience. Be choosy. As soon as you note the risky allure of sensation, protect your mind and your flow: Disengage.

GETTING STARTED: FLOW AS A LIFELINE

If you already have a flow habit, such as reading, drawing, knitting, writing, yoga, or something similar, you're ahead of the curve. When life becomes uncertain, you can return to that familiar action and let it carry you into flow.

If you don't yet have a flow habit, this moment of disruption is still a powerful place to begin. When routines fall apart and life feels unfamiliar or uncontrollable, your brain is especially open to forming new habits. You can make this situation a genuine fresh start, one rooted in self-care, kindness, and the deliberate choice to build flow into your life. If old structures disappear because of illness, isolation, confinement, or major life change, you can consciously choose to see the gap as space for something new. Ask yourself what you've always wanted to start doing.

In her book, *Art Cure* (2026, Cornerstone Press), the epidemiologist Daisy Fancourt explains the incredible health effects of engaging in the arts.

Although the arts can give you a particularly reliable place to start, flow isn't limited to artistic activities. What matters is fit. Find the activity or activities that work for you personally.

If nothing comes to mind, Part 3 and online Bonus Chapters 3, 4, 5, explore how to find flow within specific practices. In the online cheat sheet you'll also find 10 unexpected flow activities.

A word of caution: Many stories of people thriving in isolation involve individuals who already had a flow practice before crisis struck. During the COVID-19 pandemic from 2020 to 2023, some people coped by disappearing into familiar, absorbing activities, while others struggled deeply with loneliness and distress.

The real advantage comes from building a flow practice before you need it. Flow becomes most reliable when the basic skills of the activity are automated through repetition and routines. That preparation allows flow to support you through pandemics, illness, childbirth, breakups, moves, or any situation that temporarily limits connection or control.

Don't look at flow as an emergency tool only: It's a habit worth cultivating, regardless of your current situation.

Chapter **16**

Finding Flow in Stressful Times

Your brain doesn't have a Backspace key. You can't unhear, unsee, or otherwise undo cues that enter your brain through your senses. As soon as your brain determines that a cue is important enough to process, you have it there in your conscious mind. And the more threatening a cue, the more likely your brain keeps focusing on it because of a very ancient mechanism in the human brain. This mechanism keeps negative experiences at the forefront of your mind so that you can react quickly if they ever happen again.

This bad stuff circling in your mind can include experiences such as hearing an abusive comment from a customer at work, worrying that you haven't properly prepared for a teaching lesson, or getting a diagnosis of a terrible disease at the doctor's office.

This chapter is for anyone — and that's everyone — who experiences stress, be it from competition at work, caring for a loved one who has a chronic illness, juggling family with work, or dealing with physical pain. You can still find flow!

In this chapter, I describe what to do and what not to do if you want to find flow during a time of stress. Some behaviors can help your nervous system settle down and make flow more likely, while other behaviors just add fuel to the stress fire.

Understanding What Stress Does to Your Mind — and to Flow

In Chapter 4, I explain how your body, with all its systems, organs, liquids, and connections to the brain acts like a body orchestra that plays symphonies, depending on what's currently doing on — a stress symphony, sleep symphony, love symphony, and so on. With your behavior, the things that happen to you, and the things that you choose to do, you direct this body orchestra.

The basic principle of your body orchestra playing different symphonies (with the associated physical changes out and about in the body) depends on your reaction to the situation that you're in (and on your choices about what situations to put yourself in). You play the drum of your heart at a certain beat, depending on whether we're resting, playing sports, or feeling scared or angry. At the same time, your brain asks the violins of glands and organs to sprinkle their notes of hormones and neurotransmitters into your blood — prolactin after you've cried, oxytocin when you feel love, adrenaline and other stress hormones such as cortisol when you're scared or otherwise excited, dopamine when you succeed at something, and so on.

When that stress symphony is blasting from the loudspeakers, flow remains persistently elusive precisely because of these stress markers out and about in your body. They signal to your conscious mind that you need to remain alert and hooked in the moment, ready to confront whatever comes at you. The good news is: there is a way. You *can* find flow even if you have the stress-symphony ringing out in your body. Or rather, you *can* make space for flow to happen.

To change this symphony in your body to a flow-symphony, you literally need to take your body and brain and change *what you're doing* with them so that new cues enter your eight senses. This *doing* may involve to leave or change the situation you're in altogether, or you can use simple action-hacks that we will see in the next section "Changing How You Feel by What You Do — by Following the Eight Guiding Stars of Flow." Therefore, the mantra of this chapter is going to be: *change how you feel by what you do*, and flow will come.

TECHNICAL STUFF

TRAUMA AND THE MIND

The *amygdala* — the part of the brain that controls emotions and fear — checks all sensory input and classifies most of it as not relevant. Via the brain's relay station, the *thalamus,* it makes sure that the brain processes the information, but usually far out of your awareness.

Most of the stuff around you never reaches your awareness. However, for some people who have experienced a dangerous situation in the past, their amygdala goes on permanent alert, breaking your attention over and over again because of its hypervigilance. That's bad for flow.

But building a flow practice can be particularly soothing for a traumatized mind. After traumatic experiences, a person's nervous system changes — it now has a distorted sense of risk and safety. I recommend the book *The Body Keeps the Score,* by Bessel Van den Kolk (Penguin Books), if you want more information about how trauma can reflect itself in your body.

In my book *The Pathway to Flow* (Vintage), I explain emotion-regulation strategies and how to apply them to your life through the arts as a complementary tool to clinical therapy. You can see a brief overview of these in the side bar in this chapter. Exciting science shows that arts-based flow can contribute to healing your body and mind.

Changing How You Feel by What You Do — by Following the Eight Guiding Stars of Flow

You don't need a complicated or very involved flow practice at all. In looking over the following sections about the eight Guiding Stars of Flow which refer to eight behaviors (discussed in depth in Chapter 5), you will likely discover that you just need to make a few tweaks here and there to what you're already doing to get yourself on a pathway to flow.

Throughout this book, I insist that you need to build a flow practice for yourself and tailor it properly to who you are as an individual (see Chapter 3). This tailoring includes taking into account what situation you're in, including a stressful one.

In Chapter 2, I give all the details about the science of why flow feels like it does and why it's so healthy for people. Why can you have such problems getting into that state when you're stressed?

When your body plays a stress symphony (see the preceding section), you're very out of yourself and constantly focused on external things:

>> Someone else's wellness (for example, you're a carer or a parent)

>> How you can help or support someone (maybe you're a teacher)

>> How to do things right (if you're in charge of business invoicing)

>> How to please others because your income depends on them (as a business owner or professional artist)

>> Detecting any cues that might signal a threat (for example, you're a cancer patient or you work in an institution with bullies)

Within your brain, your senses are very attuned to the outside. In Chapter 2, I introduce the ten *Flow Elements* — the conditions that exist in a flow activity, such as a feeling of effortlessness, concentration, and intrinsic motivation. When you're stressed, you can struggle to achieve these conditions because your brain is in a constant state of alertness or arousal.

So, you need to work backwards, to reverse-engineer a state in your mind that's more conducive to flow. Enact the eight Guiding Stars of Flow that signal something to your brain other than *danger.*

In Part 3, I offer examples of how to collect the eight Guiding Stars through a variety of different types of flow activities.

Guiding Star of Flow 1: Movement

If you're stressed and trying to find flow, make your go-to behavior exercise. You can read the neuroscience of why everything hinges on movement in your brain in Chapter 6. But here's the takeaway: If you don't have enough exercise in your life, you find flow in any other aspect of your life hard to come by.

Movement, and especially aerobic exercise (when your heart beat goes up over 140 beats per minute) burns stress hormones, opens up mind space, and boosts mood. All of these can get your brain primed for flow. No matter how stretched for time you are, try to weave in a walk — 30 minutes a day is great. Walk up and down the stairs in your house several times. Take a dance break to your favorite music. Don't stay still when things weigh on you. Move, move, move. Perhaps check out Chapter 12, where I suggest finding flow through yoga, dance, or sports.

If you have a very physical job (builder, carer, waiter, gardener, and so on), be careful on the movement side. Your physical body may need rest instead of more movement. If you overdo it on the movement side, your mind finds it hard to find flow because you're straining your body.

Craft your flow practice to your life, and get the right amount of movement into your body. Perhaps you crave some more harmonious movement after your stressful day running about. Consider trying Tai Chi or yoga for harmonious movement practices.

Guiding Star of Flow 2: Social interaction

Psychologists agree that, in the modern world, the worst trigger for psychological problems in humans is other humans — not necessarily because the other people are bad people; the opposite is possible, too: You may worry sick about others and can't take your mind off thinking of ways to support them.

Humanity's social brain (that I explain in detail in Chapter 6) can set you up so that other people can prevent you from achieving flow. But even if your stress comes from people, your brain still needs enough positive, safe social interaction (also because of the social brain) to flick out of ruminative loops and worries, and invite flow to take hold.

Find or create a hobby community where you can collect smiles and other social nuggets to appease your social-interaction-craving brain.

Guiding Star of Flow 3: Routines and rituals

Task repetition brings relaxation to a stressed mind. Doing something repetitively (such as when you practice a tennis serve, do a drawing exercise, knit a project, or an otherwise repetitive skill) puts you en route to Flow Element 4 (compression or expansion of time). The routines that you weave into your day may also play a part in the technique practice of your flow hobby. (I talk about "Guiding Star of Flow 4: Technique practice," in the following section.)

Routines and rituals can help you forge habits in your brain that help you find flow (see the details in Chapter 7). Make sure that your mind has some fixtures during the day where it perceives well-known and loved cues within a routine, when you make your body execute the same actions over and again.

If you want to turn an action or activity into a routine or a ritual, perform it at specific times of day and include cues for your senses (sights, smells, sounds, and so on). These cues can be anything from the clicking regular beat of your knitting needles that you cheerfully extract from a beautiful carrying pouch, or a Tai Chi practice that you do in a specific corner of your office, wearing a specific scarf, with soothing music playing and the scent of incense delighting your nose.

Some people find the word *routine* prescriptive and binding in a bad way. If you feel that way, think of what you need to do to craft a flow habit as a *ritual.* Research suggests that the important words to keep in mind here are *flexible practice,* not dogma and fixed routines.

Guiding Star of Flow 4: Technique practice

If you currently live in a stressful situation, your mind is likely fixated on obtaining external goals and milestones most of the time. Whenever you reach one of these (if you reach them — because, honestly, a lot of the stress that people feel comes from not knowing whether they'll ever reach those goals), you have a strong *dopamine* discharge, where your brain gets a hit of that neurochemical. It's rewarding, and it's relieving. And, of course, you need to reach these external milestones or outcomes within whatever process you're doing. That's beyond doubt.

But *flow* feeds on the *small* and *controllable* steps of achievement. You need them in the same way that you need food — daily, one bit at a time — to maintain and perhaps even grow your self-esteem. A technique practice provides a path to making sure you always have such achievable goals at the tips of your fingers. It can give you Flow Element 2 (clear goals) and Flow Element 3 (immediate feedback about how it's going) from the activity itself. I explain how to develop a technique practice in Chapter 7 and you can see these applied to different flow options in part 3 of the book.

You don't have to set up a complicated technique practice. Simply copying (a pattern, a drawing, a dance move, a song, a painting, and so on) can get your brain to start feeling those little boosts of mastery that give you the thought, "Yes, I can do that."

And you can do technique practice whenever you want. You can always work on getting better in most hobbies. You're never done. In fact, you can keep looping through the same cycle which each element of your hobby — copy, expand, express — and then start again.

You have plenty of crafts hobbies out there to choose from, and many of them you can have with you at all times; in a pouch, a case, or a little sachet.

Guiding Star of Flow 5: Expression

If you care, *you care*. For your child, your sick loved-one, your business, your chronic pain. You have a very full mind, full of loads of things that don't directly relate to you as an individual. You may have problems finding space for what you like, want, dream, and need.

For flow, but also simply for your mental and physical health, you must set boundaries — sometimes, literal boundaries — to give your mind a break from all that caring. This separation isn't a luxury; it's a basic need. Regardless of what other people may say, according to overwhelming amounts of psychology research, you're entitled to boundaries. You need to keep them. You're allowed to take a break from the burden.

Having boundaries doesn't mean that you stop caring. It doesn't mean that you're selfish. It means that you take mental hygiene seriously — because that's what boundaries allow for. Your brain is swimming in bad stuff: sadness, information about illness, bills, feelings of overwhelm. If you go swimming in dirty water, you take a shower afterwards to clean yourself. It's part of normal hygiene. Your mind needs a clean-up sometimes, too. And although you can't remove things from your brain, you can make use of the brain's trash chute — *expression*.

REMEMBER

It's healthy to speak up about what you're feeling. Get it all out of your system. I explain in more detail what *expression* means in Chapter 7. To stay safe as you express, the section "Avoiding Mind-Hook Behaviors That Block Flow — especially, if you're stressed" later in this chapter talks about the importance of disclosing sensitive topics only to the right people if you want to find flow. It's all about regulating those conflicting emotions and sort them through healthy channels of expression; consider flow practices such as expressive writing (discussed in Chapter 14), dancing it out (covered in Chapter 12), or immersing yourself in a crafts hobby (check out Chapter 13).

You can combine your expressive practice with arts and crafts to achieve some level of emotional regulation. As you can read about in the sidebar "Regulating your emotions," in this chapter, you can use six general emotion-regulation strategies like tools to express what's happening to you and get it off your chest, which can often make you feel better.

WARNING

Some stressful processes take time. Some injuries of the soul are hard to mend, such as loss. No one-size-fits-all method of healing expression exists. But you have options. And you don't have to keep feeling the way you do. You're allowed to look ahead.

REGULATING YOUR EMOTIONS

Regulating your emotions via active hobbies that utilize your body can help you express yourself (see the section "Guiding Star of Flow 5: Expression," in this chapter, or in more detail in Chapter 7), which you need to do to clear your mind space for flow. Clinical psychology has identified six emotion regulation strategies:

- **Situation selection and modification (avoidance, escapism, setting boundaries):** You simply choose to set boundaries; you move to a different room, go to the cinema, spin a cocoon of bliss around you with your flow altar (read more about the flow altar in Chapter 10).

- **Attention deployment strategies (distraction, "pray it"):** Deploy your attention elsewhere; watch a comedy series that reflects your reality, focus your attention on your knitting needle pouch and follow the rhythmic clicking of the needles on repeat.

(continued)

(continued)

Or recite a poem with a specific intention — it doesn't have to be a religious poem, but the recital through words or song, through expressive movement as when we pray has a cathartic effect on our mind.

- **Problem-solving (incubation, inspiration, social support):** Spin a problem in your mind by using a creative activity; during incubation times, you take your mind off a problem and do something else with your body — while your mind spins the problem in the background. Or share space with non-threatening other people to give your mind a break. If you're joining a crafts community made up of fellow cancer survivors or people who have chronic pain, perhaps they have some advice for you to solve the problem that you're facing. Social support, sometimes simply having someone who listens and knows what you're feeling, does wonders for emotional regulation.

- **Cognitive change (reappraisal, acceptance):** Look for the silver lining — find the positive angle of the stressful situation. This strategy can be difficult, but you can find all kinds of movies and books that play on shifting the perspective from glass-half-empty-to-half-full.

- **Response modulation (mood induction, expressive suppression):** "Do the chameleon move" (as when you dance a happy dance, even if you feel horrible — tricking your brain into feeling lighter than before the dance, because of the movements you do); you put on a comedy series or go and watch a stand-up comedian in a bar, even if you find everything in your life right now rather terrifying. *Change how you feel by what you do.*

- **Cognitive restructuring (creative expression, self-growth):** Boost your self-esteem through skill learning, changing your perspective on what failure and mistakes mean, perhaps doing the Japanese art of *kintsugi* (golden joinery), where you rebuild a broken piece of pottery by using gold-infused lacquer, making it even prettier than it was when it was unbroken.

Guiding Star of Flow 6: The imagination

In very busy or stressful times, you can have difficulty shifting into a productive, positive imaginary space without negative thoughts intruding on the castles of your mind. But if you can do it, it provides a wonderful way to find flow.

I explain the neuroscience of the imagination in Chapter 8, but the take away for a stressful life is this: Use the imagination like a tool. Because it's so multisensory and malleable, you can make it quite all-absorbing and therefore help guide your mind into flow — especially if that mind is very full.

When you use your imagination, to paint, to draw, even to day-dream, you distract your brain from the present. This can give you a healthy retreat if you have to deal with a lot of chaos or stress in your life. You don't have to become an artist — that might actually add more stress! But you can shift your brain away from your stress and help you experience flow in a lower-stakes activity, such as reading or making jokes over coffee with a friend.

Perhaps, instead of watching a movie based on a book, you can listen to it as an audio book. Professor Joe Devlin and his team from University College London conducted a study that showed that audio-book listeners had a much more physically involving experience than if they watched the same story as a movie. It seemed that the narrative world that people built before their inner eye was stronger with the audiobook version than with the movie.

Struggling with insomnia? Audio books can act as reliable com-batants against elements of the mind that rob your sleep. Just don't listen to an audio book that you find too arousing (excit-ing, interesting, or scary) because it can wake you up. Find a good story that your mind can pleasantly flow along.

Guiding Star of Flow 7: Aesthetic emotions

Try to remember back to the last time you felt really moved, in awe or wonder. What gave you that experience? And do you remember how all-absorbing that was? Perhaps you stop at a beautiful landscape and take it all in. Or maybe it is that moment of walking through the majestic building of the Natural History Museum of your city, or as you walk about of the cinema after a great movie.

As you develop a flow practice, you benefit hugely from paying attention to the experiences and activities that evoke *aesthetic emotions* in you — feelings such as being moved, awed, or struck by wonder. These emotions deeply engage the mind, which makes them powerful flow triggers. If you are very stressed at present, such aesthetic emotions can be particularly difficult to come by. Therefore, perhaps make sure to create some reliable pathways to aesthetic emotions for next time you feel in dire straits.

When you're in flow, you often feel part of something larger than yourself and experience a strong sense of purpose. To effectively reverse-engineer flow, listen closely to these aesthetic emotions, the quiet companions of the flow experience.

In Chapter 8, you can find a short test that will help you identify the best activities that allow *you* to collect aesthetic emotions for your flow.

Guiding Star of Flow 8: Intention

You can't easily set your intention to anything besides what's stressing you. But for flow, you do need to return to the present moment and let you mind settle. Inhale, exhale, and *let the chips fall where they may* — an American idiom used to describe lumberjacks focusing on the task at hand (cutting wood), without thinking about where the small pieces of wood chips that broke off incidentally landed. You can't control a lot of things in life. And from time to time, you need to set your mind to some very small, achievable goals. Your mind needs these little boosts of achievement to feel self-sufficient, to keep your motivation up, and to feel a purpose.

A simple method to set your intention if you're really struggling right now involves counting your blessings. Focus your attention on those blessings. These positive cues can potentially become flow triggers — make them part of your habit loops. (I talk about flow triggers and habit loops in Chapter 4 and Bonus Chapter 1 at www.dummies.com/go/flowfd.) Thinking about these positive aspects of your life can distract you a little from whatever is bothering you.

You can also go basic and focus on the little cues directly available to your senses right now, as I explain in Chapter 8. Do you have a pleasant taste in your mouth from the chocolate you just ate? Can you smell the lovely scent of brewing coffee? Does the fabric of your trousers feel comfortable on your skin? You can find plenty of cues to set your intention to — *now*. In Part 3 you can find plenty of activities that can return the feeling of control to your stressed mind.

TIP

Even if it is just for 5 minutes of blissful knitting, where the next intention you need to set is the next *hoop* (clear goal — Flow Element 2), this works. You reach that goal almost instantly, and you know right away whether it went well or not (clear feedback — Flow Element 3).

Avoiding Mind-Hook Behaviors That Block Flow — Especially, If You're Stressed

When you have the stress symphony ringing through your brain and body (see Chapter 4, for more about the stress symphony), this heightened state of alert can also make you perhaps more vulnerable to even more distraction. Therefore, you're more prone to what I call the *mind–hooks* of flow (discussed in detail in Chapter 9), behaviors that can prevent you from reaching flow, personified by ancient Greek gods:

>> **Goddess Nike:** Competition. In the fight-or-flight state, your body is hyped for fighting and competing for anything.

>> **God Dionysus:** Quick pleasures. The high-calorie-consumption mode that your body goes into when you're stressed can make you very susceptible to falling into the trap of very fatty and sugary treats. Your body thinks it needs energy and compels you to accumulate it.

>> **Goddess Tyche:** Drama and risk. The high state of arousal when you're stressed also sharpens your social radar, and any emotional reactions, any drama around you makes the brain's alarm bells shrill, blocking out even the possibility of finding flow.

Any human's brain reacts strongly to competition, pleasure promises, and drama — that's an evolutionary reality, simply because humans wouldn't have survived if their brain couldn't enact competitive behaviors, chase after pleasure, and detect drama.

You can definitely enjoy hanging out with these three gods. But they make reaching flow all but impossible. They hook your mind — and if you're stressed, they have an even stronger grip.

STRESS AND FLOW: A TEACHER'S STORY

Isa Soriano, an elementary school teacher from Mallorca, Spain, has a very stressful life, doing far more for her students than can fit into her paid hours of work. She cares deeply, and to manage stress and protect her health, she maintains a clear flow practice. She collects Guiding Star of Flow 1, movement, through morning walks and Guiding Star of Flow 2, social connection, via family, friends, and students. The rest of her Guiding Stars of Flow come through arts and crafts, such as making small decorative jewelry or trinkets, and reading. Her approach shows how deliberate habits can cultivate flow, even in a busy, high-stress life.

She also deliberately avoids the three gods of mind-hooking:

- **Nike:** Isa doesn't compete to create the most beautiful necklace or to read a book the fastest — she practices at her own pace.

- **Dionysius:** Isa buys only what she needs to make the next planned piece of jewelry and limits her books to five at a time.

- **Tyche:** No social media drama; Isa shares feelings only with family and friends, avoids risky projects, and plans ahead.

Isa has also crafted an altar for her jewelry practice. At a flea market, she bought an old wooden desk that has a cabinet whose door you can close and open by using an old key. She keeps all her little beads, threads, and other utensils in that cabinet. Whenever she opens that door with the antiquated key, she sees a world of beloved cues. She treated the wood to give it a good polish before

Reducing the Behavior-Intention Gap When You're Stressed

Everyone has a ton of good intentions: Eat healthier, spend more time with friends, build a flow habit out of jewelry making. Not to be a downer, but only about 23 percent of New Year's resolutions survive over a two-year follow-up period (some studies report the number to be as low as 9 percent). People abandon resolutions for many reasons: They don't want the change enough, life gets in the way, they fall into old patterns, and so on. But what do researchers see in the data about what makes intentions stick?

For developing a flow habit in the midst of a stress-filled life, try to reduce the intention–behavior gap (which I talk about in Chapter 8):

>> **Consider when you set your intention.** Times of change make a good starting place to change old patterns. New cues enter your life, which provide great tools that you can hang a new habit on (use to start a new habit-loop, consisting of cue-action-reward, explained in Chapters 6 and 7). New Year's is a time of change, but perhaps you can make every day of your life, any day of the year one, too. So, now is a good time. Or consider setting an intention to change at the next holiday, after you move house, and so on.

>> **Chop your goals into smaller bits.** Enormous goals create a road block — your expectation. Rather, formulate smaller milestones along the way. This point relates to Guiding Star

of Flow 8 (see the section "Guiding Star of Flow 8: Intention," earlier in this chapter). It's all about setting the right intention that's close enough to where you start along the road that you can see it and have the energy to reach it. Draw a street that has all your planned milestones marked along it, and tick them off when you reach them. That gives you a visual track of how you're doing and a good excuse to boost your self-esteem by celebrating those little wins. This tracking also helps you stay accountable — which research shows can also help you keep at it.

>> **Allow for flexibility.** Nobody likes dogma. Think of the 8 Guiding Stars of Flow as guides only. Be nice to yourself. And keep a flexible mind from the outset; expect obstacles to appear in your way. Make them part of process. Maybe you missed your usual 7 a.m. expressive writing practice for flow. No problem. Do the practice at 1 p.m., before you go to lunch. Map out all the goals along the way, but at the same time keep the awareness that they may change as you progress. Flexibility is key.

The father of psychology, William James, said of humanity, "We are nothing but a heap of habits." And in a way, that's true. I explain more about habit loops in Chapter 7. You want your brain to develop many positive habit loops. Because it's so hard to set a new intention, you need to create habits so that your mind can let go.

Setting a flow habit is all about creating the environment and the right behaviors to set the settings for flow in your brain.

Craft your environment so that it can help you avoid enacting the old behaviors in relation to drama and sensation. Perhaps it's time for a change.

It's always good to start new routines and rituals such as hobbies during a time of change. Yearly festivities such as the New Year provide good moments. During a holiday, daily to-do's and chores change, and you go out of your usual habit landscape. This novelty opens the door in your brain to create new habits.

5
The Part of Tens

Discover surprising insights and lesser-known facts about flow.

Follow simple steps to identify activities that naturally draw you in to flow.

Explore new and unexpected ways to experience flow in everyday life.

Chapter **17**

10 Surprising Facts about Flow

Flow doesn't just give you a nice feeling — a flow episode may change how you think, act, and handle challenges. It boosts creativity, focus, and resilience while perhaps even opening the door to an improved version of your already wonderful *you*. In this chapter, you can discover ten surprising ways that flow can transform both life and work. Are you ready to build a flow-practice? Research shows people often fail to follow through on personal resolutions (just think of the last New Year's resolution — Where did it go?). We need motivation to keep going. Luckily, you can find many good reasons to keep working toward a flow practice. We'll look at 10 of these good reasons in this chapter. The 10 Flow Elements discussed in Chapter 2 will help you achieve these 10 benefits of flow.

Time Flies By

Your brain gives you a sense of the passage of time through dopamine markers. While you spin through your day, expectations encoded in your memory systems throughout your life about when things happen and how long they take give your brain a notion of time passing.

During activities that give you flow, you receive reliable and frequent rewards from the activity itself, which seems to mess wonderfully with your inner clock (Flow Element 4 — see Chapter 2.). That's why you experience a time warp when you're in flow. Unfortunately, this time warp can also happen when you're on social media, which explains why time flies when you scroll and scroll. See Chapters 9 and Bonus Chapter 2 (`www.dummies.com/go/flowfd`) to distinguish the differences between healthy and unhealthy absorption, and why you should.

The repetitiveness of a task helps with the time warp. Repetitive movements tease that inner clock. To increase your chances of getting into the flow state, start by focusing on the repetitive movements of the activity (the needle movements with each stitch, the steps of the dance, the rocking of the boat, and so on). (See Chapters 6 and 7 for developing the idea of how repetitive movements of the body are washing machines for minds.)

Flow-induced time-warp can be a blessing if you have to wait for something — discharge from the hospital, a war ceasefire, the end of a pandemic, and so on. Case reports suggest that people who spent time engaged in flow-activities during the COVID-19 pandemic dealt with the stress and uncertainly with more calm and felt the pandemic lasted for a shorter time than it really did.

You Feel Part of Something Bigger

The feeling of self-transcendence (Flow Element 6 — see Chapter 2), of losing yourself, of taking a break from personal worries and ruminations (Flow Elements 9 and 10 — see Chapter 2) provides a clear marker that you're in flow. Afterward you stop a flow activity, you feel like your life has new meaning and purpose; you feel like you matter because you're part of this bigger something. You may not be able to pinpoint what that something is, but that doesn't matter.

The reason for this wonderful feeling is still under investigation, but it likely involves:

>> **Aesthetic emotions:** These emotions (Guiding Star of Flow 6) shrink the ego and show you how small you are in comparison to the wonder of the universe.

>> **The generative, creative nature of flow activities:** You do flow activities by using your body, even if a lot of it takes place inside your mind, such as when you write, edit a spreadsheet, or play the piano. And you create in the sense that your mind combines information and actions in new ways. This creativity gives your brain a sense of purposefulness.

You Can't Just Let Go to Find Flow

People who are *flow-prone* (meaning they easily find flow — read more about this in Chapter 3), experience what they're doing while they find flow as letting go of their conscious mind. They feel that they let their intuitive mind take over. Some even say they feel possessed by something — they're not creating, they're just acting as the vessel. So they advise, "Just let go. Stop thinking."

But flow-prone people forget that they already have a very important ingredient firmly rooted within the neural pathways of their brain: The technique of their craft (Guiding Star of Flow 4 — Chapter 7). And they very often also have specific routines for flow in their lives (Guiding Star of Flow 3 — Chapter 7). These Guiding Stars of Flow help them let go and stop thinking.

To create a reliable path to flow, you need to practice the technique of the activity with which you want to find flow so that you can tap into the implicit-memory mechanism (which you can read about in Chapter 7). With time and repetition, you stop using the conscious, effortful, and rule-based systems of your brain and instead tap into more intuitive neural systems, making it possible to "let go" — which basically means that you disengage from attending to the sequence of movements you need to do (that's taken care of by your implicit memory systems), and instead have capacity in your mental space to focus on feelings and thoughts which you then express through the actions of your body (see more about The Guiding Star Expression in Chapter 7).

Flow Boosts Performance, Creativity, and Learning

You likely do wonderful things while you're in flow, most importantly, for your sense of self, your well-being, and your confidence. Some data suggests that if you find flow with something that you need to do, you become more creative — meaning that you find more unusual connections, more innovative ideas, and so on. Also, your productivity increases while you're in flow — up to 500 percent, according to some data. Educational research suggests that adults and children who find flow during the learning process retain what they're practicing much better than people who merely follow rules.

Use Times of Change to Start Flowing

Your brain rolls you through your days within quite fixed patterns. You have habitual cues around you that propel you into your habitual actions — both good and bad. For this reason, you can have problems developing a new practice. You may think that because you're currently in a stressful situation and in a time of change, that environment negatively impacts your ability to learn new things and to develop a flow practice. Well, it turns out that, thanks to the many new cues that changes bring to your life, you now have the opportunity to craft new habits, including that flow habit that you always wanted to start. Change can help get your brain ready for flow because you're already incorporating new routines into your life. Read more about how to do that in Chapters 15 and 16. If you're not currently going through a time of change, trick your brain into thinking that you are — change the position of the furniture in your room, recycle your clothes, change your morning routine (more on these tricks in Chapter 7).

Find Flow with (Almost) Any Activity

Almost any activity can give a person flow — you just have to find the right activity that appeals to you personally. But your flow activity does have to have a physical component. It requires action from the body, even if a very small action. I talk about the integral role of movement (Guiding Star of Flow 1) in finding flow in Chapter 6.

WARNING

Some absorbing activities give you fast, frequent, and unpredictable rewards, which can lead to compulsive or even addictive engagement with these activities. These activities definitely do not lead you to flow. (I talk about these activities in Chapters 9 and Bonus Chapter 2 at www.dummies.com/go/flowfd.) They lack important physical, creative, and self-developing opportunities that make flow so healthy and that can give you such a mood boost.

Make the Activity a Purpose in Itself

When you make what you do an aim and purpose in itself, that activity is *autotelic* for you — you find intrinsic rewards with the activity (Flow Element 5 — see Chapter 2). That's part of what makes it so rewarding and part of why you feel so good when you engage in it. Life has a meaning doing this activity! People sometimes think that either you're born autotelic (naturally being drawn to doing things just for the joy of *doing* them, instead of for extrinsic rewards), or you're not, which is completely wrong.

You can develop your flow practice so the activity becomes autotelic for you. And actually, many people have already developed a flow activity, they just might not remember doing it. Perhaps your parents took you to practice three times per week when you were in school, creating the routines (Guiding Star of Flow 3 — see Chapter 7) and technique practice (Guiding Star of Flow 4 — see Chapter 7) around the activity so that it could take hold in your brain.

The doing with your body (movement — Guiding Star of Flow 1 — see Chapter 6) can help you figure out what can become your autotelic activity; something that you do just because you love doing it. The Danish illustrator Kasper Købke (`https://kasperkobke.dk`) said it best when talking about drawing (which can apply to any flow activity): "It is not important *what* you draw but *that* you draw. The rest will come, with time and repetition."

Flow Can Bring Clarity and Control

Flow gives the mind an incredible clarity. If you work on your intention setting (Guiding Star of Flow 8 — see Chapter 8), focusing your mind's eye only a few steps ahead, this repeated reward of achievement each time you reach a little milestone gives your brain a wonderful sense of being in control. (I talk about the neurochemical aspects of this reward system in Chapter 4.) These achievements boost your self-esteem and set your mind up to have the confidence to go further — because you know that you can.

Flow Can Protect Physical and Mental Health

Research suggests that having regular flow experiences makes you less likely to develop mental health problems and even protects you from some physical ailments, such as heart disease. You can find plenty of good reasons to develop a flow practice and astutely build it into your life so that you can set boundaries for, well, life.

Some research suggests that flow-prone people are better at maintaining positive affect when faced with adversity, likely because they can disappear into their flow activity from time to time — especially in times of change, stress, and adversity — to give their body and brain a break from the gore. The regular tapping into flow can help you become more resilient. Bad things may still happen to you, yet equipped with a flow practice in your life-tool-box you, at the very least, may be better at keeping it at bay. Some days you're better at it, others you're not. Just keep going.

Chapter **18**

Ten Ways to Identify Your Flow Tool

You can find advice about all the different flow practices through schools, books, online resources, and specialist shops with specialists inside them, but the vast options may intimidate you. This chapter can assist you in finding what could be *your* flow practice. In Chapter 3, I explain in detail how much flow practices depend on who you are. So, what may work for your friend might not work for you. You need to craft your own flow activity, and you absolutely need to *like* what you're doing. Your life is full of stuff that you have to do. Flow is a moment for liking what you're doing — of connecting back to who you really are.

To help you navigate toward a possible flow activity, this chapter gives you ten prompts that you can use to identify what can give you flow.

Imagining Back to Your Childhood

Can you remember what you liked doing when you were a child? Any undertakings that you especially enjoyed? Do your parents, siblings, or friends tell stories about you being completely immersed in an activity for hours on end, where they couldn't reach you at all? Perhaps you loved drawing, or imagining with dolls, or exploring outdoors? Start a list of your childhood loves.

REMEMBER

During childhood, you're very authentically you, before you sway under social conventions and rules. Remembering back to this undisturbed joy of being delightfully immersed — and what caused it — can give you a very reliable pathway back to finding flow again.

Recalling Moments of Total Absorption

Think about any activities as an adult that completely absorbed you, where you didn't notice time flying by. What made you feel elated and self-confident, perhaps part of something bigger than you? Make a list of your strengths and most cherished activities as an adult. Perhaps working on your flower garden or fixing up your motorbike. Maybe you love solving technical problems or doing a crossword puzzle. Think about favorite subjects in school (history? literature?) or tasks at work (organizing meetings? creating guides?).

Also, make a list of any activities that you admire in others and want to learn, but never dared to explore. Ballet classes for people over 60 do exist, as do dance classes that accommodate walking aids. Don't assume you can't start something new. Your brain has neuroplasticity (neurons' ability to form new connections, in other words, *learn*) from birth to the end of our life — we *can* always learn something new and it is never too late.

Rate the different options on your lists in terms of how much they appeal to you. Whichever activity scores highest for you can provide you with a possible flow activity.

Asking Those Who Know You

Talk to people close to you — your family, friends, or colleagues — about activities that they think you seem most in flow when doing. What makes you lose touch with everything around you? Also, talk with them about what kinds of activities they engage in that they become completely absorbed in. A sport, a good book, a club they belong to. Use them as inspiration — they might introduce you to whittling or using mini pottery wheels, which may just become your thing.

Although you need to find the right flow activity that works for you personally, starting with what makes the people in your life feel flow can expand your horizons.

Testing Your Interest

You need to test activities that you think hold potential for flow to see whether they fit well with your interests and drive. Follow these steps to test out activity options:

1. **Create a list of the various options that can possibly give you flow.**

    You can use the preceding sections to help create this list, as well as Part 3 of this book and online Bonus Chapters 3, 4 and 5.

2. **Sort your list from Step 1 in terms of how much you like each activity.**

3. **Browse online resources for information about the option that you put at the top of your list in Step 2.**

4. **Time how long you research until you get bored or distracted.**

   Where your mind stays glued likely reflects an activity with which you can find flow.

5. **Repeat Steps 3 and 4 for each of the top ten activities in your list from Step 2.**

6. **Rank the activities that you researched by the most time spent researching.**

7. **For the activity at the top of Step 6's list, go to a shop related that activity.**

8. **Time how long you stay in the store, engaged in interacting with aspects of the activity.**

9. **Repeat Steps 7 and 8 for the remaining top three activities from Step 6.**

   Of these three activities, for which did you spend the longest time shopping? You probably have a strong affinity for this activity, so it can likely bring you flow. Perhaps try a taster class next?

Experimenting with Different Hobbies

Enroll (and commit) to different short classes that teach activities that might work for you. You can sign up for a short beginner's course. But you need to complete the course to get a good sense of what the activity is all about. Sometimes, the first classes feel really overwhelming or very confusing. And you see the true wonder of some activities only after some time and practice.

Analyze how you feel about the classes and the activity. Do you feel excited about doing the activity, waiting for the next class to come up? At the end of the class, do you feel happy it's over or disappointed that time's up?

Finding Your Muse

Greek Antiquity has gods, goddesses, nymphs, muses, and all kinds of creatures that personify nearly any human behavior in some way or another. Some muses, for example, personify possible flow activities. Mix and match to your heart's content, really. Consider researching a muse (or two or three), discovering the myths around them and the activities those myths associate them with; figure out which one you feel drawn to:

>> Calliope: Epic poetry

>> Thalia: Comedy/idyllic poetry

>> Terpsichore: Dance

>> Clio: History

>> Erato: Lyric/erotic poetry

>> Melpomene: *Tragedy* (meaning dramatic plays)

>> Urania: Astronomy

>> Polyhymnia: Sacred poetry/hymns

>> Euterpe: Music (specifically, she plays the flute)

Letting Your Senses Speak to You

If you have a material or fabric that you really like to feel (Sequels? Water? Dough?), you can probably find some hobby where you can incorporate it. You have eight senses (discussed in Chapter 4), so perhaps take a body scan and explore what pleases you. Perhaps you love the crackling sound of dried flowers — well, try a flower scrapbook. Does the scent of something make you feel happy? See how you can work that into an activity.

Try to find an activity by doing an online search for "different hobbies that use [material]."

Exploring the Houses of Flow

The performing arts that you watch live and in person can help you return to yourself and perhaps identify a flow practice that could work for you. I call places where you get to share space with performers or their art, in person, *Houses of Flow.* Think of a night at the ballet or a trip to a museum. Or even forms of performative art that don't restrict performers to the stage. Something about these Houses of Flow encourage people's ability to experience aesthetic emotions such as being moved, wonder, and surprise.

After you leave a House of Flow, pay attention to what you feel. Perhaps have an expressive writing session (as discussed in Chapter 14) to write down both how and what you feel. If your self-examination reveals you were affected by your experience in a House of Flow, see whether you can identify a flow practice related to it that you can try out.

Informing Yourself about Options

You have so many hobbies options that you may never have heard of. Here are some ideas:

>> **Needle arts:** Bead-embroidery, needle felting, or Macramé-knotting

>> **Woodworking:** Creating scroll saw puzzles, *fretwork* (cutting intricate designs into wood), or *pyrography* (wood burning)

>> **Visual arts:** Japanese marbling (*suminagashi*, which translates as *floating ink*) or creative collage

>> **Paper crafts:** *Quilling* (rolling and shaping paper strips into designs), *origami* (folding paper into decorative shapes), *decoupage* (decorating surfaces), paper-flower making, or scrapbooking

>> **Stories:** Poetry recitals or brush-pen calligraphy

>> **Tactile creation:** Candle making, creating stained glass art, or making jewelry

Getting Back into Your Body

People often spend too much time in their heads. Sometimes, the biggest obstacle to finding a flow activity relates to all the arousal your body sends to your brain because you're not moving enough. You can lift the cloud over and inside your head a great deal by making sure you have a physical activity that you perform regularly. That activity may even become your flow habit. Even if exercise doesn't give you flow, it does clear your mind space and calms you so that you can *feel* what it is you really want to do.

TIP

You can read more about this path to flow in Chapters 6, 10 and 13). Remember that flow is something we get from *doing* something. As explained in Chapter 6, all systems in our brain are somehow intertwined with our movement systems. Hence, simply put, by moving, you're stoking up activity in your brain. You can use this body–brain link to tap into flow.

Index

bonding hormones, release of, 122
Borhani, Khatereh, 187
BPM. *See* beats per minute (BPM)
brain
   body and environment,
      communication between, 76–77
   effects of uncertainty, 43
   functions, insula role, 74
   gray matter, 72, 153
   meaning-making portions of, 90
   memory systems, 172
   of musicians and gamers, 148–149
   neural mechanisms in
      arousal misattribution, 122
      co-representation, 121–122
      release of bonding hormones, 122
      synchronization of body's rhythms,
         122
   neuroplasticity, 35
   reward system, 34
   'things in order', 38
   white matter, 153
brain–body connection, 72–73
brain network synchrony, 38–39
Bravo, Susana, 311
Bryant, Kobe, 253

C

captivation, 183
categorical perception, 235
Catmull, Ed, 171
Christensen, Julia F., 55
cigarettes, smoking, 84
cognitive dissonance, 87
Combs, Jamie, 275
comparative neuroscientists, 160
comparative psychologists, 110
compatibilists, 193
competition, 197
competitive mindset, 228, 260

conforming as a survival strategy, 123
conscientiousness, 57–58
consciousness, 45
cortex, 72–74
   auditory, 72
   motor, 72, 154
   prefrontal, 50, 74, 150, 207
   responsible for sensory process, 72
   sensory, 72, 74, 154
   visual, 72, 74, 80
couch potato, 84–85
COVID-19 pandemic, 187, 248–249,
   306, 320, 340
Cox hazard ratio, 12
crafts, paper, 275
Csikszentmihalyi, Mihaly, 10, 19, 26–27,
   45, 67

D

dance, 246–247. *See also* athletic
   movement (sport, dance, or yoga)
dance/movement therapy (DMT), 157
dancers, 251
   ballet, 251, 254
   and neuroticism, 54
Delacroix, Eugène, 269–270
de Manzano, Örjan, Dr., 51, 52
determinists, 193
Dickens, Charles, 111
differential diagnostics, 19–20
discovering flow, 10–11
diving reflex, 119
DMT. *See* dance/movement therapy
   (DMT)
dodging language-learning mind-
   hooks, 228–233
dopamine, 50–52, 87, 88
   control, 51
   D2 receptors, 53, 64
dopamine-infused brain, 92
do's and don'ts of flow, 13–14

About the Author

Julia F. Christensen, PhD is a Danish neuroscientist and former ballet dancer. She is currently working at the Max Planck Institute for Empirical Aesthetics in Germany. Her research on emotion, flow, dance, creativity and the brain has been funded by international research institutions, including the Spanish Ministry of Science and Innovation, the British Academy, and the Max Planck Society. She publishes regularly in international scientific peer-reviewed journals and is widely featured in the international press, including *The Guardian*, the *New York Times*, the *Washington Post*, *El País*, and *Frankfurter Allgemeine Zeitung*.

Explaining science in a fun and engaging way started as a hobby during her postdoctoral training in London (U.K.), while working in different international labs (at University College London and the Warburg Institute). Today, she is an esteemed outreach speaker and is regularly featured in print, radio, and TV in Germany and the U.K. She has appeared on renowned podcasts including *Just One Thing*, *Instant Genius*, *How To Academy*, *You Magazine*, and *Well Doing*. In 2018, she co-authored the book *Dancing Is the Best Medicine* (Rowohlt) with fellow neuroscientist Dong-Seon Chang, which was published in four languages and became a bestseller in Germany. Her second trade book, *The Pathway to Flow* (Vintage) was translated into five languages. She also writes occasionally for the renowned online popular science outlet Aeon.

Dr Christensen speaks six languages and to drop her mind into flow, she draws dancers, reads spy books, writes stories about the brain while sitting in cafés, and dances Argentine tango by night. Read more about her on www.juliafchristensen.de or at @dr.julia.f.christensen (Instagram and Linkedin).

Dedication

To my mother, father and husband who know the power of flow well.

Author's Acknowledgments

This book would not have happened without fabulous Senior Acquisitions Editor Tracy Boggier at Wiley, and my magnificent agent Kate Evans from Peters Fraser + Dunlop Literary Agents, London. I thank you both so very much for your trust in me and everything else. Further appreciation and huge thanks go to project editor Tracy Brown Hamilton and copy editor Laura K. Miller, whose dilligent pens have taught me so much. With every "xxx" that you wrote, you expanded my mind into being clearer, giving more practical examples, and specifying the everyday use of a piece of scientific evidence. I've learned so much about non-fiction writing from you. I admire your skill deeply and thank you for your patience.

I also want to travel back in time for some historical thanks to Tessa David and Tim Binding from Peters Fraser + Dunlop who were the first to believe in the science of flow in 2017, after discovering my article "Let Your Soul Dangle" on Aeon. Thank you also, of course, to the wonderful team at Vintage who made my first book about flow possible, *The Pathway to Flow*, and agreed for me to write this practical book about the same topic. This thanks expands to the teams from the various foreign language editions of *The Pathway to Flow*.

Because my flow-writing happens mostly in cafés, I want to thank the gang of habituals at the café in Germany where I write — you know who you are. Thanks for the laughs, the extra seat at the tables, the appreciation and your understanding for my hour-long coffee drinking. A special thanks to the staff at Can Joan de S'Aigo in Palma, Spain, for letting me sit for hours by the old clock, for their gracious support, great coffee, and treats.

Last but not least, thank you mother, father, husband, and friends. Without you, all this would be impossible.

Publisher's Acknowledgments

Senior Acquisitions Editor:
Tracy Boggier

Project Editor:
Tracy Brown Hamilton

Copy Editor: Laura K. Miller

Senior Managing Editor:
Kristie Pyles

Managing Editor: Ajith Kumar

Production Editor:
Athiyappan Lalith Kumar

Cover Image:
© FotoMak/stock.adobe.com